Torahdike English

The Young Ben Torah's Guide to Learning English

Learning to spell

When learning to spell words, it is useful to have a strategy in place for how to learn. The following 7-step process is useful as a system to aid you in learning to spell the words you learn.

Step 1 LOOK at the word. Notice the letters, pay attention to their sounds, and observe any distinct patterns or formations.

Step 2 SAY the word. Make sure to pronounce it correctly and pay attention to the sounds that the letters make.

Step 3 SPELL the word aloud. Recite each letter distinctly with your mouth as you pay attention to what you speak with your ears. Engaging each of your senses helps you remember.

Step 4 COPY the word. As you write each letter, first look at it as it is printed and pay attention to its appearance and sound, then write it out on your paper.

Step 5 PICTURE the word in your mind. Using your mind's eye, imagine the entire word spelled before you. Focus on each letter as it appears in your mind's eye, its appearance and its sound, together with the entire word's appearance and sound,,

Step 6 Cover the word and WRITE it. Writing the word from memory forces the short-term recall area of your brain to quickly review and remember the way the word is spelled. Writing it out gives you a means of checking how well you actually remember, and helps cement what you just reviewed.

Step 7 CHECK for accuracy. Compare the word you wrote from memory to the correctly printed word in front of you. Notice any inaccuracies. If there was a mistake, repeat steps 1-6.

This work should be done for the words in each lesson to learn the spelling of the words. This is in addition to the exercises and classwork that you will be assigned each week to help you review the meanings and usages of the words.

Key Concepts
- base word
- suffix
- related forms of words
- parts of speech (noun, verb, adjective, adverb)

A **base word** is a word before any changes have been made.

A **suffix** is a word ending that changes the use of a word or its function.

Words that share the same base word, but have different prefixes or suffixes are **related forms** of the base word.

Related forms of the same base word may be different **parts of speech**. They may be nouns, adjectives, verbs, or adverbs.

There are four parts of speech used to categorize most of the spelling words in this book. **Nouns** (n.) are persons, places, or things (both things you can touch like objects, and things you cannot touch like ideas). One example of a noun is <u>apple</u>. **Adjectives** (adj.) are words that are used to modify (describe, limit, or tell you about) nouns. For example, a <u>red</u> apple. **Verbs** (v.) are actions (like eating or jumping) or states of being (like awake, alive, existing). **Adverbs** (adv.) are words that modify (describe, limit, or tell you about) verbs. For example, eating the apple <u>quickly</u>.

Lesson 1 Spelling Rule: When you add a suffix that begins with a vowel to a word that ends with silent e, drop the final e.

Suffixes used in this lesson, together with their meanings:
- -ant (that has or shows)
- -ance (act of, state of being)
- -al (of, like, act of)
- -ion (the act of, condition of, or result of)
- -ure (act or result of being, a thing or group that)
- -ial (of, like, act of)
- -ing (the action of)
- -ive (of, having the nature of)

1. PLEASE + ANT = PLEASANT
2. RESEMBLE + ANCE = RESEMBLANCE
3. PROPOSE + AL = PROPOSAL
4. PRACTICE + AL = PRACTICAL
5. IGNITE + ION = IGNITION
6. ENCLOSE + URE = ENCLOSURE
7. FINANCE + IAL = FINANCIAL
8. RESCUE + ING = RESCUING
9. RAISE + ING = RAISING
10. RELATE + IVE = RELATIVE
11. OBSERVE + ANT = OBSERVANT
12. GUIDE + ANCE = GUIDANCE
13. REHEARSE + AL = REHEARSAL
14. GLOBE + AL = GLOBAL
15. INDICATE + ION = INDICATION
16. LEGISLATE + URE = LEGISLATURE
17. RACE + IAL = RACIAL
18. ARGUE + ING = ARGUING
19. WRITE + ING = WRITING
20. COOPERATE + IVE = COOPERATIVE

Pay attention to the spelling words.

1. What eight different suffixes have been added to form spelling words? _____ _____ _____

   _____ _____ _____ _____ _____

2. Does each suffix begin with a consonant or a vowel? _____

3. Before the suffix is added, each word ends with a letter that is not pronounced. What is that

   final silent letter? _____

4. What happens to the final silent letter when the suffix is added?

   _____

When you add a suffix that begins with a vowel to a word that ends with silent **e**, drop the final **e**.

6

Spelling Dictionary

1. **ar·gue** — *v.* **–gued, –gue·ing**[1] to give reasons, to dispute, to show
2. **ar·gu·ing** — *v.* giving reasons, quarreling
3. **co·op·e·rate, co-op·e·rate**[2] — *v.* **–rat·ed, –rat·ing** to work together
4. **co·op·er·a·tive** — *adj.* Cooperating or willing to cooperate
5. **en·close** — *v.* **–closed, –clos·ing** to shut in or surround, to insert or hold in an envelope
6. **en·clo·sure** — *n.* an act of enclosing, being enclosed, something that encloses
7. **fi·nance** — *n.* the conduct of money matters *–v.*[3] **–nanced, –nancing** to supply money, to manage money
8. **fi·nan·cial** — *adj.* of finance
9. **glo·bal** — *adj.* worldwide
10. **globe** — *n.* the planet earth; a spherical shape
11. **gui·dance** — *n.* an act of guiding, a thing that guides
12. **guide** — *v.* **–guid·ed, –guid·ing** to assist, advise, or supervise *–n.* a person or thing that guides
13. **ig·nite** — *v.* **–ni·ted, –ni·ting** to set or catch on fire
14. **ig·ni·tion** — *n.* act of or means of igniting
15. **in·di·cate** — *v.* **–cat·ed, –cat·ing** point, demonstrate
16. **in·di·ca·tion** — *n.* something that indicates or shows
17. **leg·is·late** — *v.* **–lat·ed, –lat·ing** to enact laws
18. **leg·is·la·ture** — *n.* a body of persons with the power to make laws
19. **ob·serv·ant** — *adj.* paying careful attention, alert, perceptive
20. **ob·serve** — *v.* **–served, –serv·ing** to see, pay attention, obey, remark
21. **plea·sant** — *adj.* giving satisfaction or delight; agreeable
22. **please** — *v.* **pleased, plea·sing** to give satisfaction or delight
23. **plea·sing** — *adj.* giving pleasure and satisfaction; pleasant or agreeable to the senses [the *pleasing* sound of music]
24. **prac·ti·cal** — *adj.* usable, workable, useful, sensible
25. **pra·tice** — *v.* **–ticed, –ti·cing** habit, custom, action
26. **pro·po·sal** — *n.* a plan or action proposed
27. **pro·pose** — *v.* **–posed, –pos·sing** suggest
28. **race** — *n.* a group of people sharing descent, or traits
29. **ra·cial** — *adj.* of a race, between races
30. **raise** — *v.* **raised, rai·sing** to lift, to increase in force, to cause to grow
31. **rais·ing** — *n.* an act of lifting or causing to grow *–v.* lifting, causing to grow
32. **re·hearsal** — *n.* a practice performance of a show

---

[1] The dictionary will usually list related forms after the entry word. Sometimes, if the related word is significantly different from the base word it gets a separate entry. In the first few lessons, most of the related words also were listed as separate entries. Often, the dictionary abbreviates the related words and begins with the syllable that is different from the entry word. The missing first part of the word is represented by the hyphen.

[2] When there is another way to spell a word, it is called a variant, and is often listed after the entry word. More on variants in Lesson 17.

[3] The definitions are given for each word under the same entry, separated by the part of speech that it is used. The related words are listed between the part of speech and the definitions.

33. **re·hearse** v. **–hearsed, – hear·sing** to practice a performance

34. **re·late** v. **–la·ted, –la·ting** to tell, to cause or have an association
with

35. **re·la·tive** *adj.* being family with each other —*n.* a member
of the family

36. **res·cue** v. **–cued, –cu·ing** save

37. **res·cu·ing** *n.* an act of saving —*v.* saving

38. **re·sem·blance** *n.* degree of likeness, sort of likeness

39. **re·sem·ble** v. **–bled, -bling** to be like or similar to

40. **write** v. **wri·ting** to compose characters on a surface, to express
ideas in script

41. **wri·ting** *n.* something written —*v.* forming characters,
expressing ideas in script

Practicing the words

Writing

A. Answer each question with a complete sentence that uses a related form of the spelling word in the sentence by adding a suffix to the underlined word.

1. Does Herschel <u>resemble</u> his brother? _____

_____

2. Has the cast begun to <u>rehearse</u> the play? _____

_____

3. Did everyone on the team <u>cooperate</u>? _____

_____

4. Is the person you phoned <u>related</u> to you? _____

_____

5. Did Lana <u>propose</u> her idea at the last meeting? _____

_____

6. Are you going to <u>raise</u> corn in your garden? _____

_____

7. What is the name of a holiday that your family will <u>observe</u> this month? _____

_____

8. Did yesterday's weather <u>please</u> you? _____

_____

9. What <u>practice</u> does Rabbi Menasche encourage everyone to do? _____

_____

10. Who is going to <u>ignite</u> the first firework of the display? _____

_____

11. What is the next project that Mr. Reichman will <u>finance</u>? _____

_____

12. Whose pet is Tzirel about to <u>rescue</u> from the wind storm? _____

_____

13. Who will <u>guide</u> the boys as they prepare for the Shabbaton? _____

_____

14. What is causing changes in weather around the <u>globe</u>? _____

_____

15. How does a driver <u>indicate</u> in which direction he will turn? _____

_____

16. How did the zookeepers <u>enclose</u> the new group of monkeys? _____

_____

17. What new law did Congress <u>legislate</u> recently? _____

_____

18. What is your opinion with regards to discriminating against people of a different <u>race</u>?

_____

19. What is the name of someone who chose to <u>argue</u> with Korach against Moshe Rabbeinu?

_____

20. To whom will you <u>write</u> about the damaged item you received?

_____

B.   A **base word** is a word before any changes have been made. A **suffix** can be added to a base word to change the way it is used.

> Does the weather <u>please</u> you? (*please* is a verb)
> Yes, the weather is very <u>pleasing</u> today. (*pleasing* is an adjective)
> The weather has been <u>pleasant</u> for several days. (*pleasant* is an adjective)

The underlined words are **related forms** of the base word **please**. Related forms of the same base word may be different parts of speech. They may be nouns, verbs, adjectives, or adverbs. Write the base form of each word and the abbreviation of which part of speech it is[4]. Then add the suffix to the base form and write the related form, along with the abreviation of which part of speech it is. Remember to drop the final silent **e** of the base form.

	Base Form		Related Form
1. pleasing		+ ant	
2. resembling		+ ance	
3. financed		+ ial	
4. legislating		+ ure	
5. guiding		+ ance	
6. writer		+ ing	
7. argued		+ ing	
8. practicing		+ al	
9. proposing		+ al	
10. ignited		+ ion	
11. enclosing		+ ure	
12. rescued		+ ing	
13. raised		+ ing	
14. relation		+ ive	
15. observing		+ ant	
16. rehearsed		+ al	
17. globes		+ al	
18. indicated		+ ion	
19. races		+ ial	
20. cooperation		+ ive	

---

[4]   If there is more than one possibility, pick the first that is listed in the dictionary.

C. Proofreading

Cross out the misspelled words in the following paragraphs. Then rewrite them, correctly spelled on the spaces below.

I was unpleasantly surprised last week when I bumped into an old classmate of mine from elementary school. His behavior bore no resembleance to the way I remembered him as my old friend. He used to be a pleaseant, well-mannered boy who liked to help out others. But now he seems to be a very different person. He is now a politician and a member of our state's lejislacher. He told me about his proposel to enact a new law that prevents collectors from soliciting donations in synagogues. He no longer wants to see them disturb people who try to pray while they are raiseing money to help themselves out of their finantial difficulties. His new law would require all rellatives of anyone who is poor to be cooperativ in rescyuing them from their circumstances. I tried argyueing with him that this is not practickal for most people and would deprive observent Jews from fulfilling the mitzvah of charity. I am disturbed at the possibility of such an outcome. When I sought advice, I received guidence to try igniteing the outrage of the globel community, to encourage them to try riting to the lawmakers to prevent this from happening.

1. _____

2. _____

3. _____

4. _____

5. _____

6. _____

7. _____

8. _____

9. _____

10. _____

11. _____

12. _____

13. _____

14. _____

15. _____

16. _____

D. Fill in the following sentences with the appropriate spelling words.

1. That __ __ __ __ __ __ __ __ __ is intended for the animal exhibit.

2. Bird watchers are generally __ __ __ __ __ __ __ __ __ people.

3. The state __ __ __ __ __ __ __ __ __ __ __ is now in session with the required number of members.

4. I noticed the __ __ __ __ __ __ __ __ __ __ __ between the two brothers.

5. The accountant gave the new store owner __ __ __ __ __ __ __ __ __ advice.

6. Our school has a number of __ __ __ __ __ __ __ __ counselors.

7. A __ __ __ __ __ __ __ __ breeze blew along the front porch.

8. My family is proud of our __ __ __ __ __ __ heritage.

9. The senate will vote on the __ __ __ __ __ __ __ __ in the near future.

10. The firefighter received a medal for __ __ __ __ __ __ __ __ the trapped child.

11. Zalman made sure to attend every __ __ __ __ __ __ __ __ __ of the choir.

12. There is never to be any __ __ __ __ __ __ __ with a teacher.

13. We seek a __ __ __ __ __ __ __ __ __ solution to the problem?

14. The walkathon is __ __ __ __ __ __ __ money for a worthy cause.

15. Satellites enable __ __ __ __ __ __ communication.

16. In this class you will be __ __ __ __ __ __ __ some essays.

17. The driver attempted to insert the wrong key in the __ __ __ __ __ __ __ __.

18. The director of the play is a __ __ __ __ __ __ __ __ of hers.

19. Turn on your blinkers to provide __ __ __ __ __ __ __ __ __ __ of your intention to turn.

20. Cleaning up the neighborhood was a __ __ __ __ __ __ __ __ __ __ __ effort.

Key Concepts
- base word
- suffix
- related forms of words
- parts of speech (noun, verb, adjective, adverb)

A **base word** is a word before any changes have been made.

A **suffix** is a word ending that changes the use of a word or its function.

Words that share the same base word, but have different prefixes or suffixes are **related forms** of the base word.

Related forms of the same base word may be different **parts of speech**. They may be nouns, adjectives, verbs, or adverbs.

There are four parts of speech used to categorize most of the spelling words in this book. **Nouns** (n.) are persons, places, or things (both things you can touch like objects, and things you cannot touch like ideas). **Adjectives** (adj.) are words that are used to modify (describe, limit, or tell you about) nouns. **Verbs** (v.) are actions (like eating or jumping) or states of being (like awake, alive, existing). **Adverbs** (adv.) are words that modify (describe, limit, or tell you about) verbs.

Remember the old rule: **I** before **e** except after **c**; or when sounding a, as in n<u>ei</u>ghbor or w<u>ei</u>gh.

Lesson 2 Spelling Rule: When you add a suffix that begins with a consonant to a word that ends with silent e, keep the final e.

Suffixes used in this lesson, together with their meanings:
- -ity (forms a noun from an adjective; having the quality of; being in the state or condition)
- -ly (forms an adjective from a noun, or adverb from adjective; like, characteristic of, in a specified manner)
- -ing (indicates present tense of verb; forms noun from a verb)
- -ive (of; having the nature of)
- -less (without; that cannot; that does not)
- -ment (forms a noun from a verb; a result, the act or process; the state or fact)
- -ion (act, condition, or result of)
- -ory (having the function or effect of, pertaining to)

1. FESTIVE	+ ITY	= FESTIVITY	+ LY	= FESTIVELY
2. SEVERE	+ ITY	= SEVERITY	+ LY	= SEVERELY
3. TIME	+ ING	= TIMING	+ LY	= TIMELY
4. LOVE	+ ING	= LOVING	+ LY	= LOVELY
5. LIKE	+ ING	= LIKING	+ LY	= LIKELY
6. COMPLETE	+ ING	= COMPLETING	+ LY	= COMPLETELY
7. DEFINITE	+ ION	= DEFINITION	+ LY	= DEFINITELY
8. INTENSE	+ IVE	= INTENSIVE	+ LY	= INTENSELY
9. DEFENSE	+ IVE	= DEFENSIVE	+ LESS	= DEFENSELESS
10. PRICE	+ ING	= PRICING	+ LESS	= PRICELESS
11. BLAME	+ ING	= BLAMING	+ LESS	= BLAMELESS
12. AGE	+ ING	= AGING	+ LESS	= AGELESS
13. SENSE	+ ORY	= SENSORY	+ LESS	= SENSELESS
14. CONFINE	+ ING	= CONFINING	+ MENT	= CONFINEMENT
15. ENDORSE	+ ING	= ENDORSING	+ MENT	= ENDORSEMENT
16. MEASURE	+ ING	= MEASURING	+ MENT	= MEASUREMENT
17. AMUSE	+ ING	= AMUSING	+ MENT	= AMUSEMENT
18. ENGAGE	+ ING	= ENGAGING	+ MENT	= ENGAGEMENT
19. STATE	+ ING	= STATING	+ MENT	= STATEMENT
20. ACHIEVE	+ ING	= ACHIEVING	+ MENT	= ACHIEVEMENT

Pay attention to the spelling words.
1. Why is the final silent e dropped from the words in the first column to form the word in the

   middle column? _____

   _____
2. What three suffixes have been added to form the words in the last column?

   _____ _____ _____
3. Does each suffix begin with a consonant or a vowel? _____
4. What happens to the final e when a suffix beginning with a consonant is added?

   _____

> When you add a suffix that begins with a consonant to a word that ends with silent **e**, keep the final **e**. When you add a suffix that begins with a vowel to a word that ends with silent **e**, drop the final **e**.

1. **a·chieve**   *v.* **a·chieved, a·chiev·ing** to succeed in doing; to accomplish
2. **a·chieve·ment**   *n.* success; an achievement or thing achieved
3. **a·chiev·ing**   *v.* present tense of achieve
4. **age**   *n.* the time that a person or thing existed since birth or beginning *–v.* **aged, ag·ing** or **age·ing**[5] to grow old or become mature
5. **age·less**   *adj.* seemingly not growing older; eternal
6. **age·ing**   *v.* present tense of age
7. **a·muse**   *v.* **a·mused, a·mus·ing** entertain; keep pleasantly interested
8. **a·muse·ment**   *n.* the condition of being amused; something that amuses
9. **a·mus·ing**   *v.* present tense of amuse
10. **blame**   *v.* **blamed, blam·ing** to find fault with; criticize
11. **blame·less**   *adj.* not deserving to be blamed
12. **blam·ing**   *v.* present tense of blame
13. **com·plete**   *adj.* entire; whole; lacking no part *–v.* **–plet·ed, –plet·ing** to end; finish
14. **com·plete·ly**   *adv.* in a complete manner
15. **com·plet·ing**   *v.* present tense of complete
16. **con·fine**   *n.* border *–v.* **–fined , –fin·ing** to enclose; to keep shut in
17. **con·fine·ment**   *n.* a confining or being confined
18. **con·fin·ing**   *v.* present tense of confine
19. **de·fense**   *n.* protection; support
20. **de·fense·less**   *adj.* lacking defense; helpless
21. **de·fen·sive**   *adj.* feeling under attack ane needing to justify
22. **def·i·nite**   *adj.* precise and clear in meaning; certain; positive
23. **def·i·nite·ly**   *adj.* in a definite manner
24. **def·i·ni·tion**   *n.* statement of the meaning of a word or phrase
25. **en·dorse**   *v.* **–dorsed, –dors·ing** to support; to give approval
26. **en·dorse·ment**   *n.* a statement endorsing someone or thing
27. **en·dors·ing**   *v.* present tense of endorse
28. **en·gage**   *v.* **–gaged, –gag·ing** to occupy the attention of; hire; to bind by promise; to betroth
29. **en·gage·ment**   *n.* a betrothal; an appointment to meet someone or go somewhere
30. **en·gag·ing**   *v.* present tense of engage; *–adj.* attractive, charming
31. **fes·tive**   *adj.* of or for a feast or festival; joyous, merry
32. **fes·tive·ly**   *adv.* in a manner relating to a feast or festival
33. **fes·tiv·i·ty**   *n.* merrymaking, gaiety
34. **in·tense**   *adj.* occurring in a high degree; very strong
35. **in·tense·ly**   *adv.* in an intense manner
36. **in·ten·sive**   *adj.* characterized by intensity; thorough
37. **like**   *n.* preference *–v.* **liked, lik·ing** want; wish; take pleasure in
38. **like·ly** *adj.* reasonably expected; suitable; having good prospects *–adv.* probably
39. **lik·ing**   *n.* preference; taste; pleasure
40. **love**   *n.* warm feelings *–v.* **loved, lov·ing** to feel or show love

---

[5] This is a variant spelling of the word. More on that in Lesson 17

41. **love·ly**   *adj.* having qualities that inspire love
42. **lov·ing**   *adj.* feeling or showing love
43. **mea·sure**   *n.* the extent or dimensions of anything   *–v.* **–sured,**
    –sur·ing to find out or estimate the measure
44. **mea·sure·ment**   *n.* a measuring or being measured; the quantity or extent determined by
    measuring
45. **mea·sur·ing**   *v.* present tense of measure
46. **price**   *n.* amount of money asked or paid for something   *–v.* **priced,**
    pric·ing to set a price
47. **price·less**   *adj.* too valuable to be measured by price
48. **pri·cing**   *v.* present tense of price
49. **sense**   *n.* feeling; perception; understanding *–v.* **sensed, sens·ing** to perceive or
    understand
50. **sense·less**   *adj.* not showing good sense; foolish
51. **sen·so·ry**   *adj.* of the senses or sensation
52. **se·vere**   *adj.* harsh or strict; intense; difficult
53. **se·vere·ly**   *adv.* in a harsh or strict manner
54. **se·ver·i·ty**   *n.* strictness, harshness, extreme hardship
55. **state**   *n.* set of circumstances; condition   *–v.* **sta·ted, sta·ting** to set or
    establish by specifying
56. **state·ment**   *n.* the act of stating or the thing stated
57. **stat·ing**   *v.* present tense of state
58. **time**   *n.* occurrence, duration   *–v.* **timed, tim·ing** to measure duration
59. **time·ly**   *adj.* happening at a suitable time
60. **tim·ing**   *n.* arranging the time of something so as to get the best results
    –v. present tense of time

Practicing the words

A. Write the base form of each word and its abbreviated part of speech[6]. Then write the related form made by adding **ing** to the base and write its abbreviated part of speech.

		Base Form	**ing** Form
1	Achievement	_____	_____
2	Ageless	_____	_____
3	Completely	_____	_____
4	Confinement	_____	_____
5	Timely	_____	_____
6	Amusement	_____	_____
7	Engagement	_____	_____
8	Blameless	_____	_____
9	Measurement	_____	_____
10	Endorsement	_____	_____

---

[6]   If the word can be used as more than one part of speech, write the first one listed in the dictionary.

B. Proofreading
Cross out the misspelled words in these announcements. Write the words correctly

ENTERTAINMENT THIS MONTH

Here for a limited engagment!
SuperMalach 4
A marvelous achievemint in moviemaking!
Definitely one movie to see!

Add to your holiday festivety
with **Family Day** at exciting
Westernland Amusment Park.
All children free!
(You'll never read another statment like this!)

Super Circus!
Come see it all!
Vicious lions (in safe confinment)!
Death-defying acts of untold severety!
Comic clowns and amusing animals!
Music, costumes, and other sensery delights!

Super Sidewalk Sale
All merchants (by definiteon) will have
their merchandise out on the sidewalks!
All priceing will be unbelievably low,
Come and browse!

Miracle Health Club Picnic.
Defenseve about your weight?
If your measurments don't change after an
intenseve day with us, we'll give you a
year's membership free!
*Paid endorsment.

1. _____

2. _____

3. _____

4. _____

5. _____

6. _____

7. _____

8. _____

9. _____

10. _____

11. _____

12. _____

13. _____

14. _____

19

Writing

C. Answer each question with a complete sentence that uses a related form of the spelling word in the sentence by adding a suffix to the underlined word.

1. What is a festive custom that your family will do this month? _____

_____

2. What is the meaning of the severe expression on the principal's face today? _____

_____

3. What time will Yizkor be recited on Yom Kippur? _____

_____

4. Which part of Sukkos do you love most? _____

_____

5. Which of the Baalei Tefillah do you like best? _____

_____

6. How much do you expect to pay for a complete set of Arba Minim? _____

_____

7. Did Agudas Yisroel take a definite stance about the school vouchers? _____

_____

8. What part of Yom Kippur tefillos do you find very intense? _____

_____

9. What defense will you use to protect against bees or wasps in your sukkah? _____

_____

10. What determines the price of a chinuch set of Arba Minim? _____

_____

11. Who is to blame for the disruption during the tekiyos? _____

_____

12. Until what age do children eat on Yom Kippur? _____

_____

13. What is the sense of spending so much time praying if one does not understand the meaning of

his words? _____

_____

14. Why did Shmuel confine his rabbit to his backyard? _____

_____

15. Why did the Vaad endorse the Democratic candidate for town council? _____

_____

16. Do you know if it is permitted to measure a shofar on Rosh Hashanah? _____

_____

17. Does any portion of Yomim Noraim preparations amuse you? _____

_____

18. What precautions will you take not to engage in idle speech? _____

_____

19. What is the state of the shul's financial circumstances? _____

_____

20. What goals do you wish to achieve during this coming school year? _____

_____

D. Proofreading
The right base word used with the incorrect suffix or ending can make a confusing story. Mrs. Tzudreiterovits has botched up her narrative paragraph[7]. Find the ten mismatched words in her story. Then write the spelling words that could be used to replace them.

The accidental loss of the pricely ring seemed sensory. Measurement the value of the loving antique, which had been given to my great-grandmother for her engaging, was impossible. It was definition a possession that was not liking to be replaced. Our intensely search finally uncovered the culprit. He was swinging on his perch, looking completing blaming, with the ring in his beak!

1. _____

2. _____

3. _____

4. _____

5. _____

6. _____

7. _____

8. _____

9. _____

10. _____

_____

[7] A narrative paragraph is one that tells a story.

E. Fill in the following sentences with the appropriate spelling words.

1. The first night of סליחות, the בית מדרש was __ __ __ __ __ __ __ __ __ full of people.

2. No one is __ __ __ __ __ __ __ you for the mistake.

3. On Shabbos, __ __ __ __ __ __ __ __ __ __ (מדידה) is only permitted for a מצוה purpose.

4. Over the year, you will be __ __ __ __ __ __ __ __ __ great results.

5. The holiday season is a time of __ __ __ __ __ __ __ __ __.

6. The superstorm __ __ __ __ __ __ __ __ damaged the fruit trees.

7. The package will __ __ __ __ __ __ __ __ __ __ arrive by Thursday.

8. The cheese was wrapped up and stored for __ __ __ __ __.

9. What sort of __ __ __ __ __ __ __ __ park would only have four roller coasters?

10. A comedian needs good __ __ __ __ __ __ to be funny.

11. The soldiers underwent __ __ __ __ __ __ __ __ __ training.

12. This __ __ __ __ __ __ __ __ __ argument should stop immediately.

13. Mendel was looking forward to celebrating his sister's __ __ __ __ __ __ __ __ __ __.

14. The weather had been unusually __ __ __ __ __ __ for autumn.

15. The young fawn was __ __ __ __ __ __ __ __ __ __ __ without its mother.

16. Do you find the rules __ __ __ __ __ __ __ __ __?

17. The agency wrote a letter __ __ __ __ __ __ __ the options.

18. If you study diligently, you are __ __ __ __ __ __ to get a good grade.

19. We are __ __ __ __ __ __ __ the tickets below last year's costs.

20. The candidate's __ __ __ __ __ __ __ __ __ __ __ made him a popular choice.

Spelling Lesson 3

Key Concepts
- base word
- suffix
- related forms of words
- parts of speech (noun, verb, adjective, adverb)
- hard and soft sounds
- possessive form of nouns

A **base word** is a word before any changes have been made.

A **suffix** is a word ending that changes the use of a word or its function.

Words that share the same base word, but have different prefixes or suffixes are **related forms** of the base word.

Related forms of the same base word may be different **parts of speech**. They may be nouns, adjectives, verbs, or adverbs.

There are four parts of speech used to categorize most of the spelling words in this book. **Nouns** (n.) are persons, places, or things (both things you can touch like objects, and things you cannot touch like ideas). **Adjectives** (adj.) are words that are used to modify (describe, limit, or tell you about) nouns. **Verbs** (v.) are actions (like eating or jumping) or states of being (like awake, alive, existing). **Adverbs** (adv.) are words that modify (describe, limit, or tell you about) verbs.

A hard sound is one that is short and explosive, that comes out of the mouth with a popping sound. It cannot be lengthened for an appreciable amount of time. Some examples of hard sounds are **b**, **p**, and **d**.

A soft sound is one that comes out of the mouth along with air in a sort of hissing sound. It can be short or lengthened without changing its sound. Some examples of soft sounds are **ch**, **s**, and **th**.

The **possessive** form of the noun shows that something belongs to a noun. The usual way to make a possessive form is to add **'s** to the noun (girl+**'s** = girl's, men+**'s** = men's).[8]

Remember: A word that describes an action is a verb: **decorate**.
A word that names something is a noun: **decoration.**
ate is a verb ending   **ion** is a noun ending

Remember: The spelling rule from Lesson 1 was when you add a suffix that begins with a vowel to a word that ends with silent **e**, drop the final **e**.

The word ending pronounced **shun** is usually spelled **tion**. Many verbs that end with **ate** can be changed to nouns by adding the suffix **ion**. The hard **t** in **ate** becomes a soft **t** in **tion**.

Suffixes used in this lesson, together with their meanings:
- -ate (indicating a verb)
- -ion (the act of, condition of, or result of)

---

[8]   See more about possessives in Lesson 14.

1.	EQUATE	+	ION	=	EQUATION
2.	SEPARATE	+	ION	=	SEPARATION
3.	NARRATE	+	ION	=	NARRATION
4.	DECORATE	+	ION	=	DECORATION
5.	HIBERNATE	+	ION	=	HIBERNATION
6.	LEGISLATE	+	ION	=	LEGISLATION
7.	INFLATE	+	ION	=	INFLATION
8.	IRRITATE	+	ION	=	IRRITATION
9.	OBLIGATE	+	ION	=	OBLIGATION
10.	CONGREGATE	+	ION	=	CONGREGATION
11.	EVALUATE	+	ION	=	EVALUATION
12.	CREATE	+	ION	=	CREATION
13.	NAVIGATE	+	ION	=	NAVIGATION
14.	COORDINATE	+	ION	=	COORDINATION
15.	EVACUATE	+	ION	=	EVACUATION
16.	GENERATE	+	ION	=	GENERATION
17.	MANIPULATE	+	ION	=	MANIPULATION
18.	DOMINATE	+	ION	=	DOMINATION
19.	PARTICIPATE	+	ION	=	PARTICIPATION
20.	ISOLATE	+	ION	=	ISOLATION

Pay attention to the spelling words.
All of the base words on this list end with the same three letters.

1. What are those letters? _____

2. Is the final **e** pronounced or silent? _____

3. Does the letter **t** have a hard sound (ra<u>t</u>e) or a soft sound (na<u>t</u>ion)? _____

4. What are the last four letters of each word after the ion suffix is added? _____

5. What happens to the final silent e? _____

6. Does the letter t have a hard or soft sound? _____

The word ending pronounced **shun** is usually spelled **tion**. Many verbs that end with **ate** can be changed to nouns by adding the suffix **ion**. The hard **t** in **ate** becomes a soft **t** in **tion**. It might help you to remember that the noun ending ends in **n** (io<u>n</u>).

---

1. **con·gre·gate**   *v.* **–ga·ted, –ga·ting** to come together, usually for a purpose
2. **con·gre·ga·tion**   *n.* 1. a gathering of people or things   2. a group of people meeting for religious worship
3. **co·or·di·nate, co·or·di·nate**[9]   *adj.* of equal order, rank, or importance [the *coordinate* main clauses in a compound sentence]   *–v.* **–na·ted, –na·ting** to bring into proper order or relation
4. **co·or·di·na·tion, co·or·di·na·tion**   *n.* 1. a bringing into proper order; adjusting   2. harmonious or coordinated action, as of muscles
5. **co·or·di·na·tor, co·or·di·na·tor**   *n.* one who coordinates
6. **cre·ate**   *v.* **–a·ted, –a·ting** to make or cause to come into being, to bring into existence through artistic means
7. **cre·a·tion**   *n.* anything created; esp., something original created by the imagination
8. **cre·a·tor**   *n.* one who creates
9. **dec·o·rate**   *v.* **–ra·ted, –ra·ting** 1. to make more attractive by adding ornament, color, etc.   2. to award a mark of honor
10. **dec·o·ra·tion**   *n.* 1. the act of decorating   2. anything used for decorating 3. a medal, badge, or similar token of honor
11. **dec·o·ra·tor**   *n.* one who decorates
12. **dom·i·nate**   *v.* **–na·ted, –na·ting** to rule or control by superior power or influence
13. **dom·i·na·tion**   *n.* 1. social control by dominating   2. power to dominate or defeat
14. **e·quate**   *v.* **–qua·ted, –qua·ting** 1. to consider as similar or the same   2. to be equivalent or parallel, as in mathematics   3. to make the same
15. **e·qua·tion**   *n.* a statement of equality between two entities, as shown by the equal sign (=) [a quadratic *equation*]
16. **e·vac·u·ate**   *v.* **–a·ted, –a·ting** to remove (inhabitants, troops, etc.) from (a place or area), as for protective purposes
17. **e·vac·u·a·tion**   *n.* 1. the act of removing the contents of something   2. the act of evacuating; leaving a place in an ordinary fasion
18. **e·val·u·ate**   *v.* **–a·ted, –a·ting** to judge or determine the worth or quality of; appraise
19. **e·val·u·a·tion**   *n.* 1. act of determining the worth of   2. an appraisal of the value of something
20. **gen·er·ate**   *v.* **–ra·ted, –ra·ting** 1. bring into existence; produce   2. make (offspring) by reproduction
21. **gen·er·a·tion**   *n.* 1. a single stage in the history of a family [father and daughter are two *generations*] 2. the average period (about thirty years) between the birth of one generation and the birth of the next
22. **gen·e·ra·tor**   *n.* one who or that generates

---

[9]   Variant means an alternate. When a word can be spelled in more than one way, the variant spelling is listed after the first (or main) entry word. The dictionary is showing that the word can be spelled with or without a hyphen. More on variants in Lesson 17.

23. **hi·ber·nate**   *v.* **–na·ted, –na·ting** to spend the winter in a dormant or inactive state

24. **hi·ber·na·tion**   *n. 1.* the dormant or resting state in which some animals pass the winter   2. the act of retiring into inactivity

25. **in·flate**   *v.* **–fla·ted, –fla·ting** 1. to exaggerate or make bigger   2. to fill with gas or air 3. to cause prices to rise by increasing the available currency or credit

26. **in·fla·tion**   *n.* 1. the act of filling something with air   2. an increase in the amount of money in circulation that causes a fall in its value and a rise in prices

27. **ir·ri·tate**   *v.* **–ta·ted, –ta·ting** cause annoyance in; disturb, especially by minor irritations

28. **ir·ri·ta·tion**   *n.* 1. the act or condition of being irritated   2. a sore or inflamed condition

29. **i·so·late**   *v.* **–la·ted, –la·ting** place or set apart; separate

30. **i·so·la·tion**   *n.* a setting apart or being set apart from others

31. **leg·is·late**   *v.* **–la·ted, –la·ting** to make laws

32. **leg·is·la·tion**   *n.* 1. the making of a law   2. the law or laws made

33. **leg·is·la·tor**   *n.* one who legislates

34. **ma·ni·pu·late**   *v.* **–la·ted, –la·ting** 1. influence or control cleverly, shrewdly, or deviously 2. hold something in one's hands and move it

35. **ma·ni·pu·la·tion**   *n.* skillful handling or operation, clever or dishones management or control

36. **nav·i·gate**   *v.* **–ga·ted, –ga·ting** 1. travel on water   2. direct carefully and safely

37. **nav·i·ga·tion**   *n.* 1. the science of locating the position and plotting the course of ships   2. the guidance of a ship or airplane

38. **nav·i·ga·tor**   *n.* one who navigates

39. **nar·rate**   *v.* **–ra·ted, –ra·ting** 1. to recite or give a detailed account of   2. provide commentary (for a film or play)

40. **nar·ra·tion**   *n.* telling of a story or of happenings

41. **nar·ra·tor**   *n.* one who narrates

42. **ob·li·gate**   *v.* **–ga·ted, –ga·ting** 1. force somebody to do something   2. cause to be indebted

43. **ob·li·ga·tion**   *n.* a legal or moral responsibility

44. **par·ti·ci·pate**   *v.* **–pa·ted, –pa·ting** to have or take a share with others (in an activity, etc.)

45. **par·ti·ci·pa·tion**   *n.* the act of sharing in the activities of a group; involvement

46. **sep·a·rate**   *v.* **–ra·ted, –ra·ting** 1. act as a barrier   2. to force or pull apart   3. to divide

47. **sep·a·ra·tion**   *n.* 1. a dividing or coming apart   2. an arrangement by which a husband and wife live apart by agreement or court decree

Practicing the words

A. Complete each pair of sentences with a noun form (**ion**) and a verb form (**ate**) of the same word. Also write the abbreviation of which part of speech it is after writing the sentence.

1. Judges filled out _____ forms on each contestant. _____

   The teacher will _____ the results of the tests. _____

2. The soldier was awarded a _____ for bravery. _____

   Who will volunteer to _____ the gym for the party? _____

3. The lonely forest gave the campers a feeling of _____. _____

   One avalanche can _____ that mountain village for months. _____

4. The magician baffled us with the clever _____ of his props. _____

   The machine operator must _____ those levers in a certain order. _____

5. Can you _____ the boat between those rocks? _____

   The co-pilot took over the _____ of the airplane. _____

6. Does the furnace _____ generate enough heat? _____

   What music did people in our grandparents' _____ listen to? _____

7. The math teacher wrote the _____ on the whiteboard. _____

   Would you _____ being happy with being successful? _____

8. All students are expected to _____ in the class project. _____

   _____ in the sports program is voluntary. _____

9. How does one _____ the egg white from the yolk? _____

   They hung the curtain to make a _____ between men and women. _____

10. Sometimes people _____ after eating cholent on Shabbos afternoon. _____

    Bears usually find a cave for their winter _____. _____

11. Jews commemorate the 6 days of _____ by keeping Shabbos. _____

    Shimshy and Boruch will _____ a new shlok for Sukkos this year. _____

12. New _____ about how to vote is a topic full of contention. _____

    Congress will _____ a new law prohibiting vaping in public. _____

28

13. The First Amendment protects Americans' right to _____. _____

    The _____ responds to the chazzan when he recites kaddish. _____

14. The pilot needed assistance of his instruments for _____ of the flight. _____

    A kosher Waze device can help you _____ your way back home. _____

15. Shmerel's mother can help you _____ your next event. _____

    With everyone's _____, the sukkah was erected in no time. _____

16. The play director hired a professional for the _____. _____

    Your essay should _____ the family trip during summer vacation. _____

17. Sometimes the Ballooner Rebbe needs a pump to _____ balloons. _____

    Since Corona, there is _____, which signifies that Moshiach near. _____

18. When faced with _____, remember that Hashem controls everything. _____

    My mother told me not to _____ my younger sister. _____

19. The tower's shakiness spurred an _____ order by the fire department. _____

    When a hurricane nears, officials _____ tourists from the beaches. _____

20. Four nations seem to contend for _____ over the world. _____

    In the future, Hashem's Kingdom will _____ the entire world. _____

B. Unscramble the nouns in the first column. First find and circle the **ion** ending. It is not scrambled. Then unscramble the verbs in the second column. Begin by circling the **ate** ending.

1. ticapionartpi	_____	1. atetrir	_____
2. gotbionail	_____	2. sliateo	_____
3. etihbnriona	_____	3. rodcoatein	_____
4. nimdionoat	_____	4. gatergeocn	_____
5. artegenion	_____	5. sigateell	_____
6. utqionea	_____	6. atelogbi	_____
7. vucionatea	_____	7. modinate	_____
8. tionrapase	_____	8. aterec	_____
9. vanigionat	_____	9. panimateul	_____
10. veautliona	_____	10. breatehin	_____
11. rarionata	_____	11. uateqe	_____
12. attionirri	_____	12. ateatipcipr	_____
13. asionloti	_____	13. ecateord	_____
14. taionocridon	_____	14. eregaten	_____
15.iongoegncrtar	_____	15. auveatec	_____
16. elialiongst	_____	16. prateeas	_____
17. aretionc	_____	17. iatevagn	_____
18. nplaionatimu	_____	18. liatenf	_____
19. crdionaeot	_____	19. ulateeav	_____
20. liafiont	_____	20. anaterr	_____

C.

Many words that end with **ate** have a noun form that ends with **or**: narrate – narrator. Add **or** to some of the **ate** verbs from your spelling list to make nouns that match the definitions below. Then add **'s** to each noun to make a possessive form that completes each phrase. The possessive form of a noun shows that something belongs to it.

1. makes laws   _____ a _____ vote

2. tells a story   _____ the _____ voice

3. finds the way   _____ a _____ map

4. produces energy   _____ the _____ power

5. brings into being   _____ the _____ masterpiece

6. brings order   _____ the _____ plan

7. makes attractive   _____ the _____ fabrics

Now expand five of the phrases into complete sentences.

_____

_____

_____

_____

_____

_____

_____

_____

D. Complete each sentence with a spelling word.

1. Both sides of an __ __ __ __ __ __ __ must be equal.

2. To ensure __ __ __ __ __ __ __ __ __ of men and women, a mechitzah is placed.

3. His essay was a __ __ __ __ __ __ __ __ __ of the entire trip.

4. If you enhance the __ __ __ __ __ __ __ __ __ __ of your Sukkah, you are performing hiddur mitzvah.

5. When animals go into winter __ __ __ __ __ __ __ __ __ __ __, their body rests in an inactive state.

6. With new __ __ __ __ __ __ __ __ __ __ against vaping about to take effect, I know someone who is going out of business.

7. In the times of chevlei Moshiach we can expect __ __ __ __ __ __ __ __ __, as the Mishnah says that יוקר יאמיר – prices will significantly increase.

8. When faced with __ __ __ __ __ __ __ __ __ __, I remind myself that כעס is a terrible עבירה.

9. It is a positive __ __ __ __ __ __ __ __ __ __ to hear the shofar blown on Rosh Hashanah.

10. The י"ג מידות may only be said with a __ __ __ __ __ __ __ __ __ __ __ __ – when a complete minyan is present.

11. As the Yomim Norayim approach, __ __ __ __ __ __ __ __ __ of our conduct throughout the year is expected.

12. On Rosh Hashanah we celebrate the __ __ __ __ __ __ __ __ of man, when Hashem's Kingship began.

13. A map used to be essential for __ __ __ __ __ __ __ __ __, before the GPS became so widespread.

14. With the entire family's __ __ __ __ __ __ __ __ __ __ __, we erected our sukkah in no time at all.

15. As the hurricane approached, mandatory __ __ __ __ __ __ __ __ __ __ forced the vacationers away from the shore.

16. My grandparents were from a different __ __ __ __ __ __ __ __ __ __, they never owned a computer, let alone used a cell phone.

17. Students use all sorts of __ __ __ __ __ __ __ __ __ __ __ to avoid being responsible for their behavior.

18. America, China, Russia, and Iran seem to contend for __ __ __ __ __ __ __ __ __ __ over the world.

19. Everyone's __ __ __ __ __ __ __ __ __ __ __ __ is necessary to get the work done properly.

20. Unvaccinated people are sometimes kept in __ __ __ __ __ __ __ __ __ after having been exposed to contagious diseases like measles.

Key Concepts
- base word
- prefix

A **base word** is a word before any changes have been made.

A prefix is a group of letters added to the beginning of a word to change its meaning. This might alter the pronunciation of the word, but its spelling should not change.

Understanding the meaning of basic prefixes will help you understand the meaning of many new words. In addition, recognizing the prefix can help you remember how to spell the word.

Lesson Spelling Rule: A prefix can be added directly to a base word to form a new word with a different meaning. The spelling of the base word does not change when a prefix is added.

Prefixes used in this lesson, together with their meanings:
- re- means back, again, anew
- ex- means beyond, out of, thoroughly, former, previous
- in- means in, into, within, on, toward; no, not, without
- de- means away from; reverse the action of
- pro- means before in place or time; forward or ahead; supporting, favoring
- dis- means away, apart; not; opposite of
- sub- means under, beneath; lower in position; to a lesser degree; by division into smaller parts
- pre- means before in time, place or rank
- con- means with, together, or all together; very or very much
- per- means throughout; thoroughly

1.	RE	+	STRAIN	=	RESTRAIN
2.	RE	+	QUEST	=	REQUEST
3.	EX	+	PLAIN	=	EXPLAIN
4.	EX	+	CHANGE	=	EXCHANGE
5.	IN	+	JUSTICE	=	INJUSTICE
6.	IN	+	CORPORATE	=	INCORPORATE
7.	DE	+	NOTATION	=	DENOTATION
8.	DE	+	MERIT	=	DEMERIT
9.	PRO	+	CLAIM	=	PROCLAIM
10.	PRO	+	PORTION	=	PROPORTION
11.	DIS	+	SATISFIED	=	DISSATISFIED
12.	DIS	+	CHARGE	=	DISCHARGE
13.	SUB	+	STANDARD	=	SUBSTANDARD
14.	SUB	+	COMMITTEE	=	SUBCOMMITTEE
15.	PRE	+	HISTORIC	=	PREHISTORIC
16.	PRE	+	JUDGE	=	PREJUDGE
17.	CON	+	TRIBUTE	=	CONTRIBUTE
18.	CON	+	GENIAL	=	CONGENIAL
19.	PER	+	FUME	=	PERFUME
20.	PER	+	MISSION	=	PERMISSION

Pay attention to the spelling words.

1. What ten prefixes have been added to form spelling words? _____ _____ _____

   _____ _____ _____ _____ _____ _____ _____

2. Were the prefixes added to complete words? _____

3. Does the spelling of the prefix or the base word change when the two are joined? _____

4. Does the meaning of the word change when the prefix is added? _____

A prefix can be added directly to a base word to form a new word with a different meaning. The spelling of the base word does not change when a prefix is added.

35

1. **change**   *n.* a difference   *–v.* **changed, chan·ging** to make different
2. **charge**   *n.* the quantity that an apparatus is fitted to hold   *–v.* **charged, char·ging** to completely fill
3. **claim**   *n.* a request; a demand; something claimed   *–v.* **claimed, claim·ing** demand, to ask for
4. **com·mit·tee**   *n.* a group of persons appointed to perform some service or function
5. **con·gen·ial**   *adj.* similar, compatible; suited to one's needs, mood, or nature; agreeable
6. **con·tri·bute**   *v.* **–bu·ted, –bu·ting** to give to a common fund, as for charity, education, etc.
7. **cor·por·ate**   *adj.* 1. forming, of, or belonging to a corporation   2. united or combined into one
8. **de·mer·it**   *n.* a fault; mark recorded against someone for poor conduct or work
9. **de·no·ta·tion**   *n.* the basic literal meaning of a word
10. **dis·charge**   *v.* **–charged, –char·ging** to relieve of a burden; to release or remove; to let out
11. **dis·sat·is·fied**   *adj.* displeased
12. **ex·change**   *v.* **–changed, –chan·ging** to give or receive another thing for   *–n.* a giving or taking of one thing for another
13. **ex·plain**   *v.* **–plained, –plain·ing** to make plain or understandable
14. **fume**   *n.* smokelike or vaporous exhalation
15. **gen·ial**   *adj.* sympathetically cheerful
16. **his·tor·ic**   *adj.* well-known in history
17. **in·cor·po·rate**   *v.* **–ra·ted, –ra·ting** 1. to bring together into a whole, merge   2. to form into a corporation
18. **in·jus·tice**   *n.* an unjust act, injury
19. **judge**   *n.* a person qualified to decide; to pass judgment   *–v.* **judged, jud·ging** 1. to determine the result   2. to form a critical opinion of
20. **jus·tice**   *n.* lawfulness
21. **mer·it**   *n.* claim to excellence   *–v.* to deserve, be worthy of
22. **miss·ion**   *n.* 1. a group acting on behalf of government   2. a specific task that person(s) was sent to perform
23. **no·ta·te**   *v.* **–ta·ted, –ta·ting** the act of making notes in writing
24. **no·ta·tion**   *n.* written note
25. **per·miss·ion**   *n.* formal consent
26. **per·fume**   *n.* fragrance; a substance producing a pleasing odor
27. **plain**   *adj.* clear, without extras
28. **por·tion**   *n.* part of a whole   *–v.* to divide
29. **pre·his·tor·ic**   *adj.* of the period before recorded history
30. **pre·judge**   *v.* **–judged, –jud·ging** to judge beforehand, or before one knows enough to judge
31. **pro·claim**   *v.* **–claimed, –claim·ing** to announce to the public officially

32. **pro·por·tion**   *n.* comparative relation of one thing to another; pleasing arrangement; balance of parts
33. **quest**   *v.* **ques·ted, ques·ting** to search
34. **re·quest**   *v.* **–ques·ted, –ques·ting** to ask for (esp. in a polite way) *–n.* an asking for something, something asked for
35. **re·strain**   *v.* to hold back from action, to curb, to limit, restrict
36. **sa·tis·fied**   *adj.* content
37. **stan·dard**   *n.* 1. basis of comparison   2. ethics established by authority or custom *adj.* conforming to custom
38. **strain**   *v.* **strained, strain·ing** to exert, use to the utmost; injure or hurt
39. **sub·stan·dard**   *adj.* below some standard set by law or custom
40. **sub·com·mit·tee**   *n.* any of the small committees with special duties into which a main committee may be divided
41. **tri·bute**   *n.* gift; forced payment; tax

Practicing the words
A. Write the spelling word that contains each smaller word. Do not repeat a word.

1. mitt _____

2. just _____

3. aim _____

4. miss _____

5. sat _____

6. rate _____

7. but _____

8. on _____

9. it _____

10. his _____

11. port _____

12. rain _____

13. stand _____

14. not _____

15. char _____

16. lain _____

B. Crossword

Complete the crossword puzzle below

Across
6. Merge; combine with something else
8. To give
9. Exact meaning of a word
11. Ask for

Down
1. Trade
2. Consent
3. To form an opinion before having facts
4. A mark put against someone
5. Not content
7. Agreeable
10. Pleasing fragrance

C. Working with prefixes
Write at least one meaning for each of the following prefixes. Then write the spelling words that match the definitions below. To make it easier for you, the underlined word(s) correspond to the prefix.

per _____   re _____

ex _____   pre _____

pro _____   dis _____

in _____   sub _____

con _____   de _____

1. the opposite of satisfied   _____

2. hold back   _____

3. before recorded history   _____

4. combine into one   _____

5. below a measure of quality   _____

6. announce before the public   _____

7. an act that is not just   _____

8. to clear out confusion   _____

D. Fill in the following sentences with the appropriate spelling words.

1. The flowers' __ __ __ __ __ __ __ scented the night air.

2. How would you __ __ __ __ __ __ __ this Tosafos?

3. The prosecutors demanded a sentence that was beyond __ __ __ __ __ __ __ __ __ __ __.

4. The lawmakers need to address this __ __ __ __ __ __ __ __ __.

5. He was going to __ __ __ __ __ __ __ __ __ __ __ my shtickel in his new sefer.

6. The __ __ __ __ __ __ __ __ __ __ __ __ __ reported to the entire group.

7. A bad middah is a type of __ __ __ __ __ __ __ .

8. As you grow up, you must learn to __ __ __ __ __ __ __ __ your anger.

9. In olden days a town crier used to __ __ __ __ __ __ __ __ the news.

10. Let's __ __ __ __ __ __ __ __ telephone numbers.

11. The teacher is __ __ __ __ __ __ __ __ __ __ __ __ __ with lousy excuses.

12. The exact meaning is a word's __ __ __ __ __ __ __ __ __ __.

13. Those chimneys __ __ __ __ __ __ __ __ __ thick smoke.

14. We __ __ __ __ __ __ __ your presence at our simchah.

15. In a dollar store, you often find __ __ __ __ __ __ __ __ __ __ __ goods sold for discount.

16. Parental __ __ __ __ __ __ __ __ __ __ is required for the field trip.

17. We have very little reliable information about __ __ __ __ __ __ __ __ __ __ __ times.

18. It is unfair to __ __ __ __ __ __ __ __ another's actions.

19. Feel free to __ __ __ __ __ __ __ __ __ __ your ideas for consideration.

20. We are lucky to have such __ __ __ __ __ __ __ __ __ neighbors.

E. Build a word pyramid by following the code. Using your knowledge of prefixes, find the four pyramid words that match the definitions.

The word **claim** means "to call for or demand."

1. to "call out" in public

_____

2. to demand the return of something

_____

3. to "call out" as not being one's own

_____

4. shouted out loud   _____

5. unwanted   _____

		C	L	A	I	M					
	8	4	C	L	A	I	M				
7	8	6	C	L	A	I	M	3	2		
	3	12	C	L	A	I	M	3	2		
	11	5	C	L	A	I	M				
2	4	9	C	L	A	I	M				
		C	L	A	I	M	1		10		

A	D	E	I	N	O	P	R	S	T	U	X
1	2	3	4	5	6	7	8	9	10	11	12

F. Build another word pyramid by following the code. See if you can find the four pyramid words that match the definitions.

The word **tribute** means "something given or assigned."

1. can be "assigned" to a particular person or place

_____

2. to give money to

_____

3. punishment given for a wrong   _____

4. a characteristic "assigned to" a person   _____

		T	R	I	B	U	T	E				
1	12	T	R	I	B	U	T	E				
3	11	8	T	R	I	B	U	T	E			
4	6	11	T	R	I	B	U	T	E			
		T	R	I	B	U	T	1	10	13		
10	5	T	R	I	B	U	T	6	9	8		
1	12	T	R	I	B	U	T	1	2	7	5	

A	B	C	D	E	I	L	N	O	R	S	T	Y
1	2	3	4	5	6	7	8	9	10	11	12	13

G. Prefixes

You can discover or make up your own new words by combining prefixes with base words. Using your understanding of the prefixes and the base words, pick at least one word from each of the following lists and write a definition for it. If you picked a word to which you do not know the definition, get creative and manufacture your own!

- exSTRAIN   inSTRAIN   deSTRAIN   proSTRAIN   disSTRAIN
  subSTRAIN   preSTRAIN   conSTRAIN   erSTRAIN

- exQUEST   inQUEST   deQUEST   proQUEST   disQUEST
  subQUEST   preQUEST   conQUEST   rQUEST

- rePLAIN   inPLAIN   dePLAIN   proPLAIN   disPLAIN
  subPLAIN   prePLAIN   conPLAIN   rPLAIN

- reCHANGE   inCHANGE   deCHANGE   proCHANGE   disCHANGE
  subCHANGE   preCHANGE   conCHANGE   rCHANGE

- reJUSTICE   exJUSTICE   deJUSTICE   proJUSTICE   disJUSTICE
  subJUSTICE   preJUSTICE   conJUSTICE   perJUSTICE

- reCORPORATE   exCORPORATE   deCORPORATE   proCORPORATE
  disCORPORATE   subCORPORATE   preCORPORATE   conCORPORATE
  perCORPORATE

- reNOTATION   exNOTATION   inNOTATION   proNOTATION
  disNOTATION   subNOTATION   preNOTATION   conNOTATION
  perNOTATION

- reMERIT   exMERIT   inMERIT   proMERIT   disMERIT
  subMERIT   preMERIT   conMERIT   perMERIT

- reCLAIM   exCLAIM   inCLAIM   deCLAIM   disCLAIM
  subCLAIM   preCLAIM   conCLAIM   perCLAIM

- rePORTION   exPORTION   inPORTION   dePORTION   disPORTION
  subPORTION   prePORTION   conPORTION   perPORTION

- reSATISFIED
  subSATISFIED

  exSATISFIED
  preSATISFIED

  inSATISFIED
  conSATISFIED

  deSATISFIED
  perSATISFIED

  proSATISFIED

- reCHARGE
  subCHARGE

  exCHARGE
  preCHARGE

  inCHARGE
  conCHARGE

  deCHARGE
  perCHARGE

  proCHARGE

- reSTANDARD
  proSTANDARD
  perTANDARD

  exSTANDARD
  disSTANDARD

  inSTANDARD
  preSTANDARD

  deSTANDARD
  conSTANDARD

- reCOMMITTEE
  proCOMMITTEE
  perCOMMITTEE

  exCOMMITTEE
  disCOMMITTEE

  inCOMMITTEE
  preCOMMITTEE

  deCOMMITTEE
  conCOMMITTEE

- reHISTORIC
  disHISTORIC

  exHISTORIC
  subHISTORIC

  inHISTORIC
  conHISTORIC

  deHISTORIC
  perHISTORIC

  proHISTORIC

- reJUDGE
  disJUDGE

  exJUDGE
  subJUDGE

  inJUDGE
  conJUDGE

  deJUDGE
  perJUDGE

  proJUDGE

- reTRIBUTE
  disTRIBUTE

  exTRIBUTE
  subTRIBUTE

  inTRIBUTE
  preTRIBUTE

  deTRIBUTE
  perTRIBUTE

  proTRIBUTE

- reGENIAL
  disGENIAL

  exGENIAL
  subGENIAL

  inGENIAL
  preGENIAL

  deGENIAL
  perGENIAL

  proGENIAL

- reFUME
  disFUME

  exFUME
  subFUME

  inFUME
  conFUME

  deFUME
  preFUME

  proFUME

- reMISSION
  disMISSION

  exMISSION
  subMISSION

  inMISSION
  conMISSION

  deMISSION
  preMISSION

  proMISSION

Spelling Lesson 5

Key Concepts
- root
- prefix
- suffix

A **root** is a word part that cannot stand alone. It must be joined to other parts to form a word, either a prefix or a suffix. Sometimes, it will be joined with both a prefix and suffix to form a word. The final meaning of the word will usually be a combination of the meaning of the prefix, suffix, and root. When the same root is joined to different prefixes, their meaning is different enough from each other that they are not related words even though they may still have a similar meaning.

A **prefix** is a group of letters added to the beginning of a word to change its meaning. This might alter the pronunciation of the word, but its spelling should not change. A prefix can also be joined before a root to form a word.

A **suffix** is a word ending that changes the use of a word or its function. It can also be joined after a root to form a word.

When you understand the meanings of common prefixes, suffixes, and roots you can easily decipher the meanings of new words you encounter.

Prefix	+ Root	+ Suffix	Complete Word
_____	_____	_____ =	_____
re	flect	Ion	Reflection

Lesson Spelling Rule: A root can be joined with many different prefixes. Changing the prefix forms a word with a different meaning.

Roots used in this lesson, together with their meanings:
- CESS means to yield, or to move – related words have to do with moving or giving up
- STITUTE means to stand – related words have to do with conceptual STANDING in the sense of right to exist, rather than the act of staying straight up
- FLECT means to bend
- SPIRE means breath[10] – related words have to do with air or ideas
- HIBIT means to hold – refers to physical holding, as well as to supporting, showing, or maintaining
- JECT means to throw
- SUADE means to urge
- SUME means to take up, or to add – refers to physically adding, as in sums of addition; as well as to taking on ideas.

The root ject means "to throw."
>   deject = to throw down, depress
>   reject = to throw back
>   project = to throw forth or forward

---

[10]   Not to be confused with the word **spire**, which means a tall narrow part of a building. **SPIRIT** comes from this root, and it often has a metaphorical aspect in addition to the physical act of breathing.

1. RE + CESS + ION = RECESSION
2. PRO + CESS + ION = PROCESSION
3. CON + CESS + ION = CONCESSION
4. CON + STITUTE + ION = CONSTITUTION
5. SUB + STITUTE + ION = SUBSTITUTION
6. IN + STITUTE + ION = INSTITUTION
7. RE + FLECT + ION = REFLECTION
8. IN + FLECT + ION = INFLECTION
9. PER + SPIRE = PERSPIRE
10. IN + SPIRE = INSPIRE
11. EX + HIBIT = EXHIBIT
12. IN + HIBIT = INHIBIT
13. PRO + HIBIT = PROHIBIT
14. DE + JECT + ION = DEJECTION
15. RE + JECT + ION = REJECTION
16. PRO + JECT + ION = PROJECTION
17. PER + SUADE = PERSUADE
18. DIS + SUADE = DISSUADE
19. PRE + SUME = PRESUME
20. CON + SUME = CONSUME

Pay attention to the spelling words.

1. Before the prefixes and suffixes are added, are the letter group complete words? _____

2. A word part that must be joined to other word parts to for a complete word is called a _____.

3. How many different roots are used in the word list? _____

4. How many words are formed from these roots? _____

5. Do **reject**, **deject**, and **project** have the same root? _____

6. Do they have the same meaning? _____

> A root can be joined with many different prefixes. Changing the prefix forms a word with a different meaning.

1. **con·cede**   *v.* **–ce·ded, –ce·ding** to give up
2. **con·ces·sion**   *n.* 1. a conceding, or giving in   2. the right to sell food, parking space ect. on the landlord's premises
3. **con·sti·tute**   *v.* **–tu·ted, –tu·ting** to form or compose
4. **con·sti·tu·tion**   *n.* 1. the act of forming or establishing something   2. the way that something is formed   3. law determining the fundamental principles of a government
5. **con·sume**   *v.* **–sumed, –sum·ing** 1. to use up; spend or waste (time, energy, money, etc.)   2. to eat or drink up; devour
6. **de·ject**   *v.* **–jec·ted, –jec·ting** lower someone's spirits; make downhearted
7. **de·jec·tion**   *n.* a being dejected or sad; depression
8. **dis·suade**   *v.* **–sua·ded, –sua·ding** to turn (a person) aside (*from* a course of action, etc.) by persuasion or advice
9. **ex·hi·bit**   *v.* **–bi·ted, –bi·ting** to show; display   *–n.* a show; display
10. **in·flect**   *v.* **–flec·ted, –flec·ting** to change the tone of one's voice
11. **in·flec·tion**   *n.* a change in tone or pitch of the voice
12. **in·hi·bit**   *v.* **–bi·ted, –bi·ting** to hold back or keep from some action, feeling, etc. [a person *inhibited* by fear]
13. **in·spire**   *v.* **–spired, –spi·ring** to influence, stimulate, or urge, as to some creative or effective effort
14. **in·sti·tute**   *v.* **–tu·ted, –tu·ting** to establish, or to set up
15. **in·sti·tu·tion**   *n.* 1. an establishes law, custom, practice, etc.   2. an organization having a social, educational, or religious purpose, as a school, reformatory, etc.   3. the act of establishing   4. [Colloq.[11]] a person or thing long established
16. **per·spire**   *v.* **–spired, –spi·ring** to give forth {a characteristic salty moisture) through the pores of the skin; sweat
17. **per·suade**   *v.* **–sua·ded, –sua·ding** to cause to do or believe something, esp. by reasoning, urging, etc.
18. **pre·sume**   *v.* **–sumed, –sum·ing** 1. to take upon oneself without permission; venture [I wouldn't *presume* to tell you what to do]   2. to take for granted; suppose [I *presume* you know the risk you are taking]
19. **pro·cess**   *n.* 1. a particular course of action intended to achieve a result   2. a natural outgrowth from an organism   *–v.* **-cessed, -cess·ing** 1. deal with in a routine way   2. march in a procession
20. **pro·ces·sion**   *n.* a number of persons or things moving forward as in a parade, in an orderly way
21. **pro·ject**   *v.* **–jec·ted, –jec·ting** 1. extend out or protrude in space   2. put out or send forth   3. project onto a screen   *–n.* an undertaking

---

[11]   Colloq. stands for colloquialism. It is means informal speech.

22. **pro·jec·tion**   *n.* 1. something that projects or juts out   2. a prediction based on known facts, data, etc.

23. **pro·hi·bit**   *v.* **–bi·ted, –bi·ting** 1. to refuse to permit; forbid by law or by an order [smoking is *prohibited* in the building]   2. to prevent; hinder

24. **re·cess**   *n.* 1. a hidden or inner place   2. a temporary halting of work, study, etc.   *v.* **-cessed, -cess·ing** to move back or to leave

25. **re·ces·sion**   *n.* 1. a going backward; withdrawal   2. a departing procession   3. a falling off of business activity

26. **re·flect**   *v.* **–flec·ted, –flec·ting** 1. to throw or bend back   2. show an image of

27. **re·flec·tion**   *n.* 1. anything reflected or given back, such as an image   2. the act of bending back   3. serious thought; contemplation

28. **re·ject**   *v.* **–jec·ted, –jec·ting** 1. to refuse to take, agree to, use, believe, etc.   2. to discard as worthless or below standard

29. **re·jec·tion**   *n.* 1. the act of rejecting something   2. the state of being rejected

30. **sub·sti·tute**   *v.* **–tu·ted, –tu·ting** to put in place of another, switch   *–n.* a person or thing that takes the place of another

31. **sub·sti·tu·tion**   *n.* the substituting of one person or thing for another

So how do the word parts add up to the definitions? If you consider the meanings of the prefixes together with the roots, it isn't too difficult to decipher them.

RECESS The root CESS means to yield, or to move, so it has to do with moving or giving up. The prefix RE means back, or again, so to RECESS is to move back or leave. A RECESSION is the act or period of moving back.

PROCESS The root CESS means to yield, or to move, so it has to do with moving or giving up. The prefix PRO means forward, earlier, or in support of, so to PROCESS is to move forward. A PROCESSION is the act of moving forward.

CONCESSION The root CESS means to yield, or to move, so it has to do with moving or giving up. The prefix CON means with, all together, or very, so to CONCEDE is to give up. A CONCESSION is the act of giving up.

CONSTITUTE The root STITUTE means to stand, so it has to do with staying or existing. The prefix CON means with, all together, or very, so to CONSTITUTE is to make all together. CONSTITUTION is what forms something. One's constitution is what he is verily made up of. A nation's constitution is the set of principles of which it is made.

SUBSTITUTE The root STITUTE means to stand, so it has to do with staying or existing. The prefix SUB means under, lesser than, or smaller, so to SUBSTITUTE is to set something else up instead of, or under, the original. SUBSTITUTION is the act of, or the substance which is, substituting.

INSTITUTE The root STITUTE means to stand, so it has to do with staying or existing. The prefix IN means in, or not, so to INSTITUTE is to establish, or to set up. An INSTITUTION is the act of establishing or the establishment.

REFLECT The root FLECT means to bend. The prefix RE means back, or again, so to REFLECT is to bend back. A REFLECTION is the act of bending back, or the thing which is bent back.

INFLECT The root FLECT means to bend. The prefix IN means in, or not, so to INFLECT is to change the tone of one's voice and an INFLECTION is the tone of one's voice.

PERSPIRE The root SPIRE means breath. The prefix PER means throughout or thoroughly. To PERSPIRE is to sweat – because usually one is breathing heavily when they sweat, and it is as though the breathing is permeating their entire body and breathing out. PERSPIRATION is the noun and refers to the act of perspiring or the sweat itself.

INSPIRE The root SPIRE means breath. The prefix IN means in, or not. To infuse with spirit is to INSPIRE; also to move someone to action. The noun is INSPIRATION.

EXHIBIT The root HIBIT means to hold. The prefix EX means out, beyond, or former. To EXHIBIT is to hold out, to display. The noun is EXHIBITION, and refers to the act of displaying or the display itself.

INHIBIT The root HIBIT means to hold. The prefix IN means in, or not, so to INHIBIT is to hold in, to restrain. INHIBITION is the noun which refers to the act of restraining oneself, or to one's hesitations.

PROHIBIT The root HIBIT means to hold. The prefix PRO means forward, earlier, or in support of. To PROHIBIT is to give instructions earlier that hold people back from doing what is forbidden. The noun is PROHIBITION.

DEJECTION The root JECT means to throw. The prefix DE means under, away, or to undo, so to DEJECT is to feel thrown down, sad, or depressed. The noun is DEJECTION.

REJECTION The root JECT means to throw. The prefix RE means back, or again, so to REJECT is to throw back, to return, or to throw away and discard. The noun is REJECTION.

PROJECTION The root JECT means to throw. The prefix PRO means forward, earlier, or in support of, so to PROJECT is to throw forward. This can be physically, when throwing something; or conceptually, when putting forth an idea. PROJECTION is the noun for throwing forward. It also refers to something which sticks forth more than what is around it.

PERSUADE The root SUADE means to urge. The prefix PER means throughout or thoroughly, so to PERSUADE is to thoroughly urge and convince someone. The noun is PERSUASION.

DISSUADE The root SUADE means to urge. The root DIS means away, to undo. To DISSUADE is to urge someone away from something. The noun is DISSUASION.

PRESUME The root SUME means to take up, or to add. This refers to physically adding, as in sums of addition; as well as to taking on ideas. The root PRE means earlier, before., so to PRESUME is to take on an idea before you have adequate information that supports or proves it. (It is similar to ASSUME, yet it does not bear the same connotation of unsupported doubt – it reflects the likelihood of being borne out in fact.) The noun is PRESUMPTION[12].

CONSUME The root SUME means to take up, or to add. The prefix CON means with, all together, or very. To CONSUME is to take on within oneself: to eat. By extension, it refers to destruction; because fire destroys what it 'eats'. The noun is CONSUMPTION and also refers to tuberculosis, a disease which was often fatal because it led to the patient wasting away: being destroyed by it.

---

[12]   Notice the spelling change as the suffix is added. See more examples in Lesson 13

Practicing the words

A. Complete each sentence with two spelling words that have the same root and indicate which part of speech it is by its abbreviation. Some words may be used more than once.

1. The writer had feelings of _____ ____ when she received a

   _____ ____ letter from her publisher.

2. The _____ ____ of graduating students into the auditorium was

   solemn, but the _____ ____ of the same group was noisy and

   cheerful.

3. I _____ ____ you know that you should not

   _____ ____ that entire cake.

4. The actor changed the _____ ____ of his voice so that it was a

   better _____ ____ of his character's mood.

5. If I can't _____ ____ you from trying that skating stunt, can I

   at least _____ ____ you to wear knee pads and a helmet?

6. Seeing those runners _____ ____ does not

   _____ ____ me to take up jogging.

7. Moshe and Yehudis bought popcorn at the _____ ____ stand

   while they watched the _____ ____ of marching bands.

8. Writing a _____ ____ was the first order of business after the

   _____ ____ of the new town council.

9. Travel costs may _____ ____ bringing the

   _____ ____ to other countries.

10. One council member called for the _____ ____ of Plan A after

   reading a _____ ____ of the expected costs.

51

B. Proofreading

Mrs. Tzudreiterovits indulged again in her habit of mixing the wrong prefix with the right root. Help her say what she really means by changing the prefixes of the nine underlined words and writing the words correctly.

Neighbors, what do you think about the <u>constitution</u> of children delivering candy for Mishloach Manos on Purim? Some people believe that we should end this tradition. They try to <u>persuade</u> young people from joining the <u>concession</u> of bell-ringers. They point out that it may not be healthy to <u>presume</u> large amounts of candy and such treats, and that it takes too much time in traffic to deliver to every child's friend. If that is the case, then perhaps each neighborhood could consider a suitable <u>institution</u> for the practice. Maybe children should only give to people who live on their block? On the other hand, most young people would have a feeling of <u>projection</u> if they could not <u>inhibit</u> their clever costumes on Purim. Maybe a period of <u>inflection</u> would <u>perspire</u> parents to find a way to keep Purim fun for all.

1. _____   4. _____   7. _____

2. _____   5. _____   8. _____

3. _____   6. _____   9. _____

C. Fill in the following sentences with the appropriate spelling words.

1. Some people __ __ __ __ __ __ __ a lot even when it is not hot.

2. The הכנסת ספר תורה began with a gala __ __ __ __ __ __ __ __ __ __.

3. If he loses the race, I look forward to enjoying his __ __ __ __ __ __ __ __ __ __

   speech.

4. The pharmacy made a generic __ __ __ __ __ __ __ __ __ __ __ for the brand

   name medication.

5. The president keeps trying to convince voters that a __ __ __ __ __ __ __ __ __ can

   only be prevented by him.

6. You can make a קידוש השם if you __ __ __ __ __ __ __ good behavior.

7. Our school is a private __ __ __ __ __ __ __ __ __ __ and can teach Yidishe

   השקפות.

8. The moon shows a __ __ __ __ __ __ __ __ __ of the sun's light.

9. Rabbi Akiva Eiger was of delicate __ __ __ __ __ __ __ __ __ __ __.

10. Reading about the Chazon Ish should __ __ __ __ __ __ __ you to greater התמדה.

11. We may not __ __ __ __ __ __ __ חמץ on פסח.

12. Learning מוסר helps you __ __ __ __ __ __ __ your יצר הרע.

13. חז"ל __ __ __ __ __ __ __ __ moving מוקצה on שב"ק.

14. He tried to __ __ __ __ __ __ __ __ me from trying e-cigs.

15. The students expressed __ __ __ __ __ __ __ __ when they found out about the

   homework.

16. She was prepared to receive a __ __ __ __ __ __ __ __ notice when submitting a

job application.

17. The סוכה needed to be adjusted to fit the __ __ __ __ __ __ __ __ __ __ of the roof.

18. Can I __ __ __ __ __ __ __ __ you to join the nightly שיעור?

19. The __ __ __ __ __ __ __ __ __ __ of you voice needs to be changed to a question.

20. We __ __ __ __ __ __ __ all תלמידים want to achieve יראת שמים.

D. Build a word pyramid by following the code. Using your knowledge of prefixes, find the four pyramid words that match the definitions. (Inter – means in between.)

The root **jec** means "to throw."

1. an object thrown through the air

_____

2. thrown back, discarded

_____

3. thrown in between

_____

4. something thrown or jutting forward

_____

					J	E	C			
			10	3	J	E	C	11	1	2
		2	3		J	E	C	11	5	8	7
		8	1		J	E	C	11	5	7	4
	9	10	8	J	E	C	11	5	8	7
	9	10	9	J	E	C	11	5	6	3
5	7	11	1	10	J	E	C	11	3	2

B	D	E	G	I	L	N	O	P	R	T
1	2	3	4	5	6	7	8	9	10	11

E. Build another word pyramid by following the code. Using your knowledge of prefixes, find the four pyramid words that match the definitions.

The root **spir** means "breath."

			S	P	I	R			
		1	S	P	I	R	4		
	6	7	S	P	I	R	4		
9	4	10	S	P	I	R	6	7	5
11	10	1	7	S	P	I	R	4	3
2	8	7	S	P	I	R	1	2	12
10	4	S	P	I	R	1	11	6	8	7

A	C	D	E	G	I	N	O	P	R	T	Y
1	2	3	4	5	6	7	8	9	10	11	12

1. A "breathing together", or secret plotting

_____

2. to "breath" enthusiasm into

_____

3. giving forth, or "breathing" moisture through the skin _____

4. the act of breathing _____

55

Review:

Roots used in this lesson, together with their meanings:

- CESS means to yield, or to move – related words have to do with moving or giving up
  - additional words with the root **cess**: accession, excess, precess
- STITUTE means to stand – related words have to do with conceptual STANDING in the sense of right to exist, rather than the act of staying straight up
  - additional words with the root **stitute**: restitution, destitute
- FLECT means to bend
  - additional words with the root **flect**: deflection, deflect
- SPIRE means breath – related words have to do with air or ideas
  - Additional words with the root **spire**: expire, expiration, conspire
- HIBIT means to hold – refers to physical holding, as well as to supporting, showing, or maintaining
  - Additional words with the root **hibit**: disinhibit
- JECT means to throw
  - Additional words with the root **ject**: subject, subjection, conject, conjecture
- SUADE means to urge
  - Additional words with the root **suade**: persuasion, suasion, unpersuade
- SUME means to take up, or to add – refers to physically adding, as in sums of addition; as well as to taking on ideas.
  - Additional words with the root **sume**: consumption, subsume, resume, resumption

Spelling Lesson 6

Key Concepts
- compound word
- changes in language over time
- contraction
- hyphen
- apostrophe

A **compound word** is when two words are connected without any spelling changes to either word. **Compound** means having more than one part. Compound words are sometimes written as a single word, with no space in between them. Other times, they are hyphenated – joined with a hyphen in between them. Language can be really confusing in that way. Not only that, language changes over time and the way words are spelled shifts. How are you supposed to know which words are spelled which way? Generally, when a compound word begins to be used, it needs a hyphen to connect them to prevent confusion because not everyone recognizes the compound word. After a long period of usage, the hyphen begins to be dropped and the compound word is written as a single word. You can consult a dictionary to determine the correct spelling for a compound word. If a good dictionary does not contain an entry for the compound word, you can assume the word is still relatively new and still requires a hyphen.

What is a hyphen, anyway? A **hyphen** is a horizontal line in middle of the height of the line, similar to a dash, but has no space before an after it. It is used the same way you would use a letter in middle of the word – you would not leave an extra space in middle of the word. The difference between a hyphen and a dash is that the dash always has a space both before and after it. The dash is not used as a letter, it is used as a punctuation mark in middle of a sentence. A hyphen is used as a letter – to connect parts of a word to form a single word.

A **contraction** is formed when parts of a word are left out. To contract means to shrink. A longer word can drop some of its letters to form a contraction. Sometimes multiple words drop letters and combine to form a single contraction. But how is the reader to know that you dropped some of the letters? You indicate the missing letters with an apostrophe. Beware a common error – the apostrophe does not necessarily go between the original words, it only goes in place of the missing letters.

An **apostrophe** is a mark that looks like a floating comma. It hovers just above the letters and indicates that some letters were dropped. It also has another function – to indicate possession of a noun.

Lesson Spelling Rule: Complete words can be combined to form other words in several different ways.
When two words are simply connected with no changes in either word, the word formed is called a compound word.
Words joined by a hyphen are another type of compound word.
When an apostrophe is used to show that one or more letters have been omitted the word is called a contraction.

1. BACK + GROUND	= BACKGROUND
2. NET + WORK	= NETWORK
3. SCORE + BOARD	= SCOREBOARD
4. ROOM + MATE	= ROOMMATE
5. ELSE + WHERE	= ELSEWHERE
6. OTHER + WISE	= OTHERWISE
7. WHO + EVER	= WHOEVER
8. ANY + ONE	= ANYONE
9. PROOF + READ	= PROOFREAD
10. FIRE + PROOF	= FIREPROOF
11. LIFE + TIME	= LIFETIME
12. MEAN + WHILE	= MEANWHILE
13. EVERY + WHERE	= EVERYWHERE
14. WHEN + EVER	= WHENEVER
15. SELF + ADDRESSED	= SELF-ADDRESSED
16. BROTHER + IN + LAW	= BROTHER-IN-LAW
17. GREAT + AUNT	= GREAT-AUNT
18. WERE + NOT	= WEREN'T
19. HAVE + NOT	= HAVEN'T
20. SHOULD + HAVE	= SHOULD'VE

Pay attention to the spelling words.

1. In the first thirteen words, are any changes made when the two smaller words are joined? _____

2. Why does **roommate** have two **m's**? _____

3. Why does **background** have a **g**? _____

4. In words 15-17, what punctuation is added to join the words? _____

5. Does the spelling of either word change when the words are joined with the hyphen? _____

6. In the last three words, what punctuation is added to join the pairs of words?

_____

7. What does the apostrophe replace in these words? _____

1. **air·craft**   *n.* any machine designed for flying, whether heavier or lighter than air; airplane, balloon, helicopter, etc.
2. **an·y·one**   *pron*[13]. any person; anybody
3. **back·ache**   *n.* an ache or pain in the back
4. **back·ground**   *n.* 1. the part of a scene or picture toward the back   2. a position that is unimportant or attracts no attention [try to stay in the *background*]
5. **book·keep·er**   *n.* someone who records the transactions of a business
6. **broad·mind·ed**   *adj.* tolerant of other people's opinions and behavior; not bigoted; liberal
7. **broth·er-in-law**   *n., pl.* **broth·ers**[14]**-in-law** 1. the brother of one's husband or wife   2. the husband of one's sister   3. the husband of the sister of one's wife or husband
8. **else·where**   *adv.* in or to some other place; somewhere else
9. **eve·ry·where**   *adv.* in or to every place
10. **fire·proof**   *adj.* that does not burn
11. **great-aunt**   *n.* a sister of any of one's grandparents
12. **have·n't**   have not
13. **life·time**   *n.* the length of time that one lives
14. **make-be·lieve** *n.* a pretending or imagining, as in play   *–adj.* pretended; imagined [a *make-believe* friend]
15. **mean·while**   *adv.* at the same time
16. **net·work**   *n.* 1. netting; mesh   2. an interconnected system of things or people 3. (broadcasting) a chain of transmitting station operated as a unit   4. (electronics) a system of interconnected electronic components
17. **oth·er·wise**   *adj.* 1. in another manner; differently   2. in other circumstances; often used as a conjunction meaning "or else" [please help me; *otherwise* I'll be late]
18. **proof·read**   *v.* **–read·ing** to read and mark corrections on
19. **room·mate**   *n.* a person with whom one shares a room or rooms
20. **score·board**   *n.* a large board for posting the score and other details of a game, as in a baseball stadium
21. **self-ad·dressed**   *adj.* addressed to oneself [a *self-addressed* envelope]
22. **should·'ve**   should have
23. **south·west**   *n.* the direction halfway between south and west; 45° west of due south   *–adj.* in, of, to, or from the southwest
24. **two-tone**   *adj.* having two colors
25. **up·date**   *n.* 1. information or facts that update   2. the act of updating
        –v. **–dat·ed, –dat·ing** to bring up to date; make agree with the most recent facts, methods, ideas, etc.

---

[13]   Pron. stands for pronoun. A pronoun is a part of speech and stands in place of a noun.
[14]   When a noun is made of a hyphenated compound word, the plural is formed by adding **s** to the main noun instead of the end of the compound word.

26. **well-known**   *adj.* widely or generally known; famous
27. **weren't**   were not
28. **when·ev·er**   *adv.* at whatever time
29. **who·ev·er**   *pron.* any person that; whatever person [*whoever* wins gets
    a prize]

Complete words can be combined to form other words in several different ways.
When two words are simply connected with no changes in either word, the word formed is called a compound word.
Words joined by a hyphen are another type of compound word.
When an apostrophe is used to show that one or more letters have been omitted the word is called a contraction.

Practicing the words
A. Find the two or three words in each sentence that can be combined to form a
compound spelling word. Write the word.

1. Where else should we search for the missing boat? _____

2. Have you ever met the cousin who always writes to you? _____

3. The ground in back of the shed needs clearing. _____

4. The coach wrote the score on the board. _____

5. Is one day this week any more convenient than another? _____

6. My brother hopes to work in a good law office. _____

7. Catching the fish with a net was a lot of work. _____

8. It would be wise to postpone the picnic to some other day. _____

9. The mate to that sock is in the laundry room. _____

10. Meshulam was having the time of his life raking the leaves. _____

11. What proof do you have that fire has more than a single color? _____

12. Sarah's aunt sent her a great box of candy for Chanukah. _____

13. While Yaakov worked very hard, Lavan was very mean by switching his wages.

   _____

14. Have you ever wondered when is the ideal time to light Chanukah neiros?

   _____

15. I addressed the speech to my very own self. _____

B. Writing

Compose a sentence using each set of spelling words. You may use the words in any order. Write it on the lines after each set.

  1. scoreboard, should've, roommate_____

_____

_____

  2. anyone, brother-in-law, fireproof_____

_____

_____

  3. weren't, proofread, meanwhile_____

_____

_____

  4. network, elsewhere, whoever_____

_____

_____

  5. otherwise, lifetime, great-aunt_____

_____

_____

C. Proofreading
Cross out the misspelled words that appear in Helpful Hymie's newspaper column. Write the words correctly.

Dear Helpful Hymie: My yeshivah roomate is a very risky fellow. He thinks that his tzitzis are fire-proof and likes to dance around and shake them as he burns his fingernails each Friday afternoon. Meenwhile, any-one who watches him is frightened for his safety. We are worried that his tzitzis might catch fire and transfer the flames elsewere. My brother in-law told me that this is pikuach nefesh and I cannot remain silent in the backround doing nothing about it. What do I do?

Cautious and Concerned

Dear C and C: As long as your friend has not yet gotten burned you were'nt too late. I applaud your efforts for public safety. My grate-aunt always used to say that whooever sees danger has to do something about it whenever they can. You should gather your network of friends and confront the person who is careless with fire. Tell him that there are many opinions that hold it is okay to flush the nails down the toilet. In my entire life-time, I have known only a few people who actually burn theirs. If he still wants to make a fire, he cannot dance around with his strings hanging out. Either he tucks them in or doesn't dance. Otherwize you will have to take matters into your own hands and call the fire department the next time there is danger.

Helpful Hymie

1. _____ 5. _____ 9. _____

2. _____ 6. _____ 10. _____

3. _____ 7. _____ 11. _____

4. _____ 8. _____ 12. _____

D. Using compound words

The following word parts have been joined the same way to make nonsense words. Using your detective skills, re-match them to make compound or hyphenated compound words. Change only the underlined parts. Cross out each part as you use it. The hyphens are provided for you in the sentences as a hint to help you determine how to combine the words.

1. book<u>tone</u> _____
6. south<u>ache</u> _____

2. back<u>west</u> _____
7. well<u>keeper</u> _____

3. broad<u>known</u> _____
8. make<u>craft</u> _____

4. air<u>minded</u> _____
9. up<u>believe</u> _____

5. two<u>date</u> _____

Then use each of the new words to complete the following sentences:

1. The tour bus takes visitors to see the homes of _____-_____ personalities.

2. The _____ found an error in last month's billing.

3. The children were scared, although they knew the story was _____-_____.

4. Jeff suffered from a constant _____ after his accident.

5. I couldn't decide between blue or white, so I got _____-_____ shoes.

6. My parents are _____, so I know they will listen to both sides of the problem.

7. We got lost by going northeast instead of _____.

8. The _____ seemed sturdy, but Alex was still nervous about flying.

9. Radio stations gave an _____ on the situation every hour.

E. Fill in the blanks with the proper spelling word. A space for a hyphen or an apostrophe has also been marked.

1. You will need to __ __ __ __ __ __ __ __ your essay.

2. The Cheder walls are __ __ __ __ __ __ __ __ __.

3. My parents saw many technological changes in their __ __ __ __ __ __ __ __.

4. Torah is being learned __ __ __ __ __ __ __ __ __ across the globe.

5. My __ __ __ __ __ __ __ __ __ __ passed away about seven years ago.

6. Call me __ __ __ __ __ __ __ you are ready.

7. Include a __ __ __ __ __ __ __ __ __ __ __ __ __ envelope with your

    application.

8. The __ __ __ __ __ __ __ __ __ of the painting was light blue.

9. The Alter of Novardok made a large __ __ __ __ __ __ __ of Yeshivos across

    Russia.

10. The football league has a new electronic __ __ __ __ __ __ __ __ __ __.

11. The Rosh Yeshivah was my __ __ __ __ __ __ __ __ when we used to be in

    Yeshivah.

12. If the park is full, we will go __ __ __ __ __ __ __ __ __ to play ball.

13. Unless I tell you __ __ __ __ __ __ __ __ __, you should have the work done in

    class.

14. __ __ __ __ __ __ __ needs help should quietly raise their hand.

15. Has __ __ __ __ __ __ completed the essay yet?

16. __ __ __ __ __ __ __ __ __, all we can do is wait for Moshiach.

17. My __ __ __ __ __ __ __ __ __ __ __ __ __ __ is a choshuveh Yungerman.

18. I __ __ __ __ __ __ yet finished learning Shas.

19. We __ __ __ __ __ __ able to join the chaburah.

20. We __ __ __ __ __ __ __ __ tried harder to make it on time to seder.

Key Concepts
- compound words
- hyphens
- contractions
- apostrophe
- homonyms
- pronouns
- possessive

A **compound word** is when two words are connected without any spelling changes to either word. **Compound** means having more than one part. Compound words are sometimes written as a single word, with no space in between them. Other times, they are hyphenated – joined with a hyphen between them.

A **hyphen** is a horizontal line in middle of the height of the line, similar to a dash, but has no space before and after it. It is used the same way you would use a letter in middle of the word – you do not leave an extra space in middle of the word.

A **contraction** is formed when parts of a word are left out. To contract means to shrink. A longer word can drop some of its letters to form a contraction. Sometimes multiple words drop letters and combine to form a single contraction. The missing letters are indicated with an apostrophe. Beware a common error – the apostrophe does not necessarily go between the original words, it only goes in place of the missing letters.

An **apostrophe** is a mark that looks like a floating comma. It hovers just above the letters and indicates that some letters were dropped. It also has another function – to indicate possession of a noun.

Homonyms are words that sound alike even though they are not spelled the same way.

A **pronoun** is a word that stands in place of a noun. It is treated by the language nearly identically as a noun (adjectives are used for them) – except for possession, and the same pronoun might be used for different nouns.

Possessive is the form of a noun or pronoun that is used to show ownership – that the noun or pronoun owns something. In this respect there is a difference between nouns and pronouns. Possessive nouns have an apostrophe, pronouns do not.

Lesson Spelling Rule: A hyphen is always used when writing out a fraction or when writing compound numbers from twenty-one to ninety-nine.

Possessive pronouns do not contain an apostrophe.

1. ONE + QUARTER	=	ONE-QUARTER
2. TWO + THIRDS	=	TWO-THIRDS
3. FOURTEEN		
4. NINETY + FOUR	=	NINETY-FOUR
5. FORTY + EIGHT	=	FORTY-EIGHT
6. THEIR		
7. THERE		
8. THEY + ARE	=	THEY'RE
9. HERE		
10. HEAR		
11. IT + IS	=	IT'S
12. ITS		
13. THEIRS		
14. THERE + IS or THERE + HAS	=	THERE'S
15. WHOSE		
16. WHO + IS or WHO + HAS	=	WHO'S
17. YOU + ARE	=	YOU'RE
18. YOUR		
19. WEATHER		
20. WHETHER		

A hyphen is always used when writing out a fraction or when writing compound numbers from twenty-one to ninety-nine. Possessive pronouns do not contain an apostrophe.

Pay attention to the spelling words.

1. What punctuation mark is used in between the numbers when writing out fractions? _____

2. Is there a space before or after the hyphen? _____

3. What punctuation mark us used to connect the compound numbers?

    _____

4. Is a hyphen used when writing out numbers that are teens?

    _____

5. What change is made in the spelling of the number four when it is multiplied by ten?_____

6. How many sets of similar-sounding words are in this list?

    _____

7. What are sets of similar-sounding words called? _____

1. **for·ty-eight**   *n.* the number that is the sum of forty-seven and one *–adj.* being more than orty-seven

2. **four·teen**   *n.* the number that is the sum of thirteen and one *–adj.* being more than thirteen

3. **nine·ty-four**   *n.* the number that is the sum of ninety-three and one *–adj.* being more than ninety-three

4. **hear**   *v.* to perceive or sense (sounds) by the ear

5. **here**   *adv.* at, in, or to this place   *–n.* this place or point

6. **it's**   it is

7. **its**   *pron.* (attributive) belonging to it

8. **one-quar·ter**   *n.* a fourth; one of four equal parts

9. **their**   *adj.* of, belonging to, made by, or done by them [*their* books]

10. **theirs**   *pron.* (attributive) belonging to them

11. **there**   *adv.* at, in, or to that place   *–n.* that place or point [we left *there* at six]

12. **there's**   1. there is   2. there has

13. **they're**   they are

14. **two-thirds**   *n.* two of three equal parts

15. **wea·ther**   *n.* atmospheric conditions comprising of the temperature, wind, sun, clouds, and precipitation   *–v.* face and withstand with courage

16. **whe·ther**   *conj*[15]. used to introduce two or more possibilities

17. **whose**   *pron.* that or those belonging to whom [*whose* is this?] *–adj.* of, belonging to, made by, or done by whom or which [the woman *whose* car was stolen]

18. **who's**   1. who is   2. who has

19. **your**   *pron.* (attributive) belonging to you

20. **you're**   you are

---

[15] Conj. stands for conjugation. It is a part of speech that is used to connect or join words or phrases to each other.

Practicing the words
A. Crossword

Complete the crossword puzzle below

Across

3. Listen
4. Belonging to whom
5. Belonging to it
6. Belonging to you
7. Face or withstand with courage
9. This place

Down

1. If
2. 12 plus 2
8. That place

B. Find the two words in each sentence that can be combined to form a compound spelling word. Write the word.

1. Two of the hearty eaters even asked for thirds.

   _____

2. Eight out of forty members were absent from the meeting.

   _____

3. Are you ever going to visit the Kosel Hamaaravi?

   _____

4. Has one got a quarter he can lend me?

   _____

5. Four students scored above ninety on the test.

   _____

6. Is it going to rain today?

   _____

7. Has there been snow this year?

   _____

8. Has someone found out who won the election yet?

   _____

C. Fractions, numbers, and hyphens

The rule for using hyphens when writing out fractions applies only when "translating" the numerical fraction into English words. For example, when writing 2/5 in words, use a hyphen: two-fifths. Even if you are only writing out 1/4, you use a hyphen: one-quarter. However, if you are referring to a single part of a fraction and not writing out the number, then no hyphen is used. For example if you are referring to a half, that is the way it is written – without a hyphen. The same when referring to a quarter, a fifth, or any other such fraction. When you are not writing out the numbers of the fraction, no hyphen is needed.

The rule for compound numbers is that only the numbers from twenty-one to ninety-nine require a hyphen (27 = twenty-seven, 53 = fifty-three, etc.).

Ones and teens are written as a single word (1 = one, 2 = two, 6 = six, 11 = eleven, 15 = fifteen, etc.).

When combining hundreds, thousands, or above with ones, teens, or multiples of ten no hyphen is used between them (106 = one hundred six, 4330 = four thousand three hundred thirty, 2,000,006,019 = two billion six thousand nineteen, etc.)

However, the numbers from twenty-one to ninety-nine require a hyphen between them even when combined with higher numbers. (For example: 252 = two hundred fifty-two, s7029 = even thousand twenty-nine, 8,000,044 = eight million forty-four, etc.)

In addition, when compound numbers that require a hyphen are used to count a higher amount they still require a hyphen (3200 = thirty-two hundred, 87,000 = eighty-seven thousand, etc.).

4322 can be written either four thousand three hundred twenty-two
                        or forty-three hundred twenty-two

Write out the following numbers.

   1. 1/8_____

   2. 7/13_____

   3. 82_____

   4. 17_____

   5. 212_____

   6. 4529_____

   _____

   7. 2700_____

   _____

8. 2/5_____

9. 4/7_____

10. 53,283_____

_____

11. 87,245_____

_____

12. 139,452_____

_____

13. 256,018_____

_____

14. 8/11_____

15. 9/16_____

D. Homonyms

Homonyms are words that sound alike but are spelled differently. Use your understanding of the words to help you complete these sentences with the correct homonyms. It can be very helpful to try and think whether the word is really a contraction of two shorter words. If it is, you can remember to use the apostrophe in place of the missing letters. If it is not a contraction, chances are that there is no need for an apostrophe together with the pronoun.

Complete the following sentences with the correct homonyms:

1. there/they're/their   _____ seems no reason _____ happy about _____ loss.

2. who's/whose   _____ going to the event, and _____ car will he use?

3. wear/where   _____ in the world can I _____ this silly sweater?

4. your/you're   _____ cousin is coming to the siyum _____ making tonight.

5. here/hear   If we _____ the shofar from their minyan, it disturbs over _____.

6. there/they're/their   _____ hats were left _____ in the car with the windows open – _____ going to get ruined in the rain.

7. who's/whose   _____ going to remove the stinky squash _____ smell really disturbs us?

8. wear/where   _____ the handsome sweater, and hang up the ugly one _____ I told you.

9. your/you're   _____ going to be in trouble if you don't put _____ clothes away.

74

10. here/hear   If you _____ the radio over _____, please

    let me know.

11. there/they're/their   _____ looking for _____ car over

    _____.

12. who's/whose   _____ the person _____ portrait is on the

    wall?

13. wear/where   _____ is the shirt I wanted to _____?

14. your/you're   _____ ruining _____ new shoes.

15. here/hear   Can you _____ the music over
    _____?

Associating certain words with one another helps you to remember them. To decide whether to use **hear** or **here**, for example, associate these words:

     Hear goes with ear.   Here goes with there.

Can you find a way to associate other pairs of homonyms that give you trouble?

E. Fill in the blanks with the appropriate spelling word. The space for a hyphen or an apostrophe has also been marked.

1. If you get __ __ __ __ __ __ __ __ __ __ __ on your test, it isn't too bad.

2. Only __ __ __ __ __ __ __ __ __ __ __ of the class stays for Mishmor.

3. __ __ __ __ getting closer to Chanukah.

4. I'm not sure __ __ __ __ __ __ __ there will be mishmor next week.

5. __ __ __ __ __ is a minhag to say selichos on Bahab.

6. Can you __ __ __ __ the chazzan from where you are standing?

7. __ __ __ place is next to the windowsill.

8. The bus popped __ __ __ __ __ ball.

9. __ __ __ __ __ __ going to be a big mesibah.

10. You forgot __ __ __ __ sefer on the bus.

11. __ __ __ __ is the place to light your menorah.

12. Impeaching the president requires a __ __ __ __ __ __ __ __ __ majority of the Senate to convict.

13. The __ __ __ __ __ __ __ is very comfortable this week.

14. Even in Eretz Yisroel, Rosh Hashanah is __ __ __ __ __ __ __ __ __ __ __hours.

15. __ __ __ __ __ __ __ nearly always learning Torah.

16. The job of arranging who will lein was __ __ __ __ __.

17. __ __ __ __ __ trying to complete the entire masechta?

18. __ __ __ __ __ ball did I hit out of the yard?

19. A Bar Mitzvah boy is when he enters year __ __ __ __ __ __ __ __.

20. __ __ __ __ __ __ sure to succeed if you daven for siyata dishemaya.

Key Concepts
- silent partners
- vowels
- syllables
- mnemonics
- synonyms

Every letter is sometimes silent in the English language. There are a number of letter combinations in which a pair of letters are spelled together but only one of them is pronounced. (Think of the word **combination** – how pronounced is the **b**?) These pairs have a **silent partner** – the letter which is silent.

A vowel is a sound that is made with the throat and mouth opened and can be extended for a while. In other words, a vowel is a נְקוּדָה. It functions to help the other sounds of the words come out smoothly and tells you how to pronounce them.

A **syllable** is a word part that has a single vowel sound. It might have a number of vowels (**boat**) or not even a single vowel (dan**g**ling). The key is that it is pronounced as a distinct part of the word separate from the other parts – usually with a separate motion of your mouth. A hint to distinguish the different syllables is to pay attention to your chin as you clearly pronounce the word. Each distinct movement of your chin marks a separate syllable. Sometimes an entire words is a single syllable. This is even true of long words such as **brought**.

Mnemonics is the system of improving memory. A mnemonic device is a memory aid.

A **synonym** is a word that has a similar meaning to another word.

Lesson Spelling Rule: Silent partners are letters which are silent in certain combinations.

1. DESI**GN**ER
2. ALI**GN**MENT
3. CAMPAI**GN**
4. **GN**AWED
5. INDE**BT**ED
6. DOU**BT**FUL
7. **PS**ALMS
8. **PS**YCHOLOGY
9. SPA**GH**ETTI
10. **GH**ETTO
11. SOLE**MN**
12. COLU**MN**
13. CONDE**MN**
14. AUTU**MN**
15. QUA**LM**S
16. CA**LM**LY
17. PLU**MB**ING
18. NU**MB**ED
19. RHYTHMIC
20. RHYMED

Pay attention to the spelling words. Loot at the underlined letters in each word. Only one of the two letters is pronounced. The other letter is a "silent partner." Think about how each word is pronounced.

1. Which letter is silent in each combination? gn _____ bt _____ ps _____

   gh _____ mn _____ lm _____ mb _____ rh _____

2. Write the combinations in which only the **m** is pronounced. _____

   _____ _____

3. Write the letter that is silent in one combination and pronounced in

   another combination. _____

4. Write the letters that are silent in more than one combination. _____

   _____

   > A few consonants are silent in certain combinations.
   >
   > gn bt ps gh mn lm mb rh

78

Spelling Dictionary

1. **a·lign·ment**   *n.* arrangement in a straight line
2. **au·tumn**   *n.* season between summer and winter; fall
      –adj. of or like autumn [*autumn* leaves]
3. **be·nign**   *adj.* 1. good-natured [a *benign* smile]   2. (*medicine*) doing little or no harm [a *benign* tumor]
4. **calm**   *n.* 1. lack of wind or motion; stillness   2. serenity
      –adj. 1. still   2. not excited   **–calm·ly**[16] *adv.*
      –calm·ness *n.*
SYN[17]. **–calm,** basically applied to the weather, suggests a lack of movement or excitement [a *calm* sea]; **serene** suggests a dignified tranquility, as of a person who is at peace with himself; **peaceful** suggests feedom from disorder or from a show of strong feelings [a *peaceful* gathering]
–ANT. –stormy, agitated
5. **calm·ly**   *adv.* in a calm manner   *–adj.* 1. still   2. not excited
6. **cam·paign**   *n.* series of organized actions for particular purpose
      –v. **–paigned, –paign·ing** to participate in a campaign
7. **col·umn**   *n.* 1. a slender, upright structure; pillar   2. vertical sections of printed matter lying side by side on a page
8. **con·demn**   *v.* **–demned, –demn·ing** 1. to strongly disapprove 2. to convict
9. **con·sign·ment**   *n.* a shipment of goods sent to an agent for sale or safekeeping
10. **de·sign·er**   *n.* person who designs or makes original sketches, patterns, etc.
11. **doubt·ful**   *adj.* 1. not sure   2. questionable
12. **ghet·to**   *n.* any section of a city in which many members of some minority group live, or are forced to live
13. **gnaw**   *v.* **gnawed, gnaw·ing** 1. to bite and wear away bit by bit   2. to torment, as by constant pain, fear, etc.
14. **in·debt·ed**   *adj.* 1. in debt   2. obliged; owing thanks
15. **ma·lign**   *v.* **–ligned, –lign·ing** to say damaging or unfair things about; slander

---

[16]   The dictionary often lists related words under the entry of the base word. So far, we've only had related words that were also defined. Sometimes the definition is self-understood so long as you know the part of speech. In this case, the dictionary merely states the word in the same font (type of letters) as an entry word and shows which part of speech it is. **Calmly** is an adverb that modifies a verb (it describes the act being done in a calm manner), and **calmness** is a noun – the state of being still.

[17]   Syn. stands for synonymy, or list of synonyms (words that have similar meanings). See Lesson 11 for more information. Ant. stands for antonyms (the opposite of synonyms).

16. **mort·gage**   *n.* an agreement in which a person borrowing money gives the lender a claim to a certain piece of property as a pledge that the debt will be paid
17. **numb**   *adj.* deprived of the power of feeling or moving; deadened [*numb* with cold]
18. **plumb·ing**   *n.* the pipes and fixtures with which a plumber works
19. **poign·ant**   *adj.* sharply painful to the feelings; drawing forth pity, compassion, etc.
20. **psalms**   *n.* a sacred song or poem
21. **psy·cho·lo·gy**   *n.* the science that studies the mind and the reasons for the ways people think and act
22. **pto·maine**   *n.* any of a class of alkaloid substances, some of which are poisonous, formed in decaying animal or vegetable matter by bacteria
23. **qualms**   *n.* a sudden feeling of uneasiness or doubt
24. **rheu·ma·tism** *n.* any of various painful conditions in which the joints and muscles become inflamed and stiff
25. **rhyme**   *n.* likeness of sounds at the ends of words or lines of verse   *–v.* **rhymed, rhym·ing** to form a rhyme
26. **rhythm**   *n.* flow or movement having a regularly repeated pattern of accents, beats, etc.
27. **rhythmic**   *adj.* in a manner of rhythm
28. **sold·er**   *n.* a metal alloy used when melted to join or path metal parts or surfaces   *–v.* **–ered, –er·ing** to join or patch (things) with solder
29. **sol·emn**   *adj.* serious; deeply earnest
30. **spa·ghet·ti**   *n.* long, thin strings of pasta
31. **sub·tle**   *adj.* 1. not open or direct; sly; clever [a *subtle* hint]   2. delicate [a *subtle* shade of red]

Silent partners are letters which are silent in certain combinations.

Practicing the words
A. Syllables
A **syllable** is a word part that has a single vowel sound. It might have a number of vowels (**boat**) or not even a single vowel (dan**g**ling). The key is that it is pronounced as a distinct part of the word separate from the other parts – usually with a separate motion of your mouth. A hint to distinguish the different syllables is to pay attention to your chin as you clearly pronounce the word. Each distinct movement of your chin marks a separate syllable. Sometimes an entire words is a single syllable. This is even true of long words such as **brought**.

1. Write the five one-syllable spelling words.

_____   _____   _____

_____   _____

2. Write the ten two-syllable spelling words. Draw a line between the syllables.

_____   _____   _____

_____   _____   _____

_____   _____

_____   _____

3. Write the four three-syllable words. Draw a line between the syllables.

_____   _____   _____

4. Write the spelling word that remains. _____

    How many syllables does it have? _____

In לשון הקודש a syllable is called either a יתד or a תנועה. In very many of the פיוטים and שירים from the Spanish and African Rishonim, the basis of the verses were written in a format based on these syllables. There is a slight difference between syllables in לשון הקודש and English. In לשון הקודש, the sound of שוא is not a separate syllable, even though it is pronounced with a different movement of the jaw.

A יתד is a syllable that begins with a שוא נא or its assistants (חטף קמץ, חטף פתח, חטף סגול) and continues with the next נקודה. It continues until the following נקודה, which begins the next syllable.

A תנועה is a syllable that begins with a true נקודה on the letter that begins the syllable. It might just be that letter, or up to three letters, all the letters that are pronounced with that נקודה. A שוא cannot begin a תנועה. If it is a נח שוא, it might end the תנועה if the following letter has a new נקודה or a נע שוא; or the תנועה will continue if the following letter is also a שוא נח. [There are two types of שוא נח – one is pronounced and is called נח נראה (visible), the other is not pronounced and is called נח נסתר (hidden). In the word בראשית, the ת is called a נח נראה because its sound is pronounced, but the א and י are נח נסתר because their sounds are not pronounced.]

For example, in the song for Shabbos day, דרור יקרא, the pattern is יתד ושני תנועות. The first stanza of the song is דרור יק·רא לבן עם בת וְיִנ·צָר·כֶם כְּמוֹ בָ·בַת נְעִים שִמ·כֶם וְלֹא יֻש·בַּת שְבוּ וְנוּ·חוּ בְּיוֹם שַ·בָּת. The יתד's have been underlined and bolded. Syllables in a single word have been separated with the dot.

B. Mnemonics

Mnemonics is the system of improving memory. (Cover the first silent letter and say it *nemonics*.)

A mnemonic device is a memory aid.

For example, the word **HOMES** can help you to remember the names of the five Great lakes.

Huron
Ontario
Michigan
Erie
Superior

The word **FACE** tells you the four notes in the spaces of a musical staff.

Invent your own mnemonic devices for words that are difficult spelling problems.

Sometimes putting a group of words together in a nonsense sentence or phrase helps you to remember them.

1. Write the four spelling words that have been used in the "silent b" sentence.

Be indebted, doubtful, and numb about plumbing.

_____

2. Make up your own sentence for "silent n" words. solemn, column, condemn, autumn

_____

_____

3. Make up your own sentence for "silent g" words. designer, campaign, alignment, gnawed

_____

_____

4. Make up your own sentence for "silent h" words. spaghetti, rhythmic, rhymed

_____

_____

C. Synonyms

Synonyms are words that have a similar meaning to each other. They may have other meanings that are not similar, but the meanings that they share make them synonyms.

The list below contains three spelling words and four of their synonyms. Write a spelling word from the list at the top of each column. Under each spelling word, write its four synonyms.

somber	solemn	uncertain	unsure	serious
skeptical	questionable	serenely	placidly	peacefully
tranquilly	grave	earnest	doubtful	calmly

_____   _____   _____

_____   _____   _____

_____   _____   _____

_____   _____   _____

_____   _____   _____

D. Find nine new silent letter words. Begin with the word sign and find your way out of the maze. Write each word. The beginning of some of the harder words have been provided to help you.

sign

1. _____

2. p_____

3. _____

4. s_____

5. _____

6. p_____

7. _____

8. _____

9. _____

N								
G	E	P	T	O	M	A	I	N
I	G	A	N	T	M	A	L	E
N	A	N	N	S	I	G	I	R
E	G	G	O	S→	I↓	N	G	H
B	T	I	C	N	◄G	M	N	E
R	R	O	P	T	N	E	S	U
E	O	M	E	L	T	B	U	M
D	L	O	S	M	S	I	T	A

Rewrite each sentence, using one of the new words in place of the underlined words. Circle the silent letter.

1. We were moved by the <u>very affecting</u> story.

   _____

2. The stranger gave me a <u>sly, mysterious</u> smile.

   _____

3. Mark is known for his <u>good-natured</u> attitude.

   _____

4. Does the drugstore stock an ointment for <u>stiff muscles</u>?

   _____

5. An electrician should <u>fuse</u> two wires.

   _____

6. Which salesperson sold that <u>assigned shipment</u> of food?

    _____

7. The candidate tried to slander his opponent.

    _____

8. Can one contract a case of alkaloid poisoning from mushrooms?

    _____

9. Our neighbors got a second financial agreement on their house.

    _____

E. Fill in the blanks with the appropriate spelling word.

1. His sister is a graphic __ __ __ __ __ __ __ __ and helped him make his business

    card.

2. The lined margin assists the __ __ __ __ __ __ __ __ __ of your words when

    writing a list.

3. The tzedakah __ __ __ __ __ __ __ brought in a lot of revenue.

4. Reuvein __ __ __ __ __ __ a spoon when he was lost in thought.

5. I am __ __ __ __ __ __ __ __ to the Rov for helping me out.

6. I am __ __ __ __ __ __ __ __ whether this class is interesting.

7. Eino Yehudim call Tehillim __ __ __ __ __.

8. Recently, __ __ __ __ __ __ __ __ __ __ has become a popular field.

9. I do not relish having __ __ __ __ __ __ __ __ __ for supper.

10. Most of us had ancestors who were forced to live in a __ __ __ __ __ __.

11. Tisha B'Av is a very __ __ __ __ __ __ day.

12. The spelling words should be written in a __ __ __ __ __ __, not across the page.

13. We __ __ __ __ __ __ __ the recent rise of anti-Semitism hate crimes.

14. As the days grow shorter, __ __ __ __ __ __ draws to a close.

15. We have no __ __ __ __ __ __ openly displaying ourselves as Yiddin when we

    walk in the street.

16. As I get provoked, I remind myself to reply __ __ __ __ __ __ to avoid becoming

    angry.

17. I have a friend who does __ __ __ __ __ __ __ __ for a living.

18. My hand was __ __ __ __ __ __ because I had been writing tefillin for so long.

19. I enjoy listening to his __ __ __ __ __ __ __ __ voice as he prepares the parshah

for leining.

20. Many of the פיוטים __ __ __ __ __ __ well and were therefore easier to read.

Key Concepts
- single tense
- plural tense
- irregular
- vowel
- consonant
- Words ending in y
- present tense
- past tense
- helping verb

When referring to a single noun, surprisingly enough, it is called **singuar**. Even if you are referring to a large group of things or people, if you are treating them as a whole group it is a singular noun. When referring to more than one noun, and not treating them as a collective unit, you need to change to the **plural** form. Most nouns become plural by merely adding **s** to the end of the word. (There are a number of exceptions where **es** is added and other times that the plural form is **irregular**. Irregular means that the word is an exception and does not follow regular rules.) Usually, no change needs to be made to the noun, but there are some exceptions. When the last letter of the noun is **y**, and the letter before the **y** was a consonant, the **y** gets changed to **ie**.

A **vowel** is a sound that is made with the open mouth or throat and works like a נקודה to tell you how to pronounce the other letters. A **consonant** it any letter sound that is not a vowel.

This same rule also applies to nearly all words that end with y when a suffix beginning with a vowel is added to the word – the **y** changes to **ie** (**toy** + **ed** becomes **toyed**, and **baby** + **ed** becomes **babied**[18]). The suffix **ing** is an exception (just like **toy** + **ing** becomes **toying**, **baby** + **ing** becomes **babying**). If the suffix begins with a consonant, no change is made to the **y** (**baby** + **hood** becomes **babyhood**). This pattern regarding suffixes causing changes to the final letter of the base word is similar to the rule you learned in lessons 1 and 2 – if the suffix begins with a vowel it causes the change, but not if it begins with a consonant.

Verbs can be in a number of different forms, called tenses. Some of the easier tenses are past, present, and future. **Past tens**e talks about having done the verb in the past. **Present tense** refers to doing the verb now. Future tense means that the verb is going to be done later. Most verbs take the present tense by merely adding an **s** to the verb (**help** becomes **helps**). Most verbs are changed to past tense by adding **ed** to the verb (**help** becomes **helped**). The way to write future tense in English is to use **helping verbs** that show that it will or might be done later. Examples of helping verbs are **might**, **could**, **should**, **will**, **would**, etc.

Lesson Spelling Rule: If the letter before a final **y** is a vowel, do not change the **y** when you add a suffix. If the letter before the final **y** is a consonant, change the **y** to **i** before you add any suffix except **ing**. The **y** never changes before **ing**.

---

[18]   Even though the suffix added is **ed**, the e is not doubled. **Babied** instead of babieed.

		+ s	+ ed	+ ing
1.	SWAY	SWAYS	SWAYED	SWAYING
2.	CONVEY	CONVEYS	CONVEYED	CONVEYING
3.	DEFRAY	DEFRAYS	DEFRAYED	DEFRAYING
4.	DISMAY	DISMAYS	DISMAYED	DISMAYING
5.	EMPLOY	EMPLOYS	EMPLOYED	EMPLOYING
6.	DECOY	DECOYS	DECOYED	DECOYING
7.	SUBWAY	SUBWAYS		
8.	MEDLEY	MEDLEYS		
9.	ATTORNEY	ATTORNEYS		
10.	EMPLOY	EMPLOYS		
11.	APPLY	APPLIES	APPLIED	APPLYING
12.	DEFY	DEFIES	DEFYED	DEFYING
13.	ENVY	ENVIES	ENVIED	ENVYING
14.	TALLY	TALLIES	TALLIED	TALLYING
15.	MODIFY	MODIFIES	MODIFIED	MODIFYING
16.	CELEBRITY	CELEBRITIES		
17.	CENTURY	CENTURIES		
18.	PENALTY	PENALTIES		
19.	GALLERY	GALLERIES		
20.	AGENCY	AGENCIES		

Pay attention to the spelling words.

1. How many of the words in the first column have a vowel before the final **y**?_____

2. What happens to the **y** when a suffix is added? _____

3. When the letter before the final **y** is a consonant, what happens to the final **y** when the suffixes **es** or **ed** is added? _____

4. When **ing** is added to any final **y** word what happens to the **y**? _____

> If the letter before a final **y** is a vowel, do not change the **y** when you add a suffix. If the letter before the final **y** is a consonant, change the **y** to **i** before you add any suffix except **ing**. The **y** never changes before **ing**.

90

Spelling Dictionary

1. **a·gen·cy**   *n.* the work or place of work of any person, firm, authorized to act for another [an insurance *agency*]

2. **ap·ply**   *v.* **–plied, –ply·ing** 1. to put on [to *apply* salve] 2. to make a formal request [to *apply* for a job] 3. to be suitable or relevant [this rule *applies* to everyone]

3. **at·tor·ney**   *n.* any person having the legal power to act for another; esp. a lawyer

4. **ce·leb·ri·ty**   *n.* a famous person

5. **cen·tu·ry**   *n.* any period of 100 years

6. **con·vey**   *v.* **–veyed, –vey·ing** 1. to take from one place to another; transport; carry [the cattle were *conveyed* in trucks to the market] 2. to make known; communicate [writing a note to *convey* his sympathy]

7. **de·coy**   *n.* an artificial bird or animal used to lure game to a place where it can be shot   *–v.* **–coyed, –coy·ing** to lure with false promise

8. **de·fray**   *v.* **–frayed, –fray·ing** to pay (the cost or expenses)

9. **de·fy**   *v.* **–fied, –fy·ing** 1. to resist or oppose boldly or openly [to *defy* the law] 2. to resist completely in a confusing way [the puzzle *defied* solution]

10. **dis·may**   *v.* to make discouraged at the prospect of trouble; fill with alarm   *--n.* a loss of courage when faced with trouble or danger

11. **em·ploy**   *v.* **–ployed, –ploy·ing** 1. to make use of; use [she *employs* skill in her work] 2. to engage the services or labor of for pay; hire

12. **en·vy**   *n.* feeling of discontent and ill will because another has advantages, possessions, etc. that one would like to have   *–v.* **–vied, –vy·ing** to feel envy toward, at, or because of

13. **gal·le·ry**   *n.* a room, building, or establishment for showing or selling art works

14. **med·ley**   *n.* a musical piece made up of tunes or passages from various works

15. **mod·i·fy**   *v.* **–fied, –fy·ing** to change or alter, especially slightly

16. **pe·nal·ty**   *n.* 1. a punishment fixed by law, as for a crime 2. any disadvantage, put on one side in a contest for breaking a rule

17. **pul·ley**   *n.* small wheel with a grooved rim in which a rope or chain runs, as to raise a weight attached at one end by pulling on the other end

18. **sub·way**   *n.* an underground electric railway in some large cities

19. **sway**   *v.* **swayed, –sway·ing** 1. to swing or move from side to side or to and fro [the flowers *swayed* in the breeze] 2. to lean or go to one side; veer [the car *swayed* to the right]

20. **tal·ly**   *n.* an account, reckoning, or score [keep a *tally* of what you spend] *–v.* **–lied, –ly·ing** to count [usually with *up*] [*tally* up the score]

Practicing the words

A. Writing

The singular form of a noun is usually changed to plural by simply adding **s**. However, when the last letter is **y**, sometimes a slight change needs to be made to the base word. If the letter right before the **y** is a vowel, no change is needed and simply add the **s**. If the letter preceding the **y** is a consonant, then the **y** must be changed to an **i** and **es** must be added.

When a verb is mentioned as if it is taking place right now, that is the present tense. If it will be done later, then you must use the future tense of the verb – usually by adding a helping verb that shows it will be done. To show that the verb already happened, you need to change the present tense to past tense, usually by adding the suffix **ed** to the verb.

Rewrite each sentence. Change the underlined noun to the plural form. Put the underlined verb in its past tense (**ed**) form.

1. The insurance <u>agency</u> <u>employs</u> many people._____

    _____

2. Mr. Shaw's <u>decoy</u> <u>sways</u> gently on the pond._____

    _____

3. The <u>penalty</u> <u>dismays</u> the hockey player._____

    _____

4. Our art <u>gallery</u> <u>defrays</u> the cost of the exhibit. _____

    _____

5. The <u>subway</u> <u>conveys</u> thousands of commuters._____

    _____

6. Which <u>century</u> in the past <u>defies</u> understanding?_____

    _____

7. The <u>pulley</u> <u>modifies</u> the distribution of weight._____

    _____

8. The other <u>celebrity</u> <u>envies</u> the star of the show._____

    _____

9. The singers of the <u>medley</u> <u>apply</u> new words to old tunes._____

    _____

10. Which firm's <u>attorney</u> <u>tallies</u> the results?_____

    _____

B. Limerick

A limerick is a rhymed poem of five lines, about foolishness. The first, second, and last lines end with one rhyming sound. The third and fourth lines end with a different rhyme. Although gibberish is not acceptable, a limerick only has to loosely make sense. It generally states something cute or foolish and is meant to be amusing.

Complete this limerick with five spelling words. The beginning and ending letters are given as clues.

1. The old porch swing gently was s __ __ __ __ __ g;   _____

2. Paul and Max was the swing c __ __ __ __ __ __ __ g.   _____

3. For Max's cookie Paul a __ __ __ __ __ d,   _____

4. But Max firmly d __ __ __ __ d.   _____

5. Paul's evening was truly d __ __ __ __ __ __ __ g.   _____

93

C. Writing
Some words that end with **f** or **fe** form the plural by changing **f** to **v** and adding **es**[19].
Expand each phrase into a complete sentence using the plural form of the underlined word, which will need to be made plural in this manner. Then circle the spelling word in each sentence.

1. gently swaying leaf –_____

   _____

2. defrayed the cost of new library shelf –_____

   _____

3. penalties in both half –_____

   _____

4. envied the exciting life of hatzoloh members –_____

   _____

5. traveled on the subway by themself –_____

   _____

6. attorneys who prosecuted the two thief –_____

   _____

---

[19] Although this is not a hard and fast rule, generally, it needs to be done when the letter before the **f** is a consonant or the word ends in **fe**.

D. Vowels

Is the letter **y** a consonant or a vowel? The debate continues to rage about this, but generally the rule is that when the **y** is working with another vowel and is beginning the syllable, it is considered a consonant. Think, **yellow** or **yesterday**. But when it follows a consonant and functions as the instruction for pronouncing that syllable, it is treated as a vowel. Think, **syllable** or **sky**.

Lashon Hakodesh also has vowels, called נקודות, but they are distinct from the letters. In תורה שבכתב, there are no vowels, only letters. The נקודות are part of תורה שבעל פה. One analogy that the Rishonim use (it comes from a Kabbalistic Medrash) to describe the relationship between letters and נקודות is that of the body and soul. The נקודות are like the soul of the letters, allowing them to "move" as the word is spoken.

The vowel system of Lashon Hakodesh is divided in two systems that work differently with regards to forming syllables.[20] These two systems are called תנועה קטנה and תנועה גדולה. The תנועות גדולות are regular קמץ (not חטף קמץ or קמץ קטן), חולם, חיריק מלא, צירה, and שורוק. The תנועות קטנות are חיריק חסר, סגול, פתח, קמץ קטן, and מלאופום.

[There is another group of נקודות that comprise the שוא family. They are שוא נע, שוא נח, חטף סגול, and חטף קמץ, חטף פתח. They are not called תנועות at all, and never form their own syllable. A שוא נח is always part of the syllable before it, and a שוא נע or חטף is always the beginning of the next syllable.]

---

[20] One aspect of this distinction is with regards to the שוא that follows the נקודה. If it is a תנועה גדולה, then the שוא is a שוא נע (a moving שוא that is pronounced like the **i** in **if**). If it is a תנועה קלה the שוא will usually be a שוא נח (a silent שוא) where only the letter is pronounced as part of the syllable.

Another distinction is with regards to דגש, the tiny dot that appears in middle of the letters בגדכפת. If they follow a תנועה גדולה they will not have a דגש (think דָבָר), but if they follow תנועה קטנה, they often have a דגש (think שַׁבָּת).

E. Fill in the blanks with the appropriate spelling word.

1. If you shuckel, you __ __ __ __ while davening.

2. I use sentences to __ __ __ __ __ __ the meaning of the words.

3. Moadim Lesimcha helps __ __ __ __ __ __ the cost of making Yom Tov.

4. To the class's __ __ __ __ __ __ , the teacher ended up coming.

5. The gabbai is in the __ __ __ __ __ __ of the Rebbe.

6. To ride the __ __ __ __ __ __ , you go underground.

7. You make בורא מיני בשמים over a __ __ __ __ __ __ of spices.

8. You might need an __ __ __ __ __ __ __ __ if you text and drive.

9. A __ __ __ __ __ __ makes it easier to lift.

10. The thief made a __ __ __ __ __ to cover his trail.

11. When you __ __ __ __ __ yourself, you succeed.

12. It is unacceptable to __ __ __ __ the hanhalah's authority.

13. It is very good to __ __ __ __ other people's מעשים טובים.

14. The __ __ __ __ __ of the Chanukah candles without the shamash is 36.

15. Including the shamash will __ __ __ __ __ __ the sum to 44.

16. We had a __ __ __ __ __ __ __ __ __ singer come to our mesibah.

17. We live in the 2K __ __ __ __ __ __ , otherwise known as the twenty-first.

18. The __ __ __ __ __ __ __ for writing on the wrong side of the page is being left out of the raffle.

19. The Ezras Noshim is a __ __ __ __ __ __ __ overlooking the Bais Medrash.

20. The English word for שליחות is __ __ __ __ __ __ .

Key Concepts
- adjective
- adverb
- noun
- synonym
- antonym
- analogy

A **noun** is a word that is a person, place, or thing. It might be a tangible thing, which means that you can touch it, or an intangible thing, which cannot be touched like an idea. (For example, **hunger**; it is an intangible thing.)

An **adjective** is a word that modifies, limits, or describes a noun. (For example, **worldwide** hunger; it describes where the hunger is.)

An **adverb** is a word that modifies, limits, or describes a verb. That means it tells you about the action or state of being that is the verb. (For example ate **hungrily**; the verb is ate and hungrily tells you about how he ate.)

Words that share similar meanings are **synonyms**. The opposite of a synonym is an **antonym**. It is a pair of words that have meanings that are nearly opposite of each other. An easy mnemonic to help you remember which is which, is that synonym begins with a sound that is similar to similar, which is what it means: a word that is similar. On the other hand, antonym begins with a sound that is similar to anti, which is what it means: a word that is nearly opposite, or anti, the first word.

An **analogy** is a type of comparison between two things that shows a similarity. A more sophisticated analogy draws a comparison between the relationship that one set of pairs has to do with another set of pair.

Lesson Spelling Rule: When you add the suffix **ly** to words that end with **al**, remember that one **l** belongs to the base word, and one **l** belongs to the suffix. Remember to spell the unstressed **a.**

	Adjective			Adverb				Noun
1.	LOCAL	+ LY	=	LOCALLY	+	ITY	=	LOCALITY
2.	FINAL	+ LY	=	FINAL	+	ITY	=	FINALITY
3.	LEGAL	+ LY	=	LEGAL	+	ITY	=	LEGALITY
4.	EQUAL	+ LY	=	EQUAL	+	ITY	=	EQUALITY
5.	FATAL	+ LY	=	FATAL	+	ITY	=	FATALITY
6.	ACTUAL	+ LY	=	ACTUAL	+	ITY	=	ACTUALITY
7.	REAL	+ LY	=	REAL	+	ITY	=	REALITY
8.	TOTAL	+ LY	=	TOTAL	+	ITY	=	TOTALITY
9.	MENTAL	+ LY	=	MENTAL	+	ITY	=	MENTALITY
10.	MORAL	+ LY	=	MORAL	+	ITY	=	MORALITY
11.	NATIONAL	+ LY	=	NATIONAL	+	ITY	=	NATIONALITY
12.	PUNCTUAL	+ LY	=	PUNCTUAL	+	ITY	=	PUNCTUALITY
13.	GENERAL	+ LY	=	GENERAL	+	ITY	=	GENERALITY
14.	PERSONAL	+ LY	=	PERSONAL	+	ITY	=	PERSONALITY
15.	INDIVIDUAL	+ LY	=	INDIVIDUAL	+	ITY	=	INDIVIDUALITY
16.	ORIGINAL	+ LY	=	ORIGINAL	+	ITY	=	ORIGINALITY
17.	PRACTICAL	+ LY	=	PRACTICAL	+	ITY	=	PRACTICALITY
18.	FORMAL	+ LY	=	FORMAL	+	ITY	=	FORMALITY
19.	TECHNICAL	+ LY	=	TECHNICAL	+	ITY	=	TECHNICALITY
20.	SENTIMENTAL	+ LY	=	SENTIMENTAL	+	ITY	=	SENTIMENTALITY

Pay attention to the spelling words.

1. All of the adjectives in the first column end with what two letters? _____

2. What two-letter suffix is added to change the adjective to an adverb? _____

3. When the suffix **ly** is added to words that endy with the letter **l**, is one of

   the **l**'s dropped?_____

4. What are the last *four* letters of each new adverb?_____

5. Is the unstressed **a** in this ending easy to hear and identify? _____

6. Is the letter **a** easier to hear in the words formed by adding the **ity** suffix?

When you add the suffix **ly** to words that end with **al**, remember that one l belongs to the base word, and one b belongs to the suffix. Don't drop either of the l's.

98

Remember the unstressed **a** by thinking of a related form of the word in which the accent shifts to the **a** (for example, **formally** to **formality**).

1. **ac·tu·al**   *adj.* 1. presently existing   2. essential
2. **ac·tu·al·i·ty**   *n.* 1. a reality   2. an actual thing or condition; fact
3. **ac·tu·al·ly**   *adv.* as a matter of actual fact; really
4. **e·qual**   *adj.* having the same qualities
5. **e·qual·i·ty**   *n.* state or instance of being equal, esp. of having the same political, economic, and social rights
6. **e·qual·ly**   *adv.* in an equal manner; to an equal degree
7. **fa·tal**   *adj.* 1. fateful; decisive [the *fatal* day arrived]   2. resulting in death   3. having to do with death   4. having dire consequences; bringing ruin;
8. **fa·tal·i·ty**   *n.* 1. something caused by fate   2. a death caused by disaster, as in an accident, war, etc.
9. **fa·tal·ly**   *adv.* with fatal consequences
10. **fi·nal**   *adj.* 1. at the end   2. not to be undone
11. **fi·nal·i·ty**   *n.* the quality or condition of being final, settled, or complete
12. **fi·nal·ly**   *adv.* at the end; in conclusion
13. **for·mal**   *adj.* 1. according to fixed rules, customs, etc.   2. designed for wear at ceremonies, etc. [*formal* dress]   3; refined; befitting royalty or authority
14. **for·mal·i·ty**   *n.* 1. the following of established customs, rules, ceremonies, etc.; propriety   2. a formal or conventional act or requirement; ceremony or form
15. **for·mal·ly**   *adv.* with official authorization; in a formal manner
16. **gen·er·al**   *adj.* 1. of, from, or for the whole or all; not particular or specialized   2. most common; usual [[the *general* spelling of a word]   3. applying to most members; common to the public   4. affecting the entire body   —*n.* any of various military officers ranking above a colonel
17. **gen·er·al·i·ty**   *n.* a statement, expression, etc. that is general or vague rather than definite or with details
18. **gen·er·al·ly**   *adv.* 1. to or by most people; widely [is that fact *generally* known?]   2. in most instances; usually [I *generally* go straight home]   3. in a general way; without going into details [speaking *generally*, I'd agree]
19. **in·di·vid·u·al**   *adj.* 1. separate from others   2. concerning a specific person
20. **in·di·vid·u·al·i·ty**   *n.* the qualities that set one person or thing apart from others; individual character
21. **in·di·vid·u·al·ly**   *adv.* one at a time; separately
22. **le·gal**   *adj.* of, based on, or authorized by law [*legal* studies]
23. **le·gal·i·ty**   *n.* quality, instance, or condition of being legal or lawful
24. **le·gal·ly**   *adv.* 1. by law   2. conforming to the law   3. in a legal manner
25. **lo·cal**   *adj.* related or pertaining to a specific area
26. **lo·cal·i·ty**   *n.* a place; district

27. **lo·cal·ly**   *adv.* within a given area or areas [the damage done by a tornado *locally*]

28. **men·tal**   *adj.* 1. involving the mind   2. of or for the mind

29. **men·tal·i·ty**   *n.* mental capacity, power or activity; mind

30. **men·tal·ly**   *adv.* in the mind

31. **mor·al**   *adj.* 1. related to, dealing with, or capable of distinguishing between right and wrong in conduct [a *moral* question]   2. concerned with principles or standards of behavior

32. **mor·al·i·ty**   *n.* moral quality or character; rightness or wrongness, as of an action

33. **mor·al·ly**   *adv.* with respect to moral principles; in a moral manner

34. **na·tion·al**   *adj.* related or belonging to a country or the country [*national* anthem]

35. **na·tion·al·i·ty** *n.* the status of belonging to a particular nation by birth or nationalization

36. **na·tion·al·ly**   *adv.* with regard to the nation as a whole; extending throughout a nation

37. **o·rig·i·nal**   *adj.* 1. fresh; new; novel [an *original* idea]   2. first   3. not copied

38. **o·rig·i·nal·i·ty**   *n.* 1. the quality of being original   2. the ability to be original, inventive, or creative

39. **o·rig·i·nal·ly**   *adv.* 1. before now; with reference to the beginning   2. in an original manner

40. **per·son·al**   *adj.* 1. concerning or pertaining to a specific individual   2. private

41. **per·so·nal·i·ty**   *n.* 1. all the special qualities of a person which make him different from other people   2. a person, esp. a famous person

42. **per·son·al·ly**   *adv.* 1. without the help of others; in person [to attend to a matter *personally*]   2. in one's own opinion   3. as though directed at oneself [to take a remark *personally*]

43. **prac·ti·cal**   *adj.* 1. usable; workable; useful and sensible [*practical* proposals]   2. concerned with actual use or practice   3. being actual nearly in every respect [a *practical* failure]

44. **prac·ti·cal·i·ty**   *n.* the quality of being concerned with actual use rather than theoretial possibility

45. **prac·ti·cal·ly**   *adv.* 1. in a practical way   2. in effect; really; virtually [*practically* a dictator]   3. [Colloq.[21]] nearly [we're *practically* home]

46. **punc·tu·al**   *adj.* acting or arriving exactly at the appointed time; on time; prompt

47. **punc·tu·a·li·ty**   *n.* the quality or habit of adhering to an appointed time

48. **punc·tu·al·ly**   *adv.* at the expected or proper time

49. **real**   *adj.* 1. occuring in fact   2. essential

---

[21]   Colloq. stands for colloquialism. It is means informal speech.

50. **re·al·i·ty**   *n.* the quality or fact of being real **–in reality** in fact; actually

51. **re·al·ly**   *adv.* 1. in reality; in fact   2. truly or genuine [*really* hot]

52. **sen·ti·men·tal** *adj.* 1. having or showing tender or gentle feelngs, often in a foolish way [a *sentimental* song]   2. of or resulting from sentiment [to save a picture for *sentimental* feelings]   3. given to sentiment; overly emotional

53. **sen·ti·men·tal·i·ty**   *n.* the quality or condition of being sentimental, especially in a foolish way

54. **sen·ti·men·tal·ly**   *adv.* in a sentimental manner

55. **tech·ni·cal**   *adj.* 1. of or used in a specific science, art craft, etc. [*technical* terms]   2. relating to technique; showing skill   3. concerned with machinery   4. strictly adhering to rules

56. **tech·ni·cal·i·ty**   *n.* 1. a technical point, term, method, etc.   2. a minute, formal point or detail

57. **tech·ni·cal·ly**   *adv.* with regards to techniques; according to the exact meaning

58. **to·tal**   *adj.* 1. making up the (or a) whole; entire [the *total* amount is ten dollars]   2. complete; utter [a *total* loss]

59. **to·tal·ity**   *n.* 1. the fact or condition of being total   2. the total amount or sum

60. **to·tal·ly**   *adv.* completely; entirely

Practicing the words

A.Use the adjective, adverb, and noun forms of a spelling word to complete each set of phrases. An adjective modifies a noun and an adverb modifies a verb. A phrase containing no verb can only have an adjective or a noun. If the phrase contains a verb and a noun, chances are that the spelling word is an adjective or adverb.

1. _____ habits

take a remark _____

a public _____

2. demand _____ time

_____ difficult options

racial _____

3. a _____ song

looked at old photos _____

a story full of _____

4. a _____ invitation

were _____ introduced

a mere _____

5. the _____ moments of

the game

_____ admitted she was

wrong

spoke with _____

6. an _____ idea

_____ came from Toronto

an award for _____

7. _____ time

_____ grown honey

moving to a new _____

8. a _____ document

_____ valid

a mere _____

9. a _____ accident

a _____ important

decision

the _____ of war

10. _____ fact

we _____ won

it became an _____

11. _____ time

_____ neat idea

turn your dream into

_____

12. the _____ was 85

_____ prepared

the _____ of all the parts

B. Proofreading
Cross out the misspelled word or words in each sentence and rewrite them correctly.

1. The judge finaly dismissed the case because of a legal tecnicality.

   _____

   _____

2. Yanina's punctuality and individuallity are realy appreciated by everyone. _____

   _____

3. The senator's generallity about the economy was technicaly incorrect. _____

   _____

4. Originaly, all our vegetables were grown localy. _____

   _____

5. Practicaly every nationalety was represented at the conference. _____

   _____

6. I personaly think that Chana's answer had a note of finallity about it. _____

   _____

7. Actualy, we were never formalley introduced. _____

   _____

8. Generaly, the chores are equaley divided among the campers. _____

   _____

C. Synonyms and antonyms

SYNONYMS are words that have almost the same meaning

ANTONYMS are words that have the opposite meaning

A. Write the adverb (**ly**) form of a spelling word that is a synonym (**S**) or an antonym (**A**) for each word in the first column. Write a noun (**ity**) form of a spelling word that is a synonym or antonym for each word in the second column.

1. completely (**S**)	_____	1. site (**S**)	_____
2. physically (**A**)	_____	2. death (**S**)	_____
3. lastly (**S**)	_____	3. inequality (**A**)	_____
4. promptly (**S**)	_____	4. entirety (**S**)	_____
5. locally (**A**)	_____	5. unreality (**A**)	_____
6. lawfully (**S**)	_____	6. lawfulness (**S**)	_____
7. unitedly (**A**)	_____	7. informality (**A**)	_____
8. really (**S**)	_____	8. intelligence (**S**)	_____
9. unethically (**A**)	_____	9. immorality (**A**)	_____
10. lethally (**S**)	_____	10. reality (**S**)	_____

D. Analogies

An **analogy** is a type of comparison between two things that shows a similarity. A more sophisticated analogy draws a comparison between the relationship that one set of pairs has to do with another set of pairs.

Complete each analogy with a spelling word. Use the form of the spelling word that is the same part of speech as the word with which it is paired: use a noun with a noun an adjective with an adjective.

1. **oak** is to **tree** as **specifically** is to _____

2. **body** is to **mind** as **physically** is to _____

3. **tall** is to **short** as **tardiness** is to _____

4. **Atlantic** is to **ocean** as **Italian** is to _____

5. **jeans** is to **tuxedo** as **casualness** is to _____

6. **some** is to **all** as **partially** is to _____

7. **sport** is to **tennis** as **emotion** is to _____

8. **first** is to **last** as **originally** is to _____

E. Fill in the blanks with the appropriate spelling word.

1. Our Cheder is __ __ __ __ __ __ __ known to be one of the best mosdos.

2. We use punctuation marks to show __ __ __ __ __ __ __ __ to our statements.

3. Serving liquor to minors is not __ __ __ __ __ __ permitted.

4. Racial __ __ __ __ __ __ __ __ is not necessarily a Torah ideal.

5. President Lincoln was __ __ __ __ __ __ __ shot by the assassin.

6. In __ __ __ __ __ __ __ __ __, it seems Congress is headed to Impeaching the

   president.

7. It is __ __ __ __ __ __ going to happen.

8. The __ __ __ __ __ __ __ __ of Yiddin comprise 600,000 neshamos.

9. Most of our students are __ __ __ __ __ __ __ __ gifted.

10. The __ __ __ __ __ __ __ __ of the דור המבול was in terrible condition.

11. Jared Kushner is a __ __ __ __ __ __ __ __ __ __ renowned Jew.

12. Our class can improve our __ __ __ __ __ __ __ __ __ __.

13. __ __ __ __ __ __ __ __ speaking, this class is well-behaved.

14. His work-driven __ __ __ __ __ __ __ __ __ __ helps him achieve.

15. Every student must take the test __ __ __ __ __ __ __ __ __ __ __.

16. Many boys surprised me with their __ __ __ __ __ __ __ __ __ __ __ when

    writing their essay.

17. The 'a' sound is __ __ __ __ __ __ __ __ __ __ not pronounced when it comes

    between c and l.

18. Many times we say 'I'm sorry' merely as a __ __ __ __ __ __ __ __, without

   meaning it.

19. An incomplete stop at the stop sign is __ __ __ __ __ __ __ __ __ __ __ a

   violation of the law.

20. Too much __ __ __ __ __ __ __ __ __ __ __ __ __ during a speech can make

   the audience uncomfortable.

Key Concepts
- changing verbs to adjectives
- changing verb to nouns
- changing adjectives to adverbs
- synonyms
- synonymy

Many verbs can be changed to an adjective by adding the suffix **able/ible**. When added to the verb, the adjective means "able to be or do the verb."

Verbs can also be changed to nouns by adding the suffix **ance/ence**. Remember that nouns can be intangible[22] things like ideas, and this noun will mean "the idea of the verb."

Another way to form an adjective is to add the suffix **ant/ent**, which will mean "that which has or shows the base or root."

Many adjectives can be changed to adverbs by adding the suffix **ly**, which will mean "in the manner of the adjective."

Synonyms are words that have similar meanings. A **synonymy** is a section of the dictionary that lists synonyms of the word and might contain short words or phrases to explain differences between their meanings

Lesson Spelling Rule: The suffixes **able** and **ance** are more commonly added to complete words than to roots. The suffixes **ible**, **ence**, and **ent** are more commonly added to roots than to complete words.

The suffix **able/ible** forms adjectives meaning **able to be**.

The suffixe **ance/ence** is a noun ending that converts a verb to a noun.

The suffix **ant/ent** can form adjectives meaning **that which has or shows**.

Prefixes used in this lesson, together with their meanings:
- sus[23]- means under
- ex- means beyond, out of, thoroughly, former, previous
- im- means no, not, without
- in- means no, not, without
- pro- means before in place or time; forward or ahead
- pre- means before in time, place or rank
- com[24]- means with, together, or all together; very or very much
- per- means throughout; thoroughly
- ad- means toward

Suffixes used in this lesson, together with their meanings:
1. -ant/ent (that has or shows)
2. -ance/ence (act of, state of being)
3. -able/ible (able to be or do)
4. -ly (in the manner of)

---

[22]   Intangible means that cannot be touched.
[23]   In a later lesson you will learn that it really is a form of the prefix sub, meaning under.
[24]   In a later lesson you will learn that it really is a form of the prefix con, meaning all together.

BASE WORD	SUFFIX			SUFFIX		
1. DEPEND	+ ABLE	= DEPENDABLE		+ LY	= DEPENDABLY	
2. ACCEPT	+ ABLE	= ACCEPTABLE		+ LY	= ACCEPTABLY	
3. APPROACH	+ ABLE	= APPROACHABLE				
4. OBTAIN	+ ABLE	= OBTAINABLE				
5. DETECT	+ ABLE	= DETECTABLE				
6. CLEAR	+ ANCE	= CLEARANCE				
7. RESEMBLE	+ ANCE	= RESEMBLANCE				
8. IGNORE	+ ANCE	= IGNORANCE	+ ANT	= IGNORANT		
9. COMPLY	+ ANCE	= COMPLIANCE	+ ANT	= COMPLIANT		
10. ALLY	+ ANCE	= ALLIANCE				

PREFIX	ROOT	SUFFIX		SUFFIX		
1. COM	+ PAT	+ IBLE	= COMPATIBLE	+ LY	= COMPATIBLY	
2. SUS	+ CEPT	+ IBLE	= SUSCEPTIBLE			
3. PER	+ MISS	+ IBLE	= PERMISSIBLE	+ LY	= PERMISSIBLY	
4. IM	+ POSS	+ IBLE	= IMPOSSIBLE	+ LY	= IMPOSSIBLY	
5. IN	+ CRED	+ IBLE	= INCREDIBLE	+ LY	= INCREDIBLY	
6. EX	+ PERI	+ ENCE	= EXPERIENCE			
7. IN	+ GREDI			+ ENT	= INGREDIENT	
8. PRO	+ MIN	+ ENCE	= PROMINENCE	+ ENT	= PROMINENT	
9. PER	+ MAN	+ ENCE	= PERMANENCE	+ ENT	= PERMANENT	
10. AD	+ JAC			+ ENT	= ADJACENT	

Pay attention to the spelling words.

1. What four suffixes are added to complete words? _____
   _____ _____ _____
2. What happens to the final silent **e** words when a suffix beginning with a vowel is added to these words? _____
3. What happens to the words that end with a **y** preceded by a consonant? _____
4. Are the suffixes **ible**, **ence**, and **ent** added to complete words or to roots? _____
5. Which suffix corresponding to **ent** is added to complete words? _____

> The suffixes **able** and **ance** are more commonly added to complete words than to roots. The suffixes **ible**, **ence**, and **ent** are more commonly added to roots than to complete words.
> The suffix **able/ible** forms adjectives meaning **able to be**.
> The suffixe **ance/ence** is a noun ending that converts a verb to a noun.
> The suffix **ant/ent** can form adjectives meaning **that which has or shows**.

1. **ac·cept**   *v.* **–cep·ted, –cept·ing** to take; receive willingly
2. **ac·cept·a·ble**   *adj.* worth accepting; satisfactory, or sometimes, merely adequate
3. **ac·cept·ab·ly**   *adv.* in an acceptable (but not outstanding) manner
4. **ad·ja·cent**   *adj.* near or close (*to* something); adjoining
5. **al·li·ance**   *n.* a close association for a common goal, as of nations, parties, etc.
6. **al·ly**   *n.* 1. a friendly nation   2. an associate who provides assistance or cooperation   *–v.* **–lied, –ly·ing** become an ally or associate, as by a treaty or marriage
7. **ap·proach**   *v.* **–proached, –proach·ing** 1. move towards 2. come near or verge on   *–n.* 1. ideas or actions intended to deal with a problem or situation 2. the act of drawing closer to something
8. **ap·proach·a·ble**   *adj.* capable of being approached; accessible
9. **clear**   *adj.* 1. free from confusion or doubt   2. affording free passage or view   *–v.* **cleared, clear·ing** 1. remove   2. rid of obstructions   3. grant authorization or clearance for
10. **clear·ance**   *n.* 1. an act or process of clearing: as (a) a sale to clear out stock (b) authorization   2. the clear space between things
11. **com·pat·i·ble**   *adj.* capable of living together in harmony or getting along well together
12. **com·pat·ib·ly**   *adv.* in a compatible manner
13. **com·pli·ance**   *n.* a complying by giving in to a request, demand, etc. or following a rule or requirement
14. **com·pli·ant**   *adj.* inclined to comply
15. **com·ply**   *v.* **–plied, –ply·ing** act in accordance with someone's rules, commands, or wishes
16. **de·pend**   *v.* **–pen·ded, –pend·ing** 1. have faith or confidence in   2. be determined by conditions or circumstances   3. hang
17. **de·pend·a·ble** *adj.* that can be depended on
    SYN[25]. – **dependable** refers to a person or thing that can be depended on as in an emergency and often suggest personal loyalty, levelheadedness, or steadiness [she is a *dependable* friend]; **reliable** is used of a person or thing that can be counted upon to do what is expected or required [his *reliable* assistant]; **trusty** applies to a person or thing that has in the past always been trustworthy or dependable [his *trusty* horse]
18. **de·pend·ab·ly** *adv.* in a faithful manner
19. **de·tect**   *v.* **–tec·ted, –tect·ing** to discover (something hidden or not easily noticed) [to *detect* a slight flaw in an argument]
20. **de·tect·a·ble**   *adj.* 1. capable of being detected   2. easily seen or noticed
21. **ex·per·i·ence**   *n.* the act of living through an event or events [*experience* teaches us much]
22. **ig·nor·ance**   *n.* lack of knowledge
23. **ig·nor·ant**   *adj.* 1. uneducated; lacking knowledge   2. unaware because of a lack of relevant information or knowledge

---

[25] Syn. stands for synonymy. It is a list of synonyms found at the end of the entry in some words in a dictionary.

24. **ig·nore**   *v.* **–nored, –nor·ing** 1. refuse to acknowledge   2. fail to notice
    3. be ignorant of
25. **im·poss·i·ble**   *adj.* not possible; not capable of being or happening
26. **im·poss·ib·ly**   *adv.* to a degree not possible of achieving
27. **in·cred·i·ble**   *adj.* 1. not credible; unbelievable [an *incredible* story]   2. so
    great, unusual, etc. as to seem impossible [*incredible* speed]
28. **in·cred·ib·ly**   *adv.* 1. not easy to believe   2. exceedingly; extremely
29. **in·gred·i·ent** *n.* any of the things that a mixture is made of [sugar is a basic *ingredient*
    of candy]
30. **ob·tain**   *v.* **–tained, –tain·ing** to get possession of by effort
31. **ob·tain·a·ble**   *adj.* capable of being obtained
32. **per·ma·nence** *n.* the idea of being able to exist for an indefinite duration
33. **per·ma·nent**   *adj.* lasting, or intended to last indefinitely or for a long time
34. **per·miss·i·ble** *adj.* that can be permitted; allowable
35. **per·miss·ib·ly** *adv.* in a permissible manner
36. **pro·mi·nence**   *n.* 1. the state of being prominent; widely known or eminent   2.
    relative importance   3. something that bulges out or protrudes from its surroundings
37. **pro·mi·nent**   *adj.* 1. noticeable at once; conspicuous [a bird with *prominent*
    markings]   2. widely and favorably known [a *prominent* artist]
    SYN. –prominent refers to that which stands out from or as from its background or
    setting [a *prominent* nose; a *prominent* author]; **noticeable** is applied to that which is
    likely to be noticed or worth noticing [a *noticeable* improvement]; **remarkable** applies
    to that which is noticeable because it is unusual or exceptional [*remarkable* features;
    remarkable strength]; **striking** is used of something so out of the ordinary that it leaves
    a sharp impression on the mind [a *striking* contrast; a *striking* design]
38. **re·sem·blance** *n.* a point, degree, or sort of likeness
    SYN. –resemblance usually implies being alike in a superficial way or only seeming
    alike, as in looks [the *resemblance* between a diamond and a zircon]; **likeness** implies
    being closely alike in appearance, qualities, nature, etc. [her remarkable *likeness* to her
    brother]; **similarity** suggest a being alike only in a certain way or to some extent [your
    problem bears a certain *similarity* to mine]
39. **re·sem·ble**   *v.* **–bled, –bl·ing** appear like; be similar or bear a likeness to
40. **sus·cep·ti·ble**   *adj.* easily affected emotionally; having sensitive feelings
       –susceptible to easily influenced by or affected with

Practicing the words
A. Finish each incomplete spelling word with the correct ending. Write the complete words after the sentence and indicate which part of speech it is by writing the abbreviation next to each word.

1. The resembl____ between the sisters was incred____.

_____

2. The ambassadors hoped for a perman____ alli____ between the two compat____ countries.

_____

3. Clear____ for that project was not immediately obtain____.

_____

4. This ingredi____ is easily detect____.

_____

5. Compli____ with that difficult rule was nearly imposs____.

_____

6. His ignor____ of the important issues makes discussion almost imposs____.

_____

7. Your paper on your camping experi____ is not accept____.

_____

B.

Find the spelling words that are needed to complete the story.

Charley's family lived in an old house that was ___1___ to a small forest. His house was ___2___ only by walking through the forest. However, in the hot, dry summer months, the forest was ___3___ to fires. Fire marshals had posted signs in ___4___ places to warn people of the danger. Campfires were not ___5___ in the summer.

One August day, Charley and his dog Fido were on their way home. Suddenly, the smell of smoke was clearly ___6___. Charley assumed that some picnickers were not in ___7___ with the law. Gradually, the smell grew stronger. All at once, Charley and Fido seemed surrounded by an amazing, ___8___ wall of smoke. Fido, who was usually ___9___ in an emergency, started to run away. Charley called her, but she was soon out of sight. Charley froze and didn't know which way to go. Then Fido reappeared and motioned for Charley to follow. She had found a way out! Together, they escaped, but Charley knew he would never forget his frightening ___10___.

1. _____

2. _____

3. _____

4. _____

5. _____

6. _____

7. _____

8. _____

9. _____

10. _____

C. Synonym

A synonymy is a special section at the end of some word entries in a dictionary. It contains a list of synonyms for the entry word. Short phrases or sentences may be included to show the slight differences between the word meanings.

Look up dependable, resemblance, and prominent in your spelling dictionary. Read the synonymy at the end of each entry. Write the synonyms for each word.

dependable _____ _____

prominent _____ _____

resemblance _____ _____ _____

Now complete each sentence with the entry word or synonym that best fits the meaning.

1. The knight rode into battle on his _____ horse.

2. My pony has _____ strength for her size.

3. Leora drew a _____ of her father.

4. We listened to a reading by a _____ poet.

5. Did you notice the _____ between the cousins' faces?

6. Our doctor is always _____ in an emergency.

7. The performer wore a _____ Purim costume.

8. There is a _____ in the weather between the two states.

9. The store owner has a _____ manager who keeps the shop

   running.

10. There was a _____ drop in attendance at today's game.

D. Some **able** adjectives can be changed to adverbs by switching the final **e** for a **y**. Complete each phrase by writing the adverb form of the underlined spelling word.

1. <u>acceptable</u> dress   dressed _____

2. <u>compatible</u> playmates   played _____

3. <u>dependable</u> behavior   behaved _____

4. <u>impossible</u> task   _____ difficult

5. <u>incredible</u> strength   _____ strong

Now write a complete sentence using the new phrase.

1._____

_____

2._____

_____

3._____

_____

4._____

_____

5._____

_____

E. Fill in the blanks with the appropriate spelling word.

1. This is a class of __ __ __ __ __ __ __ __ __ young adults.

2. It is __ __ __ __ __ __ __ __ __ to write in colored pens in this class.

3. The principal is very __ __ __ __ __ __ __ __ __ __ __ __.

4. A great mark is __ __ __ __ __ __ __ __ __ __ when you pay attention.

5. Your effort is often __ __ __ __ __ __ __ __ __ __ in your work.

6. People are __ __ __ __ __ __ __ __ __ __ when they get along together.

7. If you are __ __ __ __ __ __ __ __ __ __ __ to colds, wear a scarf.

8. It is __ __ __ __ __ __ __ __ __ __ __ if it complies with the rules.

9. It is __ __ __ __ __ __ __ __ __ __ to entirely eradicate all germs.

10. The __ __ __ __ __ __ __ __ __ Dreidel of Feitel Van Zeidel used to be my favorite.

11. After the season, old styles go on __ __ __ __ __ __ __ __ __ sales.

12. Yaakov Avinu bore no __ __ __ __ __ __ __ __ __ __ __ to Eisav.

13. __ __ __ __ __ __ __ __ __ of the law is no excuse.

14. It is permissible if it is in __ __ __ __ __ __ __ __ __ __ with the regulations.

15. Eisav tried an __ __ __ __ __ __ __ __ with Yishmael to overcome Yaakov Avinu.

16. I have some __ __ __ __ __ __ __ __ __ __ with using good grammar.

17. Perseverance is one __ __ __ __ __ __ __ __ __ __ of success.

18. A __ __ __ __ __ __ __ __ __ feature is very noticeable.

19. Repeating a good practice makes a __ __ __ __ __ __ __ __ __ good habit.

20. The Ezras Noshim is __ __ __ __ __ __ __ __ to the Bais Medrash.

Key Concepts
- preposition
- prefix
- syllables

A **preposition** is a type of word that is placed before a word to show that word's relation to another word in the sentence. It is placed in position before (pre) the word and it tells about the relationship of the following word to the part that came earlier. Some examples of preposition words are between, through, beside, from, to, at, etc.

A prefix can often carry the meaning of a preposition before the rest of the word. It comes before the rest of the word and can tell you about the relationship of the rest of the word to the other parts of the sentence. Understanding the meanings of prefixes can help better remember the meanings of words and can help you discover the meaning of new words better.

A **syllable** is a word part that has a single vowel sound. It might have a number of vowels (**boat**) or not even a single vowel (dan**g**ling). The key is that it is pronounced as a distinct part of the word separate from the other parts – usually with a separate motion of your mouth. A hint to distinguish the different syllables is to pay attention to your chin as you clearly pronounce the word. Each distinct movement of your chin marks a separate syllable. Sometimes an entire words is a single syllable. This is even true of long words such as **brought**.

Lesson Spelling Rule: A prefix often carries the meaning of a preposition before the word.

Prefixes used in this lesson, together with their meanings:
- inter- means between
- para- means alongside
- per- means throughout; thoroughly
- ab- means down or away from
- de- means under or away from

1. <u>INTER</u>MISSION
2. <u>INTER</u>VIEW
3. <u>INTER</u>STATE
4. <u>INTER</u>PRETER
5. <u>INTER</u>CEPTION
6. <u>INTER</u>RUPT
7. <u>INTER</u>NATIONAL
8. <u>PARA</u>MEDIC
9. <u>PARA</u>LLEL
10. <u>PARA</u>PHRASE
11. <u>PER</u>ENNIAL
12. <u>PER</u>COLATE
13. <u>PER</u>FORATED
14. <u>PER</u>PETUAL
15. <u>PER</u>SEVERANCE
16. <u>AB</u>DICATE
17. <u>AB</u>SENCE
18. <u>DE</u>STRUCTION
19. <u>DE</u>PRIVED
20. <u>DE</u>PLETED

Pay attention to the spelling words.

1. The prefix inter means "between." What word refers to events that occur

   between nations? _____

2. The prefix para means "beside." What word refers to a person who is not a

   doctor, but who works alongside of or assists medical people?

   _____

3. The prefix per means "through" or "throughout." What word refers to

   flowers that bloom throughout the year? _____

4. What two prefixes mean "down from" or "away from"?

   _____

> A prefix often carries the meaning of a preposition before a word to show you the relationship of the word with regards to time and place.

Spelling Dictionary

1. **ab·di·cate**   *v.* **–cat·ed, –cat·ing** to give up formally (a high office, etc.)
2. **ab·sence**   *n.* 1. the state of being away   2. the fact of being without; lack [in the *absence* of proof]
3. **con·tra·dic·tion**   *n.* a statement in opposition to another; denial
4. **de·plete**   *v.* **–plet·ed, –plet·ing** to make less by gradually using up (funds, energy, etc.)
5. **de·prive**   *v.* **–prived, –priv·ing** to keep from having, using, or enjoying [*deprived* of the comforts of life by poverty]
6. **de·struc·tion**   *n.* a destroying or being destroyed; ruin [the earthquake caused much *destruction*]
7. **e·dict**   *n.* an official public order or law put forth by a ruler or other authority; decree
8. **in·de·struct·i·ble** *adj.* that cannot be destroyed
9. **in·struc·tion**   *n.* a message describing how something is to be done; direction [*instructions* for a test]
10. **in·ter·cept**   *v.* **–cept·ed, –cept·ing** to seize, stop, or interrupt on the way; cut off [to *intercept* a message]
11. **in·ter·cep·tion**   *n.* 1. the act of intercepting; preventing something from proceeding or arriving   2. (American football) the act of catching a football by a player on the opposing team
12. **in·ter·mis·sion**   *n.* an interval of time between periods of activity; pause, as between acts of a play
13. **in·ter·na·tion·al** *adj.* between or among nations [an *international* treaty]
14. **in·ter·pre·ter**   *n.* a person whose work is translating things said in another language
15. **in·ter·rupt**   *v.* **–rupt·ed, –rupt·ing** 1. to break into (a discussion, etc.) 2. to break in upon (a person) while he or she is speaking, working, etc.
16. **in·ter·state**   *adj.* between or among states of the federal government [*interstate* commerce]
17. **in·ter·view**   *n.* 1. a meeting of people face to face to talk about something [an *interview* about a job] 2. a meeting in which a person is asked about his or her opinions, activities, etc., as by a reporter   *–v.* **–viewed, –view·ing** 1. to go to an interview in the hope of being hired 2. to conduct an interview
18. **pa·ral·lel**   *adj.* extending in the same direction and always at the same distance apart, so as to never meet
19. **pa·ra·med·ic**   *n.* person who assists a doctor, such as a midwife, aide, or laboratory technician
20. **pa·ra·phrase**   *n.* a putting of something spoken or written into different words having the same meaning; rewording for the purpose of clarification   *–v.* express the same message in different words

21. **per·co·late**   *v.* **–lat·ed, –lat·ing** 1. to pass (a liquid) gradually through a filter   2. to brew (coffee)
22. **per·en·ni·al**   *adj.* 1. lasting or active throughout the whole year   2. becoming active again and again; perpetual [a *perennial* problem]   3. having a life cycle of more than two years: said of plants
23. **per·for·ate**   *v.* **–at·ed, –at·ing** to make a hole or holes through, as by punching or boring, often in a pattern
24. **per·pet·u·al**   *adj.* lasting forever or for an indefinitely long time
25. **per·se·ver·ance**   *n.* persistence; steadfastness; continued, patient effort
26. **re·con·struct**   *v.* **–struc·ted, –struct·ing** to build up again, make over
27. **struc·ture**   *n.* 1. something built or constructed, as a building or dam   2. the arrangement of all the parts of a whole
28. **ver·dict**   *n.* 1. (law) the decision reached by a jury at the end of a trial   2. any decision or judgment

Practicing the words
A. Write the spelling word that matches each definition. Then circle the word in the definition that gives the meaning of the prefix. Next, indicate what part of speech it is by writing the abbreviation next to it..

1. a time of being away _____

2. punched through _____

3. between states _____

4. a tearing down _____

5. continued effort through difficulty _____

6. a coming between to stop or cut off _____

7. two or more things beside each other at an equal distance _____

8. a person who translates between languages _____

10. boil a liquid through _____

9. time in between _____

11. reword "beside" the original _____

12. to have had things taken away from _____

13. a lasting throughout time _____

14. a conversation between people _____

15. step down from a high office _____

16. to rudely break in between _____

B. Make spelling words from these sets of words. First cross out one letter in each word. Then write the remaining letters together to form a spelling word. The first one has been done for you.

intern + ace + potion =   interception

part + call + gel =   _____

perform + hated =   _____

pier + pets + dual =   _____

cab + dice + mate =   _____

winter + amiss + lion =   _____

interns + ration + gal =   _____

cab + sent + ace =   _____

ode + prim + vied =   _____

spar + came + dice =   _____

perk + severe + lance =   _____

perch + old + rate =   _____

deep + lent + red =   _____

pat + graph + raise =   _____

C. A syllable is a portion of a word that has a single vowel sound. It might have no vowels or might have numerous vowels. The vowels might be written together or might be separated by consonants. All the letters that are pronounced with the same vowel SOUND make up the syllable. A hint to remember it is to feel your face change as you clearly enunciate the word. As your face changes to form a new sound segment of the word, that indicates to you that you have completed the first syllable and are beginning a new one. Find a spelling word to complete each sentence. Then write the words broken up according to its syllables. Separate each syllable with a hyphen or a line.

1. Overspending has _____ the treasury.

2. The countries signed an _____ agreement.

3. A nurse and a _____ assisted the doctor.

4. Will you _____ the coffee?

5. The rose is a _____ plant.

6. Draw two _____ lines.

7. We need an _____ for the foreign visitor.

8. The truck has an _____ route.

9. The reporter's _____ was on Kol Beramah.

10. The king had to _____ his throne.

11. The play's _____ is after Act I.

12. The paper is _____ for easy tearing.

D. In לשון הקודש a syllable is called either a יתד or a תנועה. In very many of the פיוטים and שירים from the Spanish and African Rishonim, the basis of the verses were written in a format based on these syllables. There is a slight difference between syllables in לשון הקודש and English. In לשון הקודש, the sound of שוא is not a separate syllable, even though it is pronounced with a different movement of the jaw.

A יתד is a syllable that begins with a שוא נא or its assistants (חטף קמץ, חטף פתח, חטף סגול) and continues with the next נקודה. It continues until the following נקודה, which begins the next syllable.

A תנועה is a syllable that begins with a true נקודה on the letter that begins the syllable. It might just be that letter, or up to three letters, all the letters that are pronounced with that נקודה. A שוא cannot begin a תנועה. If it is a שוא נח, it might end the תנועה if the following letter has a new נקודה or a שוא נע; or the תנועה will continue if the following letter is also a שוא נח. [There are two types of שוא נח – one is pronounced and is called נח נראה (visible), the other is not pronounced and is called נח נסתר (hidden). In the word בראשית, the ת is called a נח נראה because its sound is pronounced, but the א and י are נח נסתר because their sounds are not pronounced.]

For example, in the song for Shabbos day, דרור יקרא, the pattern is יתד ושני תעועות. The first stanza of the song is **דרור** יק·רא **לבן** עם בת **וינ·צר**·כם **כמו** ב·בת **נעים** שמ·כם **ולא** יוש·בת **שבו** ונו·חו **ביום** ש·בת. The יתד's have been underlined and bolded. Syllables in a single word have been separated with the dot.

On the next page you have the beginning of the Baal Hamaor's introduction to His Sefer Hamaor on the Rif. It is printed in the Vilna Shas right before the Rif on Maseches Brachos. The parts that might have contained Shaimos have been greyed out. As it states in the beginning of the section that is visible, each verse is comprised of two stanzas, both of which contain a יתד followed by 2 תנועות, another יתד followed by 2 תנועות, a יתד and a single תנועה.

Incredibly, the Baal Hamaor is one of the most difficult Rishonim to understand, yet he writes at the top that he authored it when he was under twenty years old!

פתיחת רבינו זרחיה הלוי

מספר המאורות

כשהוחל החבור הזה היה מחברו בן תשע עשרה שנה ופתח בו בבתים האלה :

לְדִילָה. וּגְבוּרְתָּא.

וכתב על זה אביו החכם רבי יצחק הלוי זל בר זרחיה זל:

שיר לרבינו זרחיה הלוי זל מרובע ופשוט

closing stanza · opening stanza · שני תנועות · comprised

שיר מרכב מיתד ב״ת ויתד וב״ת ויתד ותנועה בדלת וכן בסוגר

קְחָה סֵפֶר כְּמוֹ צֹהַר תְּקוּמוּ ,   וְכַבֵּר אֶל נְתִיבָתְךָ תְּשִׂימוּ .
לִיצָהֲרֵי זְרַחְיָה בְּמִגְדָּל   יְרָחֵי חִבְּרוּ לַגַּם הֲרִימוּ .
לְזֹאת מָאוֹר שְׁמוֹ קָרָא לְאוֹת פַּ .   עֲבוּר הַזְכִּיר שְׁמוֹ נָשָׂם מְקוֹמוּ .

E. Build a word pyramid by following the code. Use the spelling dictionary to find four pyramid words that match the definitions.

The root **dic** means "to say or proclaim."

1. a decision proclaimed at the end of a trial

   _____

2. to say that one gives something up

   _____

3. an official order or proclamation

   _____

4. the opposite of something said

   _____

					D	I	C				
				5	D	I	C	11			
			12	5	D	I	C	11			
			1	2	D	I	C	1	11	5	
					D	I	C	11	1	11	5	4
		9	10	7	D	I	C	11	6	8	7
3	8	7	11	10	1	D	I	C	11	6	8	7

A	B	C	D	E	I	N	O	P	R	T	V
1	2	3	4	5	6	7	8	9	10	11	12

F. Build another word pyramid. Find the four pyramid words that match the definitions. The root **struct** means "build."

1. directions on how to "build" something

   _____

2. rebuilt

   _____

3. not able to be destroyed or "unbuilt"

   _____

4. building or construction

   _____

			S	T	R	U	C	T			
			S	T	R	U	C	T	11	9	4
	4	4	S	T	R	U	C	T	5	8	
			S	T	R	U	C	T	5	8	7	10
	8	6	S	T	R	U	C	T	5	8	7
9	4	2	S	T	R	U	C	T	4	1	
5	7	1	4	S	T	R	U	C	T	5	1	6	4

B	C	D	E	I	L	N	O	R	S	U
1	2	3	4	5	6	7	8	9	10	11

126

G. Fill in the blanks with the appropriate spelling word.

1. The break between periods is only an __ __ __ __ __ __ __ __ __ __ __, not a real

   recess.

2. Part of fathers is the __ __ __ __ __ __ __ __ __ with Hanhalas Hamesivta.

3. Some __ __ __ __ __ __ __ __ __ __ highways are not long enough to actually leave the

   state.

4. Yosef Hatzadik had an __ __ __ __ __ __ __ __ __ __ __ when speaking to the rest of the

   Shevatim.

5. If an __ __ __ __ __ __ __ __ __ __ __ __ is returned for a touchdown, kids call it a 'pick

   six'.

6. The unnecessary comments __ __ __ __ __ __ __ __ __ the lesson.

7. There is __ __ __ __ __ __ __ __ __ __ __ __ __ competition between North Korea and

   the United States.

8. It took a long time for Lakewood Hatzoloh to arrange a __ __ __ __ __ __ __ __ __

   division.

9. __ __ __ __ __ __ __ __ lines do not meet.

10. I will __ __ __ __ __ __ __ __ __ __ this word if I say it a different way.

11. __ __ __ __ __ __ __ __ __ plants live throughout the year and usually bloom for a short

   period.

12. Hot water will __ __ __ __ __ __ __ __ __ through the ground beans for a brewed coffee.

13. Most notebooks are __ __ __ __ __ __ __ __ __ __ so the sheet can be detached cleanly.

14. There is __ __ __ __ __ __ __ __ __ conflict between Eisav and the Jewish people.

15. __ __ __ __ __ __ __ __ __ __ is necessary for success; it means sticking through with it.

16. The president will __ __ __ __ __ __ __ his position if he resigns.

17. Getting sick will lead to your __ __ __ __ __ __ __ from school.

18. Yaakov Avinu was shown a glimpse of the __ __ __ __ __ __ __ __ __ __ at the Mareh Hasulam.

19. Yaakov Avinu __ __ __ __ __ __ __ himself of sleep while learning in Yeshivas Shaim V'Eiver.

20. The gas tank is __ __ __ __ __ __ __ when it shows 'empty'.

Key Concepts
- assimilated prefixes
- irregular spelling

The words assimilated is similar to similar. Surprise! That's because when something becomes similar to its surroundings it becomes assimilated, just like Jews in exile become assimilated when they begin to conform to and become similar to their gentile neighbors. A prefix becomes **assimilated** when the last letter changes to match the first letter of the root. This often happens because it is easier to repeat the same letter than to switch sounds in middle of the word. The word assimilated itself contains an assimilated prefix. The prefix **ad** means "toward" and **similate** means "the same or similar." It is much easier to pronounce **assimilated** than it is to pronounce **adsimilated** (and the **d** might not be noticeable), so the **d** assimilates to **s**.

But when that happens, it also becomes easier to misspell the word because you might forget that the consonant is doubled. It can help to remember the **Mad Ad** is in disguise when it assimilates.

The prefix **ad** is assimilated more than any other prefix. It also causes more double consonant spelling problems than any other prefix.

When there are exceptions to regular spelling rules they are called **irregular spellings**. Just like prefixes become assimilated in order to make the pronunciation of the words easier, other irregular spellings happen when joining some prefixes or suffixes because it is easier to pronounce the word that way.

Lesson Spelling Rule: The prefix **ad** is assimilated more than any other prefix. Remember to double the consonants because the first one is really the assimilated prefix.

Mnemonic device: Remember that one of the double consonants is really the **Mad Ad** in disguise.

Prefixes used in this lesson, together with their meanings:
- de- means under or away from
- ad- means to, towards or opposite
- re- means back or again
- pro- means forward or in support of
- ex- means out
- in- means within
- com- means with, all together

```
 1.DE  +  CELERATE   =  DECELERATE
 2.AD  +  CELERATE   =  ACCELERATE

 3.RE  +  LOCATE     =  RELOCATE
 4.AD  +  LOCATE     =  ALLOCATE

 5.PRO +  GRESSION   =  PROGRESSION
 6.AD  +  GRESSION   =  AGGRESSION

 7.DE  +  RIVE       =  DERIVE
 8.AD  +  RIVE       =  ARRIVE

 9.RE  +  SUME       =  RESUME
10.AD  +  SUME       =  ASSUME

11.EX  +  CUSE       =  EXCUSE
12.AD  +  CUSE       =  ACCUSE

13.IN  +  TENTION    =  INTENTION
14.AD  +  TENTION    =  ATTENTION

15.PRO +  NOUNCE     =  PRONOUNCE
16.AD  +  NOUNCE     =  ANNOUNCE

17.RE  +  SENT       =  RESENT
18.AD  +  SENT       =  ASSENT

19.COM +  PREHEND    =  COMPREHEND
20.AD  +  PREHEND    =  APPREHEND
```

Pay attention to the spelling words.

1.Do the words in each pair have the same root? _____ Do they have the same prefix?

_____

2.Look at the first word in each pair. Does the spelling of the prefix change when it is

added to the root? _____

3.What prefix is added to the second root in each pair? _____

4.How is the prefix spelled when it is joined to a root that begins with a **c**? _____ with an **l**?

_____ with a **g**? _____ with an **r**? _____ with an **s**? _____ with a **t**? _____ with an **n**?

_____ with a **p**? _____

5.Is it easier to pronounce **adtract** or **attract**? _____ **Adfection** or **affection**?

_____

> The prefix **ad** is assimilated more than any other prefix. Remember to double the consonants because the first one is really the assimilated prefix.

130

1. **ac·cel·er·ate**   *v.* –**at·ed, –at·ing** to increase the speed of

2. **ac·cuse**   *v.* –**cused, –cus·ing** 1. to find at fault; to blame   2. to bring a lawsuit or charge towards (or against) someone

3. **al·lo·cate**   *v.* –**cat·ed, –cat·ing** to set apart for a specific purpose [to *allocate* funds for housing]

4. **ag·gres·sion**   *n.* 1. an unprovoked attack or warlike act   2. the practice or habit of being aggressive or quarrelsome   3. (Psychiatry) forceful or hostile behavior

5. **an·nounce**   *v.* –**nounced, –nounc·ing** to give notice of publicly; proclaim [to *announce* the opening of a new store]

6. **ap·pre·hend**   *v.* –**hend·ed, –hend·ing** 1. to capture or arrest [to *apprehend* a criminal]   2. to understand [to *apprehend* a problem]

7. **ap·pre·hen·sion**   *n.* 1. capture or arrest   2. a mental grasp or understanding   3. an anxious feeling or dread

8. **ap·pre·hen·sive**   *adj.* 1. able or quick to understand   2. uneasy or fearful about the future

9. **ar·rive**   *v.* –**rived, –riv·ing** to reach one's destination; come to a place
   –**arrive at** 1. to reach by traveling   2. to reach by thinking [to *arrive* at a decision]

10. **as·sent**   *v.* –**sent·ed, –sent·ing** to say that one will accept an opinion, proposal, etc.; agree (to)

11. **as·sim·i·late**   *v.* 1. to become similar to one's environment   2. to make similar

12. **as·sume**   *v.* –**sumed, –sum·ing** 1. to take over; seize [to *assume* control]   2. to take for granted; suppose [we *assumed* that he was loyal]

13. **as·sump·tion**   *n.* 1. the act of assuming [an *assumption* of power]   2. anything taken for granted [our *assumption* of his innocence proved correct]

14. **at·tempt**   *n.* earnest and conscientious activity intended to do something   –*v.* –**tempted, –tempt·ing** 1.make an effort   2. enter into an activity

15. **at·ten·tion**   *n.* 1. the act of keeping one's mind closely on something   2. notice or observation [his smile caught my *attention*]   3. care or consideration

16. **cause**   *n.* 1. a justification for someting existing or happening   2. the event, force, or reason that generate something, or make it happen   3. a proceeding in a court of law whereby an individual seeks legal remedy
   –*v.* **caused, caus·ing** to give rise to; make happen

17. **ce·ler·i·ty**   *n.* a rate that is rapid.

18. **com·pre·hend** *v.* –**hend·ed, –hend·ing** to grasp mentally; understand

19. **com·pre·hen·sion**   *n.* the act of understanding or the power to understand

20. **com·pre·hen·sive**   *adj.* 1. including much; inclusive [a *comprehensive* survey]   2. able to comprehend fully [a *comprehensive* mind]

131

21. **con·sent**   *n.* 1. agreement   2. approval   –*v.* –**sent·ed,** –**sent·ing** 1. to agree (to do something)   2. to give permission or approval
22. **con·tend**   *v.* –**tend·ed,** –**tend·ing** 1. maintain or assert   2. argue about something; fight against
23. **de·cel·er·ate**   *v.* to slow down
24. **de·rive**   *v.* –**rived,** –**riv·ing** to get or receive [we *derive* gasoline from petroleum; many people *derive* pleasure from music]
25. **dis·lo·cate**   *v.* –**cat·ed,** –**cat·ing** to put out of place; specif., to displace (a bone) from its proper position at a joint
26. **e·gress**   *n.* the act becoming visible, aparent   –*v.* –**gressed,** –**gress·ing** to come out of
27. **ex·cuse**   *v.* –**cused,** –**cus·ing** 1. to give reasons in defense of [she *excused* herself for being late]   2. to think of as not important; overlook; pardon [They *excused* his tardiness]   –*n.* a pretended reason; pretext
28. **grade**   *n.* 1. body of students who are taught together   2. a number or letter indicating quality (esp. of a student's performance)   3. a position on a scale of intensity or amount or quality   –*v.* **graded, grad·ing** assign a rank or rating to; determine the grade of
29. **in·sen·si·tive**   *adj.* not sensitive; having little or no reaction (to) [*insensitive* to music]
30. **in·ten·tion**   *n.* aim or purpose
31. **lo·ca·tion**   *n.* position; place; situation [a fine *location* for a Seforim store]
32. **lo·co·mo·tion**   *n.* motion, or the power of moving, from one place to another
33. **nun·cius**   *n.* 1. a messenger   2. the information communicated by a messenger; message
34. **pre·sume**   *v.* –**sumed,** –**sum·ing** 1. to take upon one's self without permission; venture [I wouldn't *presume* to tell you what to do]   2. to take for granted; suppose [I *presume* you know the risk you are taking]
35. **pro·gre·ssion**   *n.* 1. a moving forward or onward   2. a succession, as of acts, happenings, etc. [a *progression* of lucky events led to his success]
36. **pro·nounce**   *v.* –**nounced,** –**nounc·ing** 1. to say or declare officially, solemnly, etc.   2. to utter in the accepted or standard manner [he couldn't *pronounce* my name]
37. **pro·nounce·ment**   *n.* a formal statement of a fact, opinion, or judgment
38. **pro·nun·ci·a·tion** *n.* 1. the act or manner of pronouncing words   2. the way a word or language is customarily spoken
39. **re·cuse**   *v.* –**cused,** –**cus·ing** to disqualify oneself (as a judge) from a particular case
40. **re·gress**   *v.* –**gressed,** –**gress·ing** to go back.
41. **re·lo·cate**   *v.* –**cat·ed,** –**cat·ing** to move to a new location
42. **rep·re·hend**   *v.* express strong disapproval of

43.**re·sent**   *v.* **–sent·ed, –sent·ing** to feel or show bitter hurt or anger at or toward [he *resented* being called a coward]

44.**re·sent·ment**   *n.* a feeling of bitter hurt or anger at being insulted, slighted, etc. [his great *resentment* at being left out]

45.**re·sume**   *v.* **–sumed, –sum·ing** 1. to take or occupy again [to *resume* one's seat]   2. to begin again or go on with after interruption [to *resume* a conversation]

46.**re·sump·tion**   *n.* the act of resuming [*resumption* of classes after vacation]

47.**ri·val**   *n.* the contestant you hope to defeat   *–v.* **–valed** or –**valled, –val·ing** or –**val·ling** 1. be equal to in quality or ability   2. be in competition with

48.**sen·sory**   *adj.* of the senses or sensation

49.**sen·ti·ment**   *n.* tender feeling or emotion

50.**sentimental**   *adj.* 1. having or showing tender or gentle feelings, often in a foolish way [a *sentimental* song]   2. of or resulting from sentiment [to save a picture for *sentimental* reasons]

51.**sum**   *n.* 1. the whole amount   2.the result gotten by adding numbers or quantities   *–v.* **–summed, –sum·ming** 1. to add up   2. to summarize

So how do the prefixes and roots all add up to the definitions?

DECELERATE   The root **celere** means "swift." Combined with **de**, which means "down, away, or undo," it means "to slow down" (the opposite of going swift).

ACCELERATE   **Ad** means "toward." So to **accelerate** is "to go toward with swiftness, or to speed up."

CELERITY is a word that shares the root **celere** and means "a rate that is rapid."

RELOCATE   The root **locare** means "place." **Re** means "back or again." So to **relocate** is "to move to another place."

ALLOCATE   The root **ad** means "toward." So to place something towards a purpose is to **allocate** it.

LOCATION is a word that shares the root **locare** and means "place."

PROGRESSION   **Gradere** means "to step, or to go." **Pro** means "forward." So to step forward is **progression**.

AGGRESSION   **Ad** can mean opposite. So to step opposite or against someone is **aggression**.

REGRESS is a word that shares the root **gradere** and means "to go back."

EGRESS is another word that shares the root **gradere** and means "exit."

GRADE, meaning level, ultimately comes from the root **gradere** and has the meaning "step".

DERIVE   The root **rive** comes from a stream or river and means "to lead or draw off." **De** means "away." So to lead away is to derive.

ARRIVE   The prefix **ad** means "toward" and to draw off toward the destination is to **arrive**. Another possibility is that it does not share the root with derive; but rather comes from the root **ripa**, meaning "shore." In that case, arriving means "going toward shore."

RIVAL, meaning opponent, ultimately comes from **rive**, and has the meaning "using the same stream as another."

RESUME   **Re** means "again" and **sumere** is "to take or add up," so to take up again is to arriving.

ASSUME   **Ad** is "toward" and **sumere** is "to take up," so to take toward an opinion before you know the evidence is to **assume**.

SUM is a word that shares the root **sumere** and means "total, or all of the parts."

PRESUME is another word that shares the root **sumere** and means to assume something before it is going to be proved.

EXCUSE   The root **causa** means "charge or lawsuit," and **ex** means "out." So to get out of being charged in a lawsuit is to **excuse**.

ACCUSE   Combining the root **causa** (lawsuit) with **ad** (against), leads to the word **accuse** meaning "to bring a lawsuit or charge towards (or against) someone."

RECUSE is a word that shares the root **causa** and joins to the prefix **re** (hold back) means to disqualify oneself from a lawsuit.

CAUSE is another word that shares the root **causa** and means a reason, or a lawsuit.

INTENTION   The root **tendere** means "to stretch," and (surprisingly!) **in** means "in"; so to stretch yourself in to doing something is **intention**.

ATTENTION   Joining the prefix **ad** (toward) to the root **tendere** (to stretch or exert) gives **attention** the meaning "to stretch yourself towards something."

CONTEND is a word that shares the root **tendere** and means to stretch together for something

ATTEMPT is another word that shares the root **tendere** [although the sounds **nd** changed to **mp**] and joined with the assimilated **ad** (toward) means "to try something."

PRONOUNCE   The root **nuntius** is "messenger," and **pro** means "forward." So when you send a message forth to the public, you **pronounce** it.

ANNOUNCE   Since the prefix **ad** (toward) is very similar to **pro** (forward) and it is joined to the root **nuntius**, the meaning is very similar to pronounce.

NUNCIUS is a word that nearly directly comes from the root **nuntius** and means "messenger or message."

RESENT   **Re** (again) joins with **sentir**, which means "to feel." So to feel pain and hurt again and again is to **resent**.

ASSENT   Ad (toward) joins with **sentir** (to feel) and gives the word **assent** the meaning "to feel towards something, to give approval towards a request."

SENTIMENT is a word that shares the root **sentir** and means feeling.

COMPREHEND   The root **prehend** is "to hold," and **com** is "together or intensely," so to hold intensely is to **comprehend**.

APPREHEND Ad (toward) joined to **prehend** (hold) gives **apprehend** the meaning "to chase towards someone and then to catch hold of them."

REPREHEND is a word that shares the root **prehend**, and means "to strongly disapprove, to hold back."

The prefix **ad** means towards (or opposite) and often *assimilates* (ad + similar) to the letter that follows it when combined with a root. That means that the **d** changes to the first letter of the root to which it is joined.

Practicing the words
A. Complete each sentence with two spelling words that have the same root.

1.When you _____ announce the winners' names, _____ each

name carefully.

2.A careful driver knows when to _____ and when to _____.

3.We _____ much pleasure from watching the ships _____ at port.

4.Do you _____ the fact that I gave my _____ to the idea?

5.The city will _____ funds to _____ the historic building.

6.You should _____ that classes will _____ on schedule.

7.No one could _____ why it is taking so long to _____ the

criminal.

8.Attracting so much _____ was not my _____.

9.An unusual _____ of events finally led to an act of _____.

10.Did Robert _____ you of making up an _____?

B. Proofreading

Mrs. Tzudreiterovits has done it again. She has mixed up the wrong prefix with the right root. Help her say what she really means by rewriting the nine underlined words correctly. Keep the root, but replace the prefix.

It has come to my <u>intention</u> that the birdbath at the corner of Maple and Second Streets is the victim of <u>progression</u>! Too many speeding cars <u>decelerate</u> as they pass the birdbath. The birds used to <u>arrive</u> great pleasure from this birdbath. But now they refuse to go near it, and we have a very dirty bird population! We can surely <u>resume</u> that they must <u>assent</u> all the noise and fumes from speeding cars. There is no <u>accuse</u> for this situation. The police have promised to <u>comprehend</u> any illegal speeders in the area. However, I suggest that the city <u>allocate</u> the birdbath to a nearby park. Remember, a happy, well-groomed bird is a fine, feathered friend!

1. _____

2. _____

3. _____

4. _____

5. _____

6. _____

7. _____

8. _____

9. _____

C. Read the meaning of the following roots. Then write the spelling words that contain these roots and match the definitions below. Checking the meaning of the prefix will help you decide if you have chosen the right word.

gress – to go   **celer** – swift   **sen** – feel   **loc** – place

1. to move to a different **place**

     _____

2. to go at a **swifter** speed

     _____

3. to **feel** agreement with   _____

4. a **going** forward to attack

     _____

5. to **feel** hurt or anger

     _____

6. **place** or set apart for a purpose

     _____

7. slow down from a **swift** speed

     _____

8. a series **going** forward   _____

D. Some words have a form that follows an irregular spelling pattern. This means that they are exceptions to the general spelling rules. The dictionary lists these words as separate entries. The following words are irregular when joined with some suffixes. Find the correct spelling and write them correctly on the line. Then answer the questions below.

1. resume + tion   _____

2. assume + tion   _____

3. comprehend + ive   _____

4. comprehend + ion   _____

5. apprehend + ive   _____

6. apprehend + ion   _____

7. pronounce + ment   _____

8. pronounce + iation   _____

9. In which four words does the d in the base form change to s? _____

_____ _____ _____

10. Which two word forms add the letter p? _____

_____

11. Which form drops an o from the base word? _____

12. In which word is the spelling regular? _____

E. Build a word pyramid by following the code. Use the spelling dictionary to find the four pyramid words that match the definitions.

The root **loc** means "place" or "put."

1.to put out of place

_____

2.to put aside for a specific purpose

_____

3.the power of moving from place to

place

_____

4.to move to a new place

_____

			L	O	C						
			L	O	C						
			L	O	C						
			L	O	C						
			L	O	C						
			L	O	C						
			L	O	C						
		A	D	E	I	L	M	N	O	R	S	T
		1	2	3	4	5	6	7	8	9	10	11

F. Build another word pyramid. Find the four pyramid words that match the definitions.

The root **sen** means "feel."

1.a feeling of hurt or anger

_____

2.of the senses or feelings

_____

3.having or showing tender feelings

_____

4.showing no feelings

_____

			S	E	N							
			S	E	N							
			S	E	N							
			S	E	N							
			S	E	N							
			S	E	N							
			S	E	N							

A	C	D	E	I	L	M	N	O	R	S	T	V	Y
1	2	3	4	5	6	7	8	9	10	11	12	13	14

140

G. Fill in the blanks with the appropriate spelling word.

1. Give yourself enough space to __ __ __ __ __ __ __ __ __ __ in time to avoid an

   accident.

2. Press on the gas to __ __ __ __ __ __ __ __ __ __ quickly.

3. When משיח comes, בתי מדרש and בתי כנסת will __ __ __ __ __ __ __ __ to Yerushalayim.

4. We __ __ __ __ __ __ __ __ מעשר money to give to צדקה.

5. The __ __ __ __ __ __ __ __ __ __ of anti-Semitic hate is frightening.

6. Yiddin rarely should show __ __ __ __ __ __ __ __ __ when dealing with gentiles.

7. If you understand the meanings of prefixes, you can easily __ __ __ __ __ __ the

   meaning of many words.

8. If you have a good GPS, you should __ __ __ __ __ __ in time.

9. After Chanukah, we __ __ __ __ __ __ our schedule of studies.

10. I __ __ __ __ __ __ that you prefer better grades.

11. There is no __ __ __ __ __ __ to misspell the words rewritten in the second column.

12. Do not __ __ __ __ __ __ anyone falsely.

13. I am sure you have __ __ __ __ __ __ __ __ __ to achieve your utmost.

14. If you pay __ __ __ __ __ __ __ __ __, you will learn more.

15. A baal koyreh must do his best to __ __ __ __ __ __ __ __ __ the words correctly.

16. During Shacharis, the gabbai does not __ __ __ __ __ __ __ __ __ 'על הניסים' because it is a

   הפסק.

17. If you __ __ __ __ __ __ something, you risk transgressing לא תטור.

18. She indicated her __ __ __ __ __ __ with a nod of her head.

141

19. When you understand prefixes, it becomes easy to __ __ __ __ __ __ __ __ __ __ the language.

20. The police will not rest until they __ __ __ __ __ __ __ __ __ the criminal.

Spelling Lesson 14

Key Concepts
- hard and soft letters
- singular and plural nouns
- noun verb agreement
- plural forms of verbs
- present tense
- possessive form of nouns

A **hard** letter sound is one that is short and explosive, that comes out of the mouth with a popping sound. It cannot be lengthened for an appreciable amount of time. Some examples of hard sounds are **b**, **d**, and **k**.

A **soft** sound is one that comes out of the mouth along with air in a sort of hissing sound. It can be short or lengthened without changing its sound. Some examples of soft sounds are **ch**, **s**, and **th**.

A number of letters have both hard and soft sounds, like **c**, **g**, and **t**. Whether a letter sound is soft or hard usually depends on the following letter. If the letter is followed by a consonant, **a**, **o**, or **u** it will usually be a hard sound, but if it is followed by an **e**, **i**, or **y** it will usually be a soft sound.[26]

A **singular** noun is one that refers to an individual or an entire group as if it were an individual. When you use a singular noun the rest of your sentence must also be in singular tense. This is called **noun verb agreement**. The verbs must be in single tense to be in harmony and "agree" with the singular noun.

Most singular nouns change to **plural** by simply adding **s** to the end of the singular form. Sometimes you need to add **es**, sometimes change the end of the singular form slightly, and sometimes there are irregular plural forms. Whenever you are using a plural noun you must make sure that you also use the plural tense of the verbs to be in agreement.

The rules for single and plural for verbs when talking about doing something in the present tense is just about the opposite of nouns. **Present tense** means doing something right now, as opposed to past tense which means that it was already done or future tense which means that it will be done later. The plain form of the verb is usually good for plural in the present tense (for example, they **give** and **take**) but **s** needs to be added to form the singular present tense (he **gives** and **takes**).

To show that something belongs to a noun you need to use the **possessive** form of the noun. Add **'s** to all singular nouns and to a plural noun that does not end in **s** to form the possessive form (girl+**'s** = girl's, men+**'s** = men's). To a plural noun that ends in **s**, just add an apostrophe after the **s** (writers+**'** = writers').

Lesson Spelling Rule: When the letters **c** and **g** have a soft sound, they are usually followed by an **e**, **i**, or a **y**.

When the letters **c** and **g** have a hard sound, they are usually followed by an **a**, **o**, **u**, or any consonant except **y**.

Mnemonic device: Many word end with the letters **cle** (recycle, miracle, vehicle) or **gle** (angle, jungle, untangle). Remember that these endings cannot be spelled **cel** or **gel** without changing the sound of **c** and **g**.

---

[26] There are always exceptions to every rule. The **g** in **get** and **give** is hard even though it is followed by **e** and **i**. The **c** in **facade** is soft even though it is followed by **a**.

1. CITIZEN
2. COURAGE
3. CONCERNED
4. URGENCY
5. LICENSE
6. MAGICIAN
7. CALENDAR
8. CATEGORY
9. CUSTOM
10. GUARANTEE
11. CEREAL
12. GUARD
13. CERTAIN
14. DIGESTION
15. CIRCUMSTANCE
16. FRAGILE
17. RECYCLE
18. GYMNASIUM
19. RELUCTANT
20. GARGLE

Pay attention to the spelling words.

In this spelling list, the letters **c** and **g** have both a hard sound (<u>c</u>ake, gavel) and a soft sound (fa<u>c</u>e, pa<u>g</u>e).

1. Find nine words that contain a soft **c**. Write the letter that follows the soft **c** in each word.

    _____ _____ _____ _____ _____ _____ _____ _____ _____

2. Find eight words that contain a hard **c**. Write the letter that follows the hard **c** in each word.

    _____ _____ _____ _____ _____ _____ _____ _____

3. Find six soft **g** sounds in the list. Write the letter that comes after every **g** that has a soft sound.

    _____ _____ _____ _____ _____ _____

4. Find five hard **g** sounds. Write the letter that follows each hard **g**.

    _____ _____ _____ _____ _____

5. Do the letters **c** and **g** have a hard or a soft sound when they are followed by a consonant?

    _____

6. By the letters **e**, **i** or **y**? _____

7. By the letters **a**, **o**, or **u**? _____

144

> When the letters **c** and **g** have a soft sound, they are usually followed by an **e**, **i**, or a **y**.
>
> When the letters **c** and **g** have a hard sound, they are usually followed by an **a**, **o**, **u**, or any consonant except **y**.
>
> Many word end with the letters **cle** (recycle, miracle, vehicle) or **gle** (angle, jungle, untangle). Remember that these endings cannot be spelled **cel** or **gel** without changing the sound of **c** and **g**.

Spelling Dictionary

1. **cal·en·dar** *n.* a table or chart that shows the days, weeks, and months of a year

2. **cat·e·go·ry** *n.* a class or division in a system of classification [biology is divided into two *categories*, zoology and botany]

3. **ce·re·al** *n.* food made from grain, esp. breakfast food, as oatmeal or cornflakes

4. **cer·tain** *adj.* 1. sure; positive [I'm *certain* she's here]   2. not named or described [a *certain* person was just here – guess who]

5. **cir·cum·stance** *n.* 1. a fact or event connected with or forming part of a situation [what were the *circumstances* that led to his arrest?]   2. (pl.[27]) conditions affecting a person, esp. financial conditions [in comfortable *circumstances*]

6. **ci·ti·zen** *n.* a member of a state or nation who owes allegiance to it and is entitled to full civil rights

7. **con·cern** *n.* 1. an anxious feeling; worry   2. something that causes anxiety   *–v.* **–cerned, –cern·ing** 1. be relevant to [there were lots of questions *concerning* his speech]   2. be on the mind of [I'm *concerned* about young people vaping]

8. **con·cerned** *adj.* 1. involved or interested   2. uneasy or anxious   *–v.* past tense of concern

9. **cour·age** *n.* a willingness to face and deal with danger, trouble, or pain; bravery   **–the courage of one's convictions** the courage to do what one thinks is right

10. **cus·tom** *n.* a usual practice or habitual way of behaving; habit

11. **di·ges·tion** *n.* the act or process of changing (food) in the stomach and intestines into a form that can be used by the body

12. **frag·ile** *adj.* easily broken, damaged, or destroyed; delicate [*fragile* china]

13. **gar·gle** *n.* 1. a liquid used for gargling   2. a gargling sound   *–v.* **–gled, –gl·ing** to rinse (the throat) with a liquid kept in motion by slowly forcing out air from the lungs

14. **guar·an·tee** *n.* a pledge that something will be replaced if it is not as represented [thirty-day *guarantee* on the vehicle]

15. **guard** *n.* 1. the act or duty of watching over, protecting, and defending   2. a person or group that guards   *–v.* **guarded, guard·ing** 1. to watch over and protect [shepherds guard their flocks by night]   2. to keep from escape or trouble

16. **gym·na·si·um** *n.* a room or building equipped for physical training and athletic sports

17. **li·cense** *n.* formal or legal permission to do something [a *license* to marry]   *–v.* **cense cense** to give a license to or for; permit formally

18. **ma·gi·cian** *n.* an expert in magic

19. **re·cy·cle** *v.* **–cled, –cl·ing** to use again and again, as a single supply of water

20. **re·luc·tant** *adj.* not wanting (*to* do something); unwilling

21. **ur·gen·cy** *n.* an urgent quality or state; need for quick action

---

[27] Pl. stands for plural. This indicates that this usage of the word is only in the plural form of the word.

Practicing the words
A. Find the missing vowels in each word. Then rewrite the word.

1. c __ t __ g __ r __   _____

2. c __ r __ __ l   _____

3. fr __ g __ l __   _____

4. c __ t __ z __ n   _____

5. g __ __ rd   _____

6. c __ st __ m   _____

7. g __ rgl __   _____

8. l __ c __ ns __   _____

9. __ rg __ nc __   _____

10. c __ rt __ __ n   _____

11. g __ mn __ s __ __ m   _____

12. c __ rc __ mst __ nc __   _____

13. c __ l __ nd __ r   _____

14. r __ l __ ct __ nt   _____

15. g __ __ r __ nt __ __   _____

16. m __ g __ c __ __ n   _____

17. c __ __ r __ g __   _____

18. r __ c __ cl __   _____

19. c __ nc __ rn __ d   _____

20. d __ g __ st __ __ n   _____

B. Plural forms of nouns

The singular form of a noun is usually changed to plural by simply adding **s**.

When the singular form of the noun ends in a sound that is similar to s, you must add es to the word.

Examples of such sounds are **ch** (bench+**es** = benches), **s** (iris+**es** = irises), **sh** (brush+**es** = brushes), **x** (fox+**es** = foxes), and **z** (blintz+**es** = blintzes).[28]

Some words that end in o also need to add es (potato + **es** = potatoes).[29]

However, when the last letter is **y**, sometimes a slight change needs to be made to the base word. If the letter right before the **y** is a vowel, no change is needed and simply add the **s**. If the letter preceding the **y** is a consonant, then the **y** must be changed to an **i** and **es** must be added.

Some words that end with **f** or **fe** form the plural by changing **f** to **v** and adding **es**[30].

Write the plural form of the following words:

1. six   _____

2. kiss   _____

3. wish   _____

4. city   _____

5. knife   _____

6. loss   _____

7. fox   _____

8. coach   _____

9. flash   _____

10. life   _____

11. switch   _____

12. wife   _____

13. company   _____

14. box   _____

15. scarf   _____

16. loaf   _____

---

[28]   If the word already ends in **e**, just add **s** (axe+**s** = axes).
[29]   Unfortunately, there is no general rule for this, each word can be checked in a dictionary for the correct form.
[30]   Although this is not a hard and fast rule, generally, this needs to be done when the letter before the **f** is a consonant or it ends in **fe**.

17. couch   _____

18. axe   _____

19. flash   _____

20. valley   _____

21. day   _____

22. miss   _____

23. watch   _____

24. country   _____

25. toy   _____

26. glass   _____

27. witch   _____

28. choice   _____

29. spice   _____

30. chimney   _____

31. splash   _____

32. half   _____

33. ditch   _____

34. perch   _____

35. horse   _____

36. cry   _____

37. party   _____

38. place   _____

39. donkey   _____

C. Possessives

The possessive form of a noun shows that something belongs to it.

Add **'s** to all singular nouns and to a plural noun that does not end in **s** to form the possessive form (boy+**'s** = boy's, women+**'s** = women's). Even if the singular noun ends in **s** or **s** sound, still add **'s**. So Pinchos+**'s** = Pinchos's and Max+**'s** = Max's.

To a plural noun that ends in **s**, just add an apostrophe after the **s** (writers+**'** = writers').

Rewrite each phrase to show the possessive form of the underlined word.

1. The tricks of the <u>magician</u>   _____

2. the ingredients of the <u>cereal</u>   _____

3. the guarantee of the <u>saleswoman</u>   _____

4. the gymnasium of the <u>home team</u>   _____

5. the rights of the <u>citizens</u>   _____

6. the calendar of the <u>secretary</u>   _____

7. the uniform of the <u>guards</u>   _____

8. the beginning of the <u>custom</u>   _____

9. the category of the <u>children</u>   _____

10. the license of the <u>driver</u>   _____

Hard and soft letters.

Languages are often similar to each other, and even though Lashon Hakodesh is from Hashem, whereas other languages were made up by humans at the time of the Dor Haflagah, there are similarities between them. Lashon Hakodesh also has soft and hard letters. The letter ק is a hard letter, and the letter ס is a soft letter. There are also some letters that are sometimes hard and sometimes soft. For example, the ב in בראשית is a hard sound. The letter ב in the word ובהו is a soft sound. The way to know whether the sound s hard or soft is to pay attention to the דגש, the little dot inside the letter. If there is no דגש, the sound is soft; with a dot, it is hard. This type of דגש is called a דגש קל.

D. Alliteration

Alliteration is the repetition of beginning consonant sounds: **P**eter **P**iper **p**icked a **p**eck of **p**ickled **p**eppers. If the same consonant is used, but its sound changes (for example from hard to soft), that is not alliteration. For example, "curved ceilings" is not an example of alliteration because one of the words is a hard **c** and the other is soft.

Write alliterative sentences like the one below, that use the sounds of the letters **c** and **g**. Use as many spelling words as possible in a single sentence. The sentence can be just as nonsensical as the example below. Thinking of the sounds, and writing the sentences will help you to remember the correct spelling. Feel free to use the spelling words more than once, and not the entire sentence needs to be the alliterative sound. Try to come up with at least two sentences for **c** and **g**, each.

Concerned **c**onsumers **c**ontinually **c**omplained, **c**laiming **c**alendar **c**ustoms **c**aused **c**onsiderable **c**onfusion.

_____

_____

_____

_____

_____

_____

_____

_____

E. Fill in the blanks with the appropriate spelling word.

1. Not every __ __ __ __ __ __ has the right to vote.

2. It takes lots of __ __ __ __ __ __ __ to change a habit.

3. Agudas Yisroel is __ __ __ __ __ __ __ __ __ about government interference with religion.

4. The __ __ __ __ __ __ __ of the situation called for immediate attention.

5. A fishing __ __ __ __ __ __ __ is not required in NJ for someone under 16.

6. My old chavrusa sometimes performs as a __ __ __ __ __ __ __ __ – Amazing Aaron.

7. Some people get a new __ __ __ __ __ __ __ for the new solar year.

8. One __ __ __ __ __ __ __ __ of נביאים is כתבי הקודש.

9. Some have a __ __ __ __ __ __ to observe ניטל נאכט in January (6-7).

10. Selling a field with אחריות means giving a __ __ __ __ __ __ __ __ __ against prior שעבודים.

11. Some kinds of __ __ __ __ __ __ never have concerns of Chodosh.

12. __ __ __ __ __ __ Your Tongue is a book about Shemiras Halashon.

13. We are __ __ __ __ __ __ __ about the truth of Torah.

14. After the time of __ __ __ __ __ __ __ __ __, one can no longer recite a ברכה אחרונה.

15. A favorable __ __ __ __ __ __ __ __ __ __ __ __ caused his rescue.

16. Menorah oil cups are __ __ __ __ __ __ __ if they are made from glass.

17. Lakewood township requires people to __ __ __ __ __ __ __ certain materials.

18. The __ __ __ __ __ __ __ __ __ is where many free periods are spent.

19. Many students are __ __ __ __ __ __ __ __ __ to spend time working on homework.

20. To fight cavities, __ __ __ __ __ __ with antiseptic mouthwash.

Spelling Lesson 15

Key Concepts
- syllable
- dividing words
- hyphen
- accented syllable
- related words
- schwa

A **syllable** is a word part that has a single vowel sound. It might have more than one vowel (coat, hope) or it might have no vowel at all (fumbling). An easy way to help you distinguish the syllables of a word is to pay close attention to your mouth and chin as you clearly enunciate the word. Each separate movement of your jaw is a distinct syllable.

Sometimes a word needs to be **divided** at the end of a line of writing because there is insufficient space to fit the entire word. The word can be divided according to its syllables, separating between complete mouth movements so the reader can easily understand what you wrote. If a word has more than two syllables, it can be divided between any two of them. As you complete the first part of the word, write a **hyphen** (-) to show that the word is not finished, then complete the rest of the word on the next line. For example, in the word psychology, from lesson 7, there are three places the word can be divided. In most dictionaries, the words are actually divided according to their syllables. This shows you how to pronounce it properly, and also how you can divide it at the end of a line. This is how it looks psycholo-gy. There is no space between the first part of the word and the hyphen.

In most words with more than a single syllable, one of the syllables is pronounced with more stress than other syllables. For example, in the word example, the main stress is on the am, (like eggs AM pull). It would seem silly for someone to stress the first syllable (EGGS am pull) or the last syllable (eggs am PULL). The stressed syllable is called an **accented syllable**.

Words that share the same base word, but have different suffixes are called **related words**. Often, the pronunciation is similar, but sometimes the accented syllable shifts to a different location in some of the words and a different syllable becomes accented. With these words you can remember how to spell the word correctly by thinking of a different related word and how it is pronounced.

A vowel sound that is barely pronounced is called a **schwa**. Surprisingly enough, it is very similar to an actual שוא, from which it is derived. It only occurs in an unstressed syllable of a word and sounds like the e sound in the word the moment. It can be represented by any vowel, or even no vowel at all. In English the schwa sound can be a syllable by itself.[31] Examples of schwa are: **a**way, el**e**phant, cous**i**n, choc**o**late, s**u**pport, vin**y**l, rhy**th**m. When you have a word that has the schwa sound, it can be difficult to distinguish which vowel it represents.

In some base words, the final syllable is not accented and sounds like a schwa. You might not remember how to spell the word. Recalling related words, when the suffix causes that syllable to become accented, will remind you how to spell that sound.

Lesson Spelling Rule: Unstressed vowels can be difficult to identify, especially before the letter r. First, think of related forms in which the mystery vowel may be stressed. Then use other clues to help you distinguish ar/or and ary/ory:

The ending ar often follows the letter l.

The ordinary ary is more common than ory and ery.

The ending or often refers to a person or occupation. Both or and ory frequently follow the letter t.

---

[31]   This is different from Lashon Hakodesh, where no שוא is its own syllable. A שוא נח is part of the syllable that begins with the נקודה before it (a תנועה) and a שוא נע begins the next syllable together with the following (יתד) נקודה.

152

1.	POPULAR	POPULARITY
2.	REGULAR	REGULARITY
3.	SOLAR	SOLARIUM
4.	FAMILIAR	FAMILIARITY
5.	SIMILAR	SIMILARITY
6.	EDITOR	EDITORIAL
7.	AUTHOR	AUTHORITY
8.	SUPERIOR	SUPERIORITY
9.	MAJOR	MAJORITY
10.	MINOR	MINORITY
11.	ORDINARY	ORDINARILY
12.	LIBRARY	LIBRARIAN
13.	TEMPORARY	TEMPORARILY
14.	SECRETARY	SECRETARIAL
15.	VOLUNTARY	VOLUNTARILY
16.	IMAGINARY	IMAGINATION
17.	NECESSARY	NECESSARILY
18.	HISTORY	HISTORICAL
19.	VICTORY	VICTORIOUS
20.	MEMORY	MEMORIAL

Pay attention to the spelling words.

1.   Before the suffixes are added, what are the last two letters of the first five base words? _____

2.   What are the last two letters of the base words 6-10? _____

3.   Can you clearly distinguish the vowel before the final **r** in these two groups of words? _____

4.   Think of how both forms of each word is pronounced. Are the vowels easier to identify before or after the suffixes are added? _____

5.   What three letters come at the end of the base words 11-17? _____

6.   What unstressed vowel becomes stressed when suffixes are added to these words? _____

7.   Think of the way the last three words are pronounced. How many syllables does each word have? _____

8.   If the unstressed vowel were not pronounced, how many syllables would these words *seem* to have? _____

> Unstressed vowels can be difficult to identify, especially before the letter r. First, think of related forms in which the mystery vowel may be stressed. Then use other clues to help you distinguish **ar/or** and **ary/ory**:
>
>   The ending **ar** often follows the letter **l**.
>   The ordin<u>ary</u> **ary** is more common than **ory** and **ery**.
>   The ending **or** often refers to a person or occupation.
>   Both **or** and **ory** frequently follow the letter **t**.

Spelling Dictionary

1. **al·le·gor·i·cal** *adj.* 1. of or characteristic of allegory   2. that is or contains allegory
2. **al·le·go·ry** *n.* a story in which people, things, and events have a hidden or symbolic meaning
3. **au·thor** *n.* the writer (*of* a book, article, etc.)
4. **au·thor·i·ty** *n.* 1. the power or right to give commands or make final decisions; jurisdiction   2. an expert whose opinion is considered reliable [an *authority* on music]
5. **def·i·nite** *adj.* 1. exact and clear in meaning   2. certain; positive
6. **de·fin·i·tive** *adj.* 1. that decides or settles in a final way; conclusive [a *definitive* answer]   2. most nearly complete and accurate [a *definitive* biography]
7. **dic·ta·tor** *n.* a ruler with absolute power and authority, esp. a tyrant or despot
8. **dic·ta·tor·i·al** *adj.* of, like, or characteristic of a dictator; autocratic; tyrannical; domineering
9. **ed·i·tor** *n.* 1. a person who prepares copy for publication by selecting, arranging, revising, etc.   2. the head of a department of a newspaper magazine, etc.
10. **ed·i·tor·i·al** *adj.* of, by, or characteristic of an editor or editors   -*n.* a statement of opinon in a newspaper, etc. or on radio, etc.
11. **fa·mil·iar** *adj.* 1. knowing about; closely acquainted (*with*) [he is *familiar* with the subject]   2. well-known; common [a *familiar* sight]
12. **fa·mil·i·ar·i·ty** *n.* 1. intimacy   2. the fact of being closely acquainted (*with* something) [his *familiarity* with the subject makes him an expert]
13. **his·tor·i·cal** *adj.* 1. of or concerned with history   2. that really existed or happened [*historical* persons and events]
14. **his·to·ry** *n.* an acount of what has happened in the life of a people, country, institution, etc.
15. **i·mag·i·na·ry** *adj.* existing only in the imagination; unreal
16. **i·mag·i·na·tion** *n.* the act or power of creating mental images of what is not actually present or of what has never been
17. **in·fi·nite** *adj.* lacking limits or bounds; extending beyond measure or comprehension; without beginning or end [the universe is not *infinite*]
18. **in·fi·ni·ty** *n.* endless or unlimited space, time, distance, amount, etc.
19. **li·brar·i·an** *n.* a person in charge of a library
20. **li·brar·y** *n.* a room or building where a collection of books, periodicals, etc. is kept for reading or reference
21. **ma·jor** *adj.* greater in size, amount, or extent [a *major* effort]; greater in importance or rank [a *major* poet]
22. **ma·jor·i·ty** *n.* the greater part or larger number; more than half [the *majority* voted to adjourn]
23. **me·mo·ri·al** *n.* anything meant to help people remember some person or event, as a statue, holiday, etc.
24. **mem·o·ry** *n.* 1. the power, act, or process of bringing to mind facts or experiences 2. a person, thing, etc. remembered [the music brought back *memories*]
    SYN. –memory refers to the ability or power of keeping in or bringing to mind past thoughts, images, ideas, etc. [to have a good *memory*]; **remembrance** applies to the act or process of having such events or things come to mind again [the *remembrance* of things in the past]; **recollection** implies a careful effort to remember the details of some event [his *recollection* of the campaign is not too clear]; **reminiscence** implies the thoughtful or nostalgic recollection of

long-past events, usually pleasant ones, or the telling of these [he entertained us with *reminiscences* of his childhood]

25. **mi·nor**   *adj*. 1. *a)* lesser in size, amount, or extent [a *minor* accident] *b)* lesser in importance or rank [a *minor* official]   2. under full legal age

26. **mi·nor·i·ty**   *n*. 1. the lesser part or smaller number; less than half [a *minority* voted for the law]   2. a racial, religious, or political group smaller than the larger, controlling group

27. **nec·es·sar·i·ly**   *adv*. as a necessary result [cloudy skies do not *necessarily* mean rain]

28. **nec·es·sar·y**   *adj*. that cannot be done without; essential; indispensable [the food *necessary* to life]

29. **or·a·to·ry**   *n*. skill in public speaking

30. **or·a·tor·i·cal**   *adj*. of or characteristic of a skilled public speaker

31. **or·di·nar·i·ly**   *adv*. usually; as a rule

32. **or·di·nar·y**   *adj*. 1. customary, usual [the *ordinary* price is $10]   2. unexceptional; common; average

33. **pe·cul·iar**   *adj*. 1. particular; special [a matter of *peculiar* interest]   2. queer; odd; strange [things look *peculiar* through these dark glasses]

34. **pe·cu·li·ar·ity** *n*. 1. a being peculiar   2. something that is peculiar, as a habit

35. **pop·u·lar**   *adj*. 1. common; widespread [a *popular* notion]   2. liked by very many people [a *popular* actor]

36. **pop·u·lar·i·ty**   *n*. the quality of being popular

37. **reg·u·lar**   *adj*. 1. usual; customary [he sat in his *regular* place]   2. consistent, habitual, steady, etc. [a *regular* customer]

38. **reg·u·lar·i·ty**   *n*. 1. the quality of being regular

39. **sec·re·tar·i·al**   *adj*. in the nature of a secretary

40. **sec·re·tar·y**   *n*. a person whose work is keeping records, taking care of correspondence, etc., as in a business office

41. **sen·a·tor**   *n*. a member of a senate

42. **sen·a·to·ri·al**   *adj*. of or relating to senators

43. **sim·i·lar**   *adj*. nearly but not exactly the same or alike

44. **sim·i·lar·i·ty**   *n*. a being nearly but not exactly the same or alike

45. **so·lar**   *adj*. 1. of or having to do with the sun   2. produced by or coming from the sun [*solar* energy]

46. **so·lar·i·um**   *n*. a glassed-in porch, room, etc. where people sun themselves

47. **su·pe·ri·or**   *adj*. 1. high or higher in order, rank, etc. [a *superior* officer]   2. above average in quality; excellent [a *superior* wine]

48. **su·pe·ri·or·i·ty**   *n*. the quality of being superior

49. **tem·po·rar·i·ly**   *adv*. in a temporary manner; not permanent

50. **tem·po·rar·y**   *adj*. lasting only for a time; not permanent

51. **vic·to·ri·ous**   *adj*. having won a victory; triumphant

52. **vic·to·ry**   *n*. 1. the decisive winning of a battle or war   2. success in any struggle [a football *victory*]

53. **vol·un·tar·i·ly**   *adv*. in a voluntary manner; of one's own free will or choice

54. **vol·un·tar·y**   *adj*. brought about by one's own free choice; given or done of one's own free will [*voluntary* gifts]

Practicing the words
A. Syllables
The following spelling words have been divided into separate syllables. Paying careful attention to the pronunciation of the words, find the accented syllable (the one that is stressed) and circle it. Then write the related spelling word and circle its accented syllable. Also indicate which part of speech it is by writing the abbreviation.

1. POP · U · LAR

_____

2. REG · U · LAR

_____

3. SO · LAR

_____

4. FA · MIL · IAR

_____

5. SIM · I · LAR

_____

6. ED · I · TOR

_____

7. AU · THOR

_____

8. SU · PE · RI · OR

_____

9. MA · JOR

_____

10. MI · NOR

_____

11. OR · DI · NAR · Y

_____

12. LI · BRAR · Y

_____

13. TEM · PO · RAR · Y

_____

14. SEC · RE · TAR · Y

_____

15. VOL · UN · TAR · Y

_____

16. I · MAG · I · NAR · Y

_____

17. NEC · ES · SAR · Y

_____

18. HIS · TO · RY

_____

19. VIC · TO · RY

_____

20. MEM · O · RY

_____

B. The words in each group are related in some way. Find and write a spelling word that fits into each group.

1. everyday, usual, common _____

2. vital, essential, required _____

3. writer, novelist, columnist _____

4. president, vice-president, treasurer _____

5. supreme, primary, leading _____

6. fanciful, unreal, mythical _____

7. geography, spelling, science _____

8. inferior, good, average _____

9. conquest, win, triumph _____

10. approved, current, liked _____

11. atomic, electric, nuclear _____

12. unimportant, lesser, trivial _____

C. Proofreading
An important part of good writing is learning to avoid wordy phrases. Improve this paragraph by substituting a spelling word for each of the eight underlined phrases.

In order to do research for a book about reporters, author Ted Bennet was spending a week at *The Daily Sun*. First, Ted met the person who makes assignments and checks the news stories. Then he was introduced to a real reporter who let him work alongside her. Ted noticed that there was a lot that was the same between writing books and news reporting. The biggest part of both writers' time is spent collecting facts. This means going on interviews, making phone calls, and checking information at the place with all the books and records. Both jobs also require skill and the ability to imagine and create things. However, most of the time the reporter is working to meet a tight deadline and is writing to fit a very strict format. Ted was not knowledgeable about or comfortable with this sort of system, and was glad that his job as as reporter was only for a short time. When the week was over, Ted returned thankfully to his book, full of admiration for the reporters he had met.

1. _____

2. _____

3. _____

4. _____

5. _____

6. _____

7. _____

8. _____

E. Writing

Find the word in each phrase that is a synonym (similar in meaning) to a spelling word. Write the spelling word. Expand each phrase into a sentence in which the synonym you found is replaced with the spelling word.

1. an expert on earthquakes   _____

_____

2. usually arrives on time   _____

_____

3. most of the students   _____

_____

4. willingly helped   _____

_____

5. a definite likeness between them   _____

_____

6. the article in Tuesday's newspaper _____

_____

7. efficient clerical staff in the office _____

_____

F. Circle the first letter of each word in the nonsense sentences below to find eight base words. Then add the suffixes.

1. Put each crocodile under lights in Avrohom's room.

   __peculiar__ + ity = __peculiarity__

2. Did Illana crochet the airplane that Osher rode?

   __dictator__ + ial = __dictatorial__

3. Sarah eats nearly all the orange radishes.

   __senator__ + ial = __senatorial__

4. Aharon lets Leah entertain giants on Reuvein's yacht.

   __allegory__ + ical = __allegorical__

5. Osniel readily accepted the old red yo-yo.

   __oratory__ + ical = __oratorical__

6. Dazzling exports frequently include natural, impressive, tremendous eggs.

   __definite__ + ive = __definitive__

7. If Nechama feels irritable, nothing is too enjoyable.

   __infinite__ + y = __infinity__

8. Perhaps ants rent little iceboxes and motorcycles, enjoy nature, travel, and raise yams.

   __parliament__ + ian = __parliamentarian__

G. Fill in the blanks with the appropriate spelling word.

1.The program's __ __ __ __ __ __ __ __ __ __ made it an instant success.

2.Keeping סדרים with __ __ __ __ __ __ __ __ __ __ is an essential habit for שטייגing.

3.A יאהרצייט candle is a type of __ __ __ __ __ __ __ __.

4.A __ __ __ __ __ __ __ __ might contain delicate plants or amphibians.

5.He addressed the דרשן with __ __ __ __ __ __ __ __ __ __ __ because they were related.

6.Making a דרשה from a __ __ __ __ __ __ __ __ __ __ is often called a בנין אב.

7.The __ __ __ __ __ __ __ __ __ __ __ duties are handled in a separate office.

8.He __ __ __ __ __ __ __ __ __ __ gave up his seat for the elderly gentleman.

9.I try to use my __ __ __ __ __ __ __ __ __ __ __ when composing these sentences.

10.They do not __ __ __ __ __ __ __ __ __ __ indicate ingenuity.

11.Using a number of pseudonyms, someone can write more than one __ __ __ __ __ __ __ __ __ in

each issue of his newspaper.

12.His extensive research made him an __ __ __ __ __ __ __ __ __ on מקוואות.

13.The __ __ __ __ __ __ __ __ __ __ of the בד"ץ עדה החרדית makes it a very sought-after השגחה.

14.The __ __ __ __ __ __ __ __ of מחמירים will usually rely on the עדה החרדית.

15.There is a __ __ __ __ __ __ __ __ of people in חוץ לארץ who still איבער-מעשר.

16.__ __ __ __ __ __ __ __ __, we do not assume the produce was imported from ארץ ישראל.

17.The __ __ __ __ __ __ __ __ is responsible for keeping track of the books

18.The library is __ __ __ __ __ __ __ __ __ __ closed for mid-winter vacation.

19.There is __ __ __ __ __ __ __ __ __ __ debate about where קריעת ים סוף actually took place.

20.If you learn תורה with all your might you will be __ __ __ __ __ __ __ __ __ __ over your יצר הרע.

Spelling Lesson 16

Key Concepts

- 1·1·1 words
- 1·1·1 doubling rule
- consonants and vowels
- VAC words or the 2·1·1 rule
- long vowels and short vowels
- idiom

The 1·1·1 doubling rule of spelling applies to **1·1·1 words**. These are short words that have a single syllable, a single vowel, and a single final consonant (for example **glad**). A syllable is a word part that has a single vowel sound and is made with a single movement of the chin and jaw. Once you determine that the word only has a single syllable, it must also have only one vowel. Words like **boat** or **hope** are not 1·1·1 words because they both contain more than one vowel. After determining that the word contains only one vowel, it must end in a single final consonant. **Help** and **lamp** are not 1·1·1 words because they end in two consonants.

A **vowel** is a sound that is made with the open throat or mouth and is like a נקודה. A **consonant** is any other letter sound.

The **1·1·1 doubling rule** means that when you add a suffix that begins with a vowel to a 1·1·1 word, you must double the final consonant of the base word (glad+**er** = gladder). This is an exception to the usual rule that when adding a suffix, no change is needed to the base word. If the suffix begins with a consonant, then there is no need to double the final letter of the base word (glad+**ly** = gladly).

If a word has more syllables, but the final syllable is accented and contains a single vowel with a single final consonant, the same rule applies. These are called VAC words: they end in a syllable that is **a**ccented, contains a single **v**owel, and a single final **c**onsonant. Another way to look at it is the 2·1·1 rule. The word has 2 (or more) syllables, the word ends in 1 consonant that is after 1 vowel and the ending is stressed (accented). For example, **commit** has more than a single syllable, but ends in 1 consonant after 1 vowel. So commit+**ing** = committed, but commit+**ment** = commitment.

A **long vowel** is a vowel sound that is made the same way as the vowel letter is called in the English language. For example, the letter **a** (sounds like eight) in the word **late** is a long vowel.

A **short vowel** is a vowel sound that is not made the same way as the vowel's letter name is. For example, the **a** in **apple** is a short vowel. Because each vowel has only one name, there is only one way to pronounce each long vowel. In contrast, there are numerous ways of pronouncing the short vowels because there are a lot of ways to be different from the long vowel. Some examples of different short **a**'s: amount, absolute; elephant; are.

The reason behind the 1·1·1 rule is because the silent e at the end of most words makes the vowel before it a long vowel. Since the usual rule for adding suffixes beginning with a vowel to a base word ending in silent e is to drop the e – remember way back in lesson 1 and 2 – it would become very confusing with 1·1·1 words (which do not have a silent final e) that also got a suffix beginning with a vowel. That is why the final consonant of the base is doubled, it clearly shows that the vowel was, and remains, a short vowel.[32]

Lesson Spelling Rule: Double the final consonant of a 1·1·1 word (or 2·1·1 word) before a suffix that begins with a vowel. Do not double before a suffix that begins with a consonant

---

[32] Because of this, if the 1·1·1 word contains a long vowel, it is an exception and you do not double the final consonant. For example, throw+ing = throwing.

Base Word	+ ED, ER	+ ING, EST, ARY, ANCE, ENCE, ENT, ABLE, AL	suffix beginning with consonant
1. FIT	FITTED	FITTING	FITNESS
2. THIN	THINNER	THINNEST	THINNESS[33]
3. MAD	MADDER	MADDEST	MADLY
4. THROB	THROBBED	THROBBING	
5. SUM	SUMMED	SUMMARY	
6. ZIP	ZIPPED, ZIPPER		
7. QUIT[34]	QUITTER	QUITTING	
8. ADMIT	ADMITTED	ADMITTANCE	
9. REMIT	REMITTED	REMITTANCE	
10. PERMIT	PERMITTED	PERMITTING	
11. OMIT	OMITTED	OMITTING	
12. SUBMIT	SUBMITTED	SUBMITTING	
13. OCCUR	OCCURRED	OCCURRENCE[35]	
14. RECUR	RECURRED	RECURRENCE	
15. CONCUR	CONCURRED	CONCURRENT	
16. REGRET	REGRETTED	REGRETTING	
17. ACQUIT	ACQUITTED	ACQUITTAL	
18. EQUIP	EQUIPPED	EQUIPPING	EQUIPMENT
19. ANNUL	ANNULLED	ANNULLING	ANNULMENT
20. COMMIT	COMMITTED	COMMITTING	COMMITMENT

> Double the final consonant of a 1·1·1 word (or 2·1·1 word) before a suffix that begins with a vowel. Do not double before a suffix that begins with a consonant.

Pay attention to the spelling words. The words on this list all fall under the 1·1·1 rule or the 2·1·1 rule.

1. Which words are 1·1·1 words? _____ Which are 2·1·1 words? _____

2. What happens to the final consonant of these words when a suffix beginning with a vowel is added? _____

3. What happens when a suffix beginning with a consonant is added? _____

4. In what three words are the letters **qu** treated as a single consonant?

   _____ _____ _____

---

[33] Since the suffix also begins with an **n**, there ends up being two **n**'s, but it is not because of the 1·1·1 rule.

[34] **Qu** is treated as a single consonant rather than a vowel. This is because the **u** tells you to add the **w** sound to the **k** of the **q**, and does not give instructions as to which way to pronounce that consonant sound of **kw**.

[35] This is an exception to the general rule that **ance** is added to complete words and that **ence** is added to roots.

1. **ac·quit**   *v.* **–quit·ted, –quit·ting** to declare not guilty of a charge
2. **ac·quit·tal**   *n.* a setting free or being set free by a court
3. **ad·mit**   *v.* **–mit·ted, –mit·ting** 1. to permit to enter and use   2. to acknowledge or confess
4. **ad·mit·tance**   *n.* 1. an admitting or being admitted   2. permission or right to enter

5. **an·nul**   *v.* **–nulled, –nul·ling** 1. to do away with   2. to make no longer binding under the law [the marriage was *annulled*]
6. **an·nul·ment**   *n.* a formal statement by a court that a marriage is no longer binding
7. **com·mit**   *v.* **–mit·ted, –mit·ting** 1. to put officially in custody or confinement [committed to prison]   2. to do or perpetrate (an offense or crime)   **–commit to paper**[36] to write down
8. **com·mit·ment**   *n.* a pledge or promise
9. **con·cur**   *v.* **–curred, –cur·ring** 1. to combine in having an effect; act together   2. to agree (*with*); be in accord (*in* an opinion, etc.)
10. **con·cur·rent**   *adj.* 1. occurring or existing at the same time   2. in agreement
11. **e·quip**   *v.* **–quipped, –quip·ping** to provide what is needed; outfit
12. **e·quip·ment**   *n.* whatever one is equipped with for some purpose; supplies
13. **fit**   *v.* **fit·ted** also **fit·ed, fit·ting** also **fit·ing** 1. to be the proper size, shape, etc. for [the coat *fits* me]   2. to make or alter so as to fit [his new suit has to be *fitted*]   *–n.* the manner of fitting [a tight *fit*]   **–fit to be tied** (Colloq.) frustrated or angry
14. **fit·ness**   *n.* 1. good physical condition; being in shape or in condition   2. the quality of being suitable or qualified
15. **mad**   *adj.* 1. mentally ill; insane   2. foolish and rash; unwise [a *mad* scheme]   3. angry (often with *at*) [she's *mad* at us for leaving]
16. **mad·der**   *adj.* comparative[37] of mad
17. **mad·dest**   *adj.* superlative[38] of mad
18. **mad·ly**   *adv.* 1. insanely   2. foolishly   3. extremely
19. **oc·cur**   *v.* **–curred, –cur·ring** 1. to present itself; come to mind [an idea *occurred* to him]   2. to take place; happen [the accident *occurred* last week]
20. **oc·cur·rence**   *n.* something that occurs; event; incident
21. **o·mit**   *v.* **–mit·ted, –mit·ting** 1. to fail to include; leave out [to *omit* a name from the list]   2. to fail to do; neglect
22. **per·mit**   *v.* **–mit·ted, –mit·ting** to allow; consent to [smoking is not *permitted*]
23. **quit**   *v.* **quit** also **quit·ted, quit·ting** to stop, discontinue, or resign from [to *quit* one's job]   **–call it quits** to break off an attempt to do something; to end
24. **quit·ter**   *n.* a person who quits or gives up easily, without trying hard
25. **re·cur**   *v.* **–curred, –cur·ring** to happen or appear again or from time to time [his fever *recurs* every few months]
26. **re·cur·rence**   *n.* happening again (esp. at regular intervals) [the *recurrence* of spring]

---

[36]   When there is a common phrase that contains a word used differently from its literal meaning (called an idiom), the dictionary often lists the phrase under the entry of that word and defines the phrase.

[37]   Comparative is a form of comparison that means more than or having more of than.

[38]   Superlative is a form of comparison that means the best at or having the most of.

27. **re·gret**   *v.* –**gret·ted,** –**gret·ting** to be sorry about or mourn for (a person or thing gone, lost, etc.)   –*n.* a troubled feeling or guilt   –**sent her regrets** a polite expression of regret as at refusing an invitation

28. **re·mit**   *v.* –**mit·ted,** –**mit·ting** 1. to make less or weaker; slacken [without *remitting* one's efforts]   2. to send (money) in payment

29. **re·mit·tance**   *n.* money sent in payment, as by mail

30. **sub·mit**   *v.* –**mit·ted,** –**mit·ting** 1. to present to others for them to look over, decide about, etc.   2. yield

31. **sum**   *n.* 1. the whole amount   2.the result gotten by adding numbers or quantities   –*v.* –**summed,** –**sum·ming** 1. to add up   2. to summarize

32. **sum·mary**   *n.* a brief report covering the main points; digest

33. **thin**   *adj.* having little fat or flesh; slender

34. **thin·ner**   *adj.* Comparative of thin

35. **thin·ness**   *n.* the property of being thin

36. **thin·nest**   *adj.* Superlative of thin

37. **throb**   *v.* **throbbed, throb·ing** to beat strongly or fast; palpitate, as the heart under exertion   –*n.* a beat or pulsation

38. **zip**   *n.* (Colloq.) energy; force   –*v.* **zipped, zip·ping** (Colloq.) 1. to act or move with speed or energy   2. to fasten or unfasten with a zipper

39. **zip·per·**   *n.* a device used to fasten and unfasten two edges of material: it consists of two rows of interlocking teeth worked by a sliding part

Practicing the words
A. Form spelling words by adding endings to the base words.

    1. permit + ed   _____

    2. fit + ness   _____

    3. submit + ing   _____

    4. mad + er   _____

    5. annul + ment   _____

    6. acquit + al   _____

    7. submit + ing   _____

    8. throb + ing   _____

    9. regret + able   _____

    10. mad + ly   _____

    11. thin + nest   _____

    12. zip + er   _____

    13. annul + ment   _____

    14. thin + ness   _____

    15. quit + er   _____

    16. recur + ed   _____

    17. regret + ed   _____

    18. concur + ent   _____

    19. omit + ed   _____

    20. sum + ary   _____

B. Answer each riddle with two spelling words that rhyme and belong in the spaces between the letters. Write the complete spelling words and the abbreviation of the part of speech.

1.   What did the criminal do when caught red-handed? ad__ed what he had com__ed

_____

2.   What did the coach give the baseball team? A com__nt to new equip__nt

_____

3.   What was the tired tailor always planning? qu__ng the f__ng

_____

4.   What would you call the second time an event happens? A re__ce of the o__ce

_____

5.   What do you call ticket money sent through the mail? The re__ce of the ad__ce

_____

6.   What was the teacher doing about overdue papers? per__ng late sub__ng

_____

7.   What did the confused judge do? co__ed the ac__ed

_____

8.   How was the astronaut prepared for his flight? He was eq__ed and z__ed

_____

9.   What did the witness say about the alleged crime? She c__ed that it o__ed

_____

C.

A **long vowel** is a sound that is the same as the vowel's name. For example, the letter **a** (sounds like eight) in the word **late** is a long vowel.

A **short vowel** is a sound that is not the same as the vowel's name. For example, the **a** in **apple** is a short vowel. Because each vowel has only one name, there is only one way to pronounce each long vowel. In contrast, there are numerous ways of pronouncing the short vowels because there are a lot of ways to be different from the long vowel. Some examples of different short **a**'s: amount, absolute; elephant; are.

Change the short vowel to a long vowel by adding a final silent **e** to each **1+1+1** word.

mad = _____   man = _____   sit = _____   dim = _____

mat = _____   plan = _____   shin = _____   rob = _____

When suffixes that begin with a vowel are added, **1+1+1** words and final silent **e** words are often confused. Write the correct **ing** form for each space.

1. grip/gripe   _____ the handlebars, he started _____ about the flat tire.

2. star/stare   Everyone was _____ at the actors who were _____ in the play.

3. scrap/scrape   Reuven considered _____ the old bicycle after _____ both fenders.

4. tap/tape   The loud _____ noise interrupted my _____ of the music.

5. wag/wage   He started _____ his finger when they spoke of _____ war.

6. mop/mope   If you don't stop _____ you'll never finish _____ the floor.

D. Idioms

An idiom is a phrase that has a meaning different from what the individual words usually mean. For instance, "flash in the pan" means "a sudden, seemingly skilled effort that fails." The meanings of idiomatic phrases are usually found in the entry for the key word of the idiom.

> **flash**   *v.* to send out a sudden, brief light, esp. at intervals
> **–flash in the pan** 1. a sudden, seemingly skillful effort that fails   2. one that fails after such an effort

Each sentence contains an idiom. The key word in each idiom is a spelling word. First find the spelling word and look it up in the spelling dictionary. Then write the idiom and the definition for it that is shown in the entry.

1. Let's call it quits for today and finish the game tomorrow.

_____

_____

2. Your clever ideas should be committed to paper.

_____

_____

3. Shoshanah sent her regrets by mail.

_____

_____

4. Whenever it rains on a Sunday I am fit to be tied.

_____

_____

E. Fill in the blanks with the appropriate spelling word.

1. The crossing guard __ __ __ __ __ __ __ __ __ the emergency vehicle to go ahead.

2. The word __ __ __ __ __ __ __ __ with alarming frequency.

3. It is not __ __ __ __ __ __ __ for a בן תורה to walk about untucked.

4. The __ __ __ __ __ __ __ __ lines are written with the point of the קולמוס.

5. __ __ __ __ __ __ __ __ unnecessary words make for smooth reading in your writing.

6. Who is still __ __ __ __ __ __ __ __ __ __ their application to Mesivta?

7. Nearly every __ __ __ __ __ __ __ __ __ __ of the word 'very' is very unnecessary.

8. He chased after them __ __ __ __ __, in hot pursuit.

9. The opinion of the entire courtroom __ __ __ __ __ __ __ __ __ with the jury's verdict.

10. The loan becomes __ __ __ __ __ __ __ __ when שמיטה arrives – unless a פרוזבול was made.

11. It takes great __ __ __ __ __ __ __ __ __ __ to stick to the דף יומי schedule.

12. Their mistake was a __ __ __ __ __ __ __ __ __ __ __ incident.

13. His finger __ __ __ __ __ __ __ __ with the pain of infection.

14. The court martial dispensed __ __ __ __ __ __ __ justice.

15. The __ __ __ __ __ __ __ is a nifty invention.

16. __ __ __ __ __ __ __ __ is not an option.

17. __ __ __ __ __ __ __ __ __ __ of questionable evidence rendered the decision unjust.

18. He __ __ __ __ __ __ __ __ a list of his expenses for reimbursement.

19. The president's __ __ __ __ __ __ __ __ __ is nearly certain.

20. Among my __ __ __ __ __ __ __ __ __ are a number of sharp blades.

Spelling Lesson 17

Key Concepts
- 2·1·1 rule
- accented syllable
- variant spelling

The **2·1·1 rule** of doubling final consonants applies to 2·1·1 words. 2·1·1 words have two or more syllables, end in a single consonant after a single vowel, and are accented on the final syllable. The 2·1·1 rule says that if you add a suffix beginning with a vowel to the 2·1·1 word, the final consonant is doubled.

An **accented syllable** is the part of the word that is stressed, or spoken with more emphasis. Another word for it is inflected syllable.

We already saw in lesson 15 that changing suffixes sometimes changes the inflection, or the accented syllable. The same thing can happen to 2·1·1 words. If adding a suffix moves the accent away from the final syllable in the base word, then the 2·1·1 rule does not apply.

Variant is another word for alternative. In language, variants are alternative forms of spelling, pronouncing, or saying a word. Some variants are just as common as each other, while others are less frequently used. The dictionary will often list the variant forms after the entry word that comes first alphabetically, or after the entry word that is used more commonly if it comes first. The way the dictionary tells you if they are just as common or one is more frequent is by using the words or and also. If it says or the variant, they are just as common. If it says also the variant, then the entry word is the more frequent one.

Sometimes variants are based on location where the language is spoken. For example Canada and Britain often differ from the United States. In this lesson, the words that end in l have variant spellings. In Canada and Britain the final l is often doubled.

Lesson Spelling Rule: The 2·1·1 rule only applies to a word that has its final syllable accented. If adding the suffix moves the accent away from that syllable, the 2·1·1 rule does not apply.

1. EXPEL	EXPELLED	EXPELLING		
2. REPEL	REPELLED	REPELLING		
3. PROPEL	PROPELLED	PROPELLING		
4. COMPEL	COMPELLED	COMPELLING		
5. DISPEL	DISPELLED	DISPELLING		
6. REFER	REFERRED	REFERRING	REFERENCE	
7. INFER	INFERRED	INFERRING	INFERENCE	
8. INFER	INFERRED	INFERRING	INFERENCE	
9. CONFER	CONFERRED	CONFERRING	CONFERENCE	
10. TRANSFER	TRANSFERED	TRANSFERING	CONFERENCE	
11. PROFIT	PROFITED	PROFITING		
12. BENEFIT	BENEFITED	BENEFITING		
13. BENEFIT	BENEFITED	BENEFITING		
14. EDIT	EDITED	EDITING		
15. LIMIT	LIMITED	LIMITING		
16. MODEL	MODELED	MODELING		
17. LABEL	LABELED	LABELING		
18. TRAVEL	TRAVELED	TRAVELING		
19. CANCEL	CANCELED	CANCELING		
20. QUARREL	QUARRELED	QUARRELING		

Pay attention to the spelling words.

> The 2·1·1 rule only applies to a word that has its final syllable accented. If adding the suffix moves the accent away from that syllable, the 2·1·1 rule does not apply.

1. What syllable is accented in the first ten words? _____

2. What syllable is accented in the last ten words? _____

3. Which words are 2·1·1 words? _____

4. What happens to the final consonant of the 2·1·1 word when a suffix beginning with a vowel is added? _____

5. Some of the 2·1·1 words use the **ence** suffix. What syllable is accented in those words? _____

6. Why isn't the final consonant of the base word doubled? _____

7. Which word has more than one way to pronounce it? _____

8. In what way would its spelling change because of its pronunciation? _____

172

Spelling Dictionary

1. **ben·e·fit**   *n.* anything helping to improve conditions [a paved road for the *benefit* of all the residents]   –*v.* to receive advantage; profit [he'll *benefit* from regular exercise]

2. **can·cel**   *v.* **–eled** or **–elled, –el·ing** or **–el·ling** 1. to cross out with lines or mark over   2. to do away with; abolish, withdraw, etc. [to *cancel* an order]

3. **chan·nel**   *n.* 1. a body of water joining two larger bodies of water   2. any means by which something moves or passes   3. the band of frequencies within which a radio or television transmitting station must keep its signal   *v.* **–eled** or **–elled, –el·ing** or **–el·ling** to send through a channel

4. **com·pel**   *v.* **–elled, –el·ling** to force or oblige to do something

5. **con·fer**   *v.* **–ferred, –fer·ring** 1. to give, grant, or bestow [to *confer* a medal upon the hero]   2. to meet for discussion

6. **con·fer·ence**   *n.* a conferring or consulting on a serious matter

7. **cred·it**   *n.* 1. praise or approval [to deserve *credit* for trying]   2. an official record that one has completed a unit or course of study   –*v.* to give credit to

8. **dis·pel**   *v.* **–elled, –el·ling** to scatter and drive away [wind *dispelled* the fog]

9. **ed·it**   *v.* 1. to prepare written material for publication by selecting, arranging, revising, etc.   2. to be in charge of what is printed in (a newspaper or periodical)

10. **ed·i·tor**   *n.* 1. a person who prepares copy for publication by selecting, arranging, revising, etc.   2. the head of a department of a newspaper, magazine, etc.

11. **e·mit**   *v.* **e·mit·ted, e·mit·ting** to send out; give forth [the kettle *emitted* steam]

12. **ex·pel**   *v.* **–elled, –el·ling** 1. to drive out by force; eject [harmful gases *expelled* through the exhaust pipe]   2. to dismiss or send away by authority [he was *expelled* from school]

13. **ex·tol**   *v.* **–elled, el·ling** to praise highly; laud

14. **im·pel**   *v.* **–elled, –el·ling** 1. to push, drive, or move forward; propel   2. to force, compel, or urge [what *impels* him to lie?]

15. **in·fer**   *v.* **–ferred, –fer·ring** to conclude by reasoning from something known or assumed

16. **in·fer·ence**   *n.* a conclusion or opinion arrived at by inferring

17. **la·bel**   *n.* 1. a card, strip of paper, etc. marked and attached to an object to show what it is   2, a descriptive word or phrase applied to a person, group, etc.   3. an identifying brand of a company   –*v.* **–eled** or **–elled, –el·ing** or **–el·ling** 1. to attach a label to   2. to classify as; call; describe

18. **lim·it**   *n.* 1. the point, line, or edge where something ends or must end [beyond the *limit* of his strength]   2. *pl.* bounds or boundaries [city *limits*]   –*v.* to set a limit to; restrict; curb

19. **mar·vel**   *n.* a wonderful or astonishing thing   *v.* **–eled** or **–elled, –el·ing** or **–el·ling** to be amazed; wonder

20. **mod·el**   *n.* 1. a small copy of an object   2. a person or thing considered as a standard of excellence to be imitated   3. a style or design [a 1984 *model*]   4. a person who poses for an artist or photographer   –*adj.* 1. serving as a model, or standard of excellence [a *model* student] 2. representative of others of the same kind, style, etc.; typical [a *model* home]   –*v.* **–eled** or **–elled, –el·ing** or **–el·ling** 1. to make a model of   2. to display (a dress, etc.) by wearing

21. **pan·el**   *n.* a flat piece forming part of the surface of a wall, door, etc.   –*v.* **–eled** or **–elled, –el·ing** or **–el·ling** to provide, decorate, etc. with panels

22. **pre·fer**   *v.* **–ferred, –fer·ring** to choose first; like better [he *prefers* baseball to football

23. **preference**   *n.* a preferring; greater liking [a *preference* for lively music]

24.   **pro·fit**   *n.* 1. advantage; benefit [it would be to his *profit* to read more]   2. *often pl.* income from money invested   *–v.* to make a profit; benefit; gain

25.   **pro·pel**   *v.* **–lled, –el·ling** to push, drive, or make go onward, forward, or ahead [a rocket *propelled* by liquid fuel]

26.   **quar·rel**   *n.* a dispute, esp. one marked by anger and resentment   *–v.* **–eled** or **–elled, –el·ing** or **–el·ling** to dispute heatedly

27.   **rav·el**   *v.* **–eled** or **–elled, –el·ing** or **–el·ling** to separate the parts, esp. threads, of; untwist

28.   **re·but**   *v.* **–but·ted, but·ting** to prove, or try to prove (someone or something) to be wrong

29.   **re·fer**   *v.* **–ferred, –fer·ring** to direct (to someone or something) for aid, information, etc.

30.   **ref·er·ence**   *n.* 1. a mention or allusion [she made no *reference* to the accident]   2. a statement giving the qualifications, abilities, etc. of someone seeking a position   3. a source of information [*reference* books]

31.   **re·pel**   *v.* **–elled, –el·ling** 1. to drive back or force back [to *repel* an attack]   2. to cause dislike in; disgust [the odor *repels* me]

32.   **trans·fer**   *v.* 1. to move, carry, send, etc. from one person or place to another   2. to change from one school, college, etc. to another   3. to change from one bus, train, etc. to another
       –n. a ticket allowing the bearer to change from one bus, train, etc. to another

33.   **trans·fer·ence**   *n.* 1. the act of transferring from one form to another   2. changing ownership

34.   **trav·el**   *v.* **–eled** or **–elled, –el·ing** or **el·ling** 1. to go from one place to another; make a journey [they *traveled* across the state]   2. (*basketball*) to move (usually more than two steps) while holding the ball

35.   **tun·nel**   *n.* 1. an underground or underwater passageway for automobiles, trains, etc.   2. an animal's burrow   *–v.* **–eled** or **–elled, –el·ing** or **–el·ling** to make a tunnel through

Practicing the words

A. Each base word in the first column is divided into syllables. Say each word to yourself and listen for the accented or inflected syllable – the one that you emphasize most. Circle the accented syllable. Then add the endings shown to the base word and write the word forms.

1. quar · rel   + ed = _____   + ing = _____

1. re · fer   + ed = _____   + ing = _____

2. prof · it   + ed = _____   + ing = _____

3. in · fer   + ed = _____   + ing = _____

4. tra · vel   + ed = _____   + er = _____

5. mod · el   + ed = _____   + ing = _____

6. con · fer   + ed = _____   + ing = _____

7. pro · pel   + ed = _____   + er = _____

8. ex · pel   + ed = _____   + ing = _____

9. ben · e · fit   + ed = _____   + ing = _____

10. pre · fer   + ed = _____   + ing = _____

11. re · pel   + ed = _____   + ent = _____

12. cred · it   + ed = _____   + ing = _____

13. can · cel   + ed = _____   + ing = _____

14. ed · it   + ed = _____   + or = _____

15. lim · it   + ed = _____   + ing = _____

B. Proofreading

Mrs. Tzudreiterovits is still combining the wrong prefix with the right root. Help her say what she really means by writing the nine underlined words correctly.

I am honored to be the keynote speaker at this year's inference on gardening. First, I feel repelled to tell you that you should grow what you like and like what you grow. My personal reference is the petunia[39]. I feel myself expelled toward any garden where precious petunias are in bloom. However, I don't want you to make the conference that I like only petunias. My preference to petunias is just an example. I love most flowers and am not propelled by any single type. I'm sure you will have no trouble conferring the idea behind my example of petunias to your own taste in flowers. I hope I have compelled any incorrect notion. Now, where was I?

1. _____

2. _____

3. _____

4. _____

5. _____

6. _____

7. _____

8. _____

9. _____

---

[39] A type of flower.

C. Read the definitions for **transfer**, **credit**, **editor**, **label**, and **travel** and use one word in each sentence below. You may add an ending to the word. Write the definition which best matches the word as you used it in the sentence.

1. When did that recording group switch to a new _____? _____

_____

2. Who is the _____ of the morning newspaper? _____

_____

3. You must take the final test to receive _____ for the course. _____

_____

4. The bus driver asked to see our _____. _____

_____

5. The referee called a penalty for _____ with the ball. _____

_____

D. Using the letter maze, begin by writing the letter I on the first line. Then count every three letters to find nine new words that are similar to the ones in this lesson. Cross out each letter as you use it. You should go around the maze three times, and there will be one letter left over. Write the words on the lines.

M ➡ I A I M R T P V T E E

M	U
Z	L
E	L
L	N
L	E
T	P
E	N
E	X
U	A
N	E
V	T
B	N
N	L

A E A R R H L L C E O

1. _____

2. _____

3. _____

4. _____

5. _____

6. _____

7. _____

8. _____

9. _____

Add **ed** or **ing** to the new words to match these definitions. Then answer the question.

1. showed wonder at   _____

2. praising highly   _____

3. forced to move forward   _____

4. directed into the proper place   _____

5. digging a passage through   _____

6. put up wall coverings   _____

7. giving off   _____

8. trying to prove something wrong   _____

9. untwisted, untangled   _____

10. Would you expect any of these forms to have a second spelling in the dictionary? Why?

_____

E. Fill in the blanks with the appropriate spelling words.

1. He __ __ __ __ __ __ __ __ his breath with a sigh of relief.

2. Mosquito __ __ __ __ __ __ __ __ __ is really useful in the summer.

3. The fan's __ __ __ __ __ __ __ __ __ broke when it got knocked over.

4. The defense's __ __ __ __ __ __ __ __ __ __ argument won the trial.

5. The clear evidence __ __ __ __ __ __ __ __ __ all doubt.

6. The עין משפט makes __ __ __ __ __ __ __ __ __ to the רמב"ם, סמ"ג, and the שולחן ערוך about the
   גמ

7. The גמ' __ __ __ __ __ __ __ __ that ריב"ל held לשמה בקיאין שאין לפי.

8. Devorah's __ __ __ __ __ __ __ __ __ was to have fleishig for supper.

9. The hanhallah is __ __ __ __ __ __ __ __ __ __ a great distinction on the מסיים.

10. He __ __ __ __ __ __ __ __ __ from one bus line to the other.

11. Shifra was __ __ __ __ __ __ __ __ __ from her experiences as a waitress.

12. The rules __ __ __ __ __ __ __ __ __ the poor workers.

13. The company __ __ __ __ __ __ __ __ her account for the spoiled merchandise.

14. If you like catching mistakes, you might want to become an __ __ __ __ __ __ __.

15. Preserve your hearing by __ __ __ __ __ __ __ __ your exposure to loud music.

16. The teacher __ __ __ __ __ __ __ __ how to do the prewriting work on the board.

17. The sefer was clearly __ __ __ __ __ __ __ with the name of its owner.

18. I met the __ __ __ __ __ __ __ __ in the Bobov Bais Medrash near the bus stop.

19. Are you __ __ __ __ __ __ __ __ __ your subscription to the newsline?

20. Usually you should not be __ __ __ __ __ __ __ __ __ __ with classmates.

Key Concepts
- hard and soft letter sounds
- adjusting suffixes to keep the hard/soft sound
- pairs of suffixes

A hard sound is one that is short and explosive, that comes out of the mouth with a popping sound. It cannot be lengthened for an appreciable amount of time. Some examples of hard sounds are **b**, **p**, and **d**.

A soft sound is one that comes out of the mouth along with air in a sort of hissing sound. It can be short or lengthened without changing its sound. Some examples of soft sounds are **ch**, **s**, and **th**.

The letter or vowel that follows **c** or **g** usually indicate whether the **c** or **g** was hard or soft. Sometimes, the usual **rules for suffixes are adjusted in order to maintain the c or g as a hard or soft letter**. There are a few **pairs of suffixes** that each work the same way, but are spelled with a different vowel. That means that if the pair changes a verb to a noun, both suffixes will function the same way, but some words will get the version of the suffix with one vowel while others will get the one with the other vowel. These are: **ant/ent**, **able/ible**, **uous/ious**, **ance/ence**. When the suffix follows the letter **c** or **g**, make sure to use the version of the suffix that will keep the sound of the **c** or **g** soft or hard as the word is pronounced.

Lesson Spelling Rule: When the letters **c** or **g** have a hard sound, they will be followed by the vowels **a**, **o**, or **u**, or a consonant. When they are soft, they will be followed by the vowels **e**, **i**, and **y**.

The pairs of suffixes follow **c** or **g** the same way.

If the **c** or **g** is hard, use the endings ance ant, able, uous.

If the **c** or **g** is soft, use the endings ence, ent, ible, ious.

Sometimes the final silent **e** is kept to protect the soft sound of **c** or **g** when a suffix is added.

1. ELE<u>G</u>ANT	5. INTELLI<u>G</u>ENT	9. OUTRA<u>G</u>EOUS
2. EXTRAVA<u>G</u>ANCE	6. NEGLI<u>G</u>ENCE	10. VEN<u>G</u>EANCE
3. NAVI<u>G</u>ABLE	7. ELI<u>G</u>IBLE	
4. AMBI<u>G</u>UOUS	8. CONTA<u>G</u>IOUS	

11. APPLI<u>C</u>ANT	15. MAGNIFI<u>C</u>ENT	19. ENFOR<u>C</u>EABLE
12. SIGNIFI<u>C</u>ANCE	16. INNO<u>C</u>ENCE	20. REPLA<u>C</u>EABLE
13. COMMUNI<u>C</u>ABLE	17. CONVIN<u>C</u>IBLE	
14. CONSPI<u>C</u>UOUS	18. SUSPI<u>C</u>IOUS	

Pay attention to the spelling words.

1. Look at the words in the first column and think about their pronunciation. Do the underlined

   letters have a hard or a soft sound? _____

2. Write the endings that follow these letters _____ _____ _____ _____

3. Look at the words in the second column and think about their pronunciation. Do the

   underlined letters have a hard or a soft sound? _____

4. Write the endings that follow these letters _____ _____ _____ _____

5. When **c** or **g** has a hard sound, it is followed by which letters? _____ or _____

6. When **c** or **g** has a soft sound, it is followed by the letters _____ or _____.

7. When a final silent **e** is followed by a suffix beginning with a vowel, what usually happens

   to the **e?** _____

8. Look at the words in the final column. If the **e** were dropped in these words what vowel

   would follow the **c** and **g**? _____ Would its sound be soft or hard? _____

9. What is done with the final **e** to maintain the appropriate sound of **c** or **g** in this case?
   _____

10. It is often difficult to choose between the following endings when you are spelling a word:
    ant/ent, ance/ence, able/ible, uous/ious. When the letter before the ending is **c** or **g**, what
    can help you remember the appropriate ending?

    _____

When the letters **c** or **g** have a hard sound, they will be followed by the vowels **a**, **o**, or **u**, or a
consonant. When they are soft, they will be followed by the vowels **e**, **i**, and **y**.
The pairs of suffixes follow **c** or **g** the same way.
If the **c** or **g** is hard, use the endings ance ant, able, uous.
If the **c** or **g** is soft, use the endings ence, ent, ible, ious.
Sometimes the final silent **e** is kept to protect the soft sound of **c** or **g** when a suffix is added.

---

1. **am·big·u·ous**   *adj.* not clear; vague
2. **app·li·cant**   *n.* a person who applies, as for employment, help, etc.
3. **ap·ply**   *v.* **–plied, –ply·ing** 1. to put on [to apply salve]   2. to make a formal request [to *apply* for a job]   3. to be suitable or relevant [this rule *applies* to everyone]
4. **com·mu·ni·ca·ble**   *adj.* 1. that can be communicated, as an idea   2. that can be transmitted, as a disease
5. **com·mu·ni·cate**   *v.* **–cat·ed, –cat·ing** to give, exchange, speak
6. **com·mu·ni·ca·tion**   *n.* a giving or exchanging of information, etc. by talk, writing, etc.
7. **con·spic·u·ous**   *adj.* easy to see or perceive; obvious [a *conspicuous* poster]
8. **con·ta·gion**   *n.* 1. the spreading of a disease by contact   2. a contagious disease
9. **con·ta·gious**   *adj.* spread by contact: said of diseases
10. **con·vince**   *v.* **–vinced, –vinc·ing** to overcome the doubts of; persuade by argument [I'm *convinced* he's telling the truth]   **—con·vin·ci·ble** *adj.* **—con·vinc·ing·ly** *adv.*
11. **con·vin·ci·ble**   *adj.* subject to convincing
12. **el·e·gant**   *adj.* having a dignified richness and grace, as of dress, style, manner, etc. **—el·e·gant·ly** *adv.*
13. **el·i·gi·ble**   *adj.* fit to be chosen, qualified by law, rules, etc. [*eligible* to hold office] **—el·i·gi·bil·i·ty** *n.*   **—el·i·gi·bly** *adv.*
14. **en·force**   *v.* **–forced, –forc·ing** to force observance of (a law, etc.) **—en·force·a·ble** *adj.*   **—en·force·ment** *n.*
15. **en·force·a·ble** *adj.* subject to being enforced
16. **ex·trav·a·gance**   *n.* a spending of more than is reasonable or necessary
17. **ex·trav·a·gant**   *adj.* 1. going beyond reasonable limits; excessive   2. costing or spending too much   **—ex·trav·a·gant·ly** *adv.*
18. **in·com·mu·ni·ca·ble**   *adj.* that cannot be communicated or told **—in·com·mu·ni·ca·bil·i·ty** *n*   **—in·com·mu·ni·ca·bly** *adv.*
19. **in·con·spic·u·ous**   *adj.* not conspicuous; attracting little attention **—in·con·spic·u·ous·ly** *adv.*   **—in·con·spic·u·ous·ness** *n*
20. **in·el·e·gant**   *adj.* not elegant; lacking refinement, good taste, grace, etc.; coarse, crude [*inelegant* manners]   **—in·el·e·gant·ly** *adv.*
21. **in·el·i·gi·ble**   *adj.* not eligible; not qualified under the rules [*ineligible* to vote] *–n.* an ineligible person   **—in·el·i·gi·bil·i·ty** *n*   **—in·el·i·gi·bly** *adv.*
22. **in·no·cence**   *n.* 1. freedom from sin or guilt   2. simplicity
23. **in·no·cent**   *n.* free from sin, evil or guilt   **—in·no·cent·ly** *adv.*
24. **in·tel·li·gence**   *n.* the ability to comprehend; to understand and profit from experience
25. **in·tel·li·gent**   *adj.* having or showing an alert mind or high intelligence; bright; clever, wise, etc.   **—in·tel·li·gent·ly** *adv.*
26. **in·sig·nif·i·cant**   *adj.* 1. having little or no importance or meaning; trivial [insignificant details]   2. small in size, amount, scope, etc. [to add an insignificant amount of salt] **—in·sig·nif·i·cance, in·sig·nif·i·can·cy** *n*   **—in·sig·nif·i·cant·ly** *adv.*
27. **mag·ni·fi·cence**   *n.* the quality of being magnificent, splendid, or grand
28. **mag·ni·fi·cent**   *adj.* beautiful in a grand or stately way; rich or splendid **—mag·ni·fi·cent·ly** *adv.*
29. **nav·i·ga·ble**   *adj.* 1. wide, deep, or free enough for ships, etc. to go through [a *navigable* river]   2. that can be steered or directed [a *navigable* balloon]

30. **nav·i·ga·tion**   *n.* 1. the science of locating the position and plotting the course of ships 2. the guidance of a ship or airplane   —**nav·i·ga·tion·al** *adj.*

31. **neg·li·gence**   *n.* the habitual failure to give proper care; laxity; inattentiveness

32. **neg·li·gent**   *adj.* 1. habitually failing to do the required thing   2. careless; lax; inattentive   —**neg·li·gent·ly** *adv.*

33. **out·ra·geous**   *adj.* so wrong or uncontrolled as to be shocking [to charge *outrageous* prices]   —**out·ra·geous·ly** *adv.*

34. **re·place**   *v.* –**placed,** –**plac·ing** 1. to put back in a former or proper position [*replace* the tools]   2. to take the place of [workers *replaced* by automated equipment]   —**re·place·a·ble** *adj.*   —**re·place·ment** *n.*

35. **re·place·a·ble** *adj.* subject to being replaced

36. **re·place·ment** *n.* a person or thing that takes the place of another that is lost, worn out, dismissed, etc.

37. **sig·nif·i·cance**   *n.* 1. meaning [the *significance* of the remark]   2. importance; consequence [a battle of great *significance*]

38. **sig·nif·i·cant**   *adj.* 1. full of meaning [a *significant* speech]   2. important; momentous [a *significant* occasion]   —**sig·nif·i·cant·ly** *adv.*

39. **sus·pi·cion**   *n.* the act of suspecting guilt, a wrong, etc. with little or no evidence

40. **sus·pi·cious**   *adj.* 1. causing or likely to cause suspicion [suspicious behavior]   2. tending to suspect evil, etc.   —**sus·pi·cious·ly** *adv.*

41. **un·am·big·u·ous**   *adj.* not indefinite or vague

42. **un·en·force·a·ble**   *adj.* 1. not able to be imposed by force   2. not able to force observance of (a law, etc.)

43. **un·in·tel·li·gent**   *adj.* 1. not having or using intelligence   2. not having or showing an alert mind or high intelligence; not bright, clever

44. **un·nav·i·ga·ble**   *adj.* 1. not wide or deep enough, or free enough from obstructions, for ships, etc. to go through   2. not able to be steered or directed

45. **un·sus·pi·cious**   *adj.* 1. not causing or likely to cause suspicion   2. not showing suspicion 3. not tending habitually to suspect evil, etc.

46. **venge·ance**   *n.* the return of an injury for an injury, in punishment; revenge

47. **venge·ful**   *adj.* seeking or wanting revenge

Practicing the words
A. Find the missing vowels for each word. Write the word and the abbreviation for its part of speech.

c_mm_n_c_bl_ —————————— — _nf_rc_ _bl_ —————————— —

_ _tr_g_ _ _s —————————— — s_gn_f_c_nc_ —————————— —

c_nv_nc_bl_ —————————— — m_gn_f_c_nt —————————— —

_l_g_nt —————————— — _xtr_v_g_nc_ —————————— —

_nn_c_nt —————————— — r_pl_c_ _bl_ —————————— —

n_v_g_bl_ —————————— — c_nsp_c_ _ _s —————————— —

c_nt_g_ _ _s —————————— — _nt_ll_g_nt —————————— —

_ppl_c_nt —————————— — s_sp_c_ _ _s —————————— —

_l_g_bl_ —————————— — _mb_g_ _ _s —————————— —

v_ng_ _nc_ —————————— — n_gl_g_nc_ —————————— —

B. Complete each sentence with a spelling word.

1. Even the huge ship was barely _____ during the storm.

2. Sarah groaned when she learned that the broken china was not _____.

3. What is the _____ of the fifty stars in the American flag?

184

4. Are porpoises more or less _____ than dogs?

5. His bright red beard made the celebrity _____ in a crowd.

6. Ruth felt that hiring a band was an unnecessary _____.

7. The police believe the new traffic law will be easily _____.

8. Due to your _____ none of the supplies will arrive on time.

9. Each _____ for the job must submit a sample of his or her writing.

10. The directions he gave us were _____ and confusing.

11. Is your skhtickl torah _____ to be printed in this zman's kovetz?

12. We had a _____ view of the mountains from our room.

13. In American courts, a jury will decide the guilt or _____ of the prisoner.

14. Shana's idea is so wild and _____ that it just might work!

C. Proofreading

Read the descriptions of the following titles. Cross out the nine misspelled words and write them correctly.

1. BORUCH'S ROPE

A sea captain promises vengeance when his magnificant, irreplaceable sailor's knot is untied by a suspicieous stranger.

2. DAYS OF OUR BRIBES

An eligable candidate for a veterinary degree must have a believable story as she protests her inocence of the charge of bribing sick dogs with milk bones.

3. ANOTHER CURL

The tragic, riches-to-rags story of elegent Ginger, who wastes her wealth on numerous outragious wigs.

4. ONE DATE AT A TIME

Yirmiyahu's feelings are ambigeous when he learns that his sore throat is neither contageous nor comunicable, but can be cured only by eating dried fruit.

1. _____

2. _____

3. _____

4. _____

5. _____

6. _____

7. _____

8. _____

9. _____

D. Follow each direction to make new forms of spelling words. Each direction can only be applied to the number of words for which there are spaces. For the last two, also use one of the new words. Use the spelling dictionary to help you.

1. Change **ence** to **ent** and add **ly**: _____ _____

2. Change **ance** to **ant** and add **ly**: _____ _____

3. Change **ious** to **ion**: _____ _____

4. Change **able** to **ment**: _____ _____

5. Change **able** to **ation**: _____ _____

6. Change **ance** to **ful**: _____

7. Add the negative prefix **un**: _____ _____

   _____ _____ _____

8. Add the negative prefix **in**: _____ _____

   _____ _____ _____

E. Fill in the blanks with the appropriate spelling word.

1. Some סופרים write very __ __ __ __ __ __ __ tefillin and mezuzos.

2. For some people it is an __ __ __ __ __ __ __ __ __ __ __ __ to eat שמורה מצה all 8 days of

   Pesach .

3. The מסילת ישרים compares עולם הזה to a __ __ __ __ __ __ __ __ __ maze – IF you get the right

   instructions.

4. The יצר הרע makes our way __ __ __ __ __ __ __ __ __ – blurring right and wrong.

5. Even __ __ __ __ __ __ __ __ __ __ people make mistakes.

6. A שומר חנם is responsible for __ __ __ __ __ __ __ __ __ __ – פשיעה.

7. Achashveirosh commanded that every __ __ __ __ __ __ __ maiden be brought to him.

8. Unlike allergies, the flu is __ __ __ __ __ __ __ __ __ __, so avoid spreading germs.

9. The __ __ __ __ __ __ __ __ __ claims by silly Democrats make me feel uncomfortable.

10. It is forbidden to take __ __ __ __ __ __ __ __ __ – it transgresses לא תקום.

11. Each __ __ __ __ __ __ __ __ hopes he gets accepted to camp.

12. It is of little __ __ __ __ __ __ __ __ __ __ __ whether you use a suitcase or duffel bag.

13. His feelings were barely __ __ __ __ __ __ __ __ __ __ __ because the words wouldn't come

    out.

14. The large letters were __ __ __ __ __ __ __ __ __ __ __, catching all eyes right away.

15. Our school is a __ __ __ __ __ __ __ __ __ __ educational organization.

16. __ __ __ __ __ __ __ __ is presumed until proven otherwise.

17. The rabble is easily __ __ __ __ __ __ __ __ __ __ __ by the fake news media.

18. The __ __ __ __ __ __ __ __ __ activity provoked investigation.

19. The תקנות of חז"ל are __ __ __ __ __ __ __ __ __ __ __ by מכת מרדות or חרם.

20. Money is __ __ __ __ __ __ __ __ __ __, but hurt emotions are difficult to repair.

Key Concepts
- assimilated prefixes
- padded sentences
- synonym
- connotation

We already learned that prefixes sometimes **assimilate**, or change to the following letter to accommodate easier pronunciation. Some prefixes always "assimilate" to **m** before the letters **b**, **m**, and **p** because it is easier to pronounce that way. The prefixes **con** and **in** both follow this pattern. They become **com** and **im** when joined to a root or base that begins with **b**, **m**, or **p**. They are spelled this way to make more compatible combinations that are easier to pronounce.

Say **in̲mediately** and **im̲mediately**. Say **con̲mute** and **com̲mute**.

This can sometimes cause a problem with tricky double consonants because one is from the prefix and one is from the root. Remembering that the prefix assimilated can help you remember to double the consonants.

A **padded sentence** has useless words or phrases. Even though it might seem to you that your writing sounds elegant, sophisticated, and elaborate because of all the extra words, it is really unnecessary to stuff your writing with extra fluff. Omit unnecessary words. The main idea should not be blurred by needless wordiness.

Synonyms are words that have similar meanings. The dictionary sometimes lists synonyms after the entry in a synonymy and explains some differences between the similar words. The exact meaning of a words is its denotation. On the other hand, a shade in meaning that is not the precise meaning of the word is its **connotation**. [In yeshivishe jargon, a connotation is the משמעות of the word.]

Lesson Spelling Rule: The prefixes **con** and **in** follow the same spelling pattern. Both are spelled with an **n** before most letters of the alphabet. Both are spelled with an **m** before roots or words that begin with the letters **b**, **m**, or **p**. Don't forget to double the consonants.

Mnemonic device: Remember co**mm**on co**mp**atible com**b**inations.

1	CON+	GRESSIONAL	=CONGRESSIONAL	11	IN+	TUITION	= INTUITION
2	CON+	SERVATIVE	= CONSERVATIVE	12	IN+	SULATION	= INSULATION
3	CON+	NOTATION	= CONNOTATION	13	IN+	NOCENT	= INNOCENT
4	CON+	MENTATOR	= COMMENTATOR	14	IN+	MUNITY	= IMMUNITY
5	CON+	MUTE	= COMMUTE	15	IN+	MORTALITY	= IMMORTALITY
6	CON+	MERCIAL	= COMMERCIAL	16	IN+	MEDIATELY	= IMMEDIATELY
7	CON+	PETITION	= COMPETITION	17	IN+	PATIENT	= IMPATIENT
8	CON+	PUTER	= COMPUTER	18	IN+	POSTOR	= IMPOSTOR
9	CON+	PROMISE	= COMPROMISE	19	IN+	PEACHED	= IMPEACHED
10	CON+	BUSTION	= COMBUSTION	20	IN+	BEDDED	= IMBEDDED

A prefix may be spelled in several different ways.
Pay attention to the spelling words.

1. Look at the first three words in each column. Are the prefixes **con** and **in** spelled

   with an **n** or an **m** when they are added to form these words? _____

2. Why do the words **connotation** and **innocent** have double consonants?_____

   _____

3. Look at the remaining words in each column. How is the prefix **con** spelled when

   it is added to roots that begin with **b**, **m**, or **p**? _____

4. How is the prefix in spelled when it is added to words or roots that begin with **b**,

   m, or **p**? ____

> The prefixes **con** and **in** become **com** and **im** when joined to a root or base that begins
> with **b**, **m**, or **p** to become easier to pronounce.
> This sometimes causes a double consonant – remember that one is from the prefix and the
> other from the base.

190

Spelling Dictionary

1. **char·la·tan**   *n.* one who pretends to have expert knowledge or skill that he does not

2. **com·bus·tion**   *n.* 1. the act or process of burning   2. rapid oxidation accompanied by heat and, usually, light   —**com·bus·tive** *adj.*

3. **com·men·ta·tor**   *n.* 1, a person who gives (a series of remarks or observations) 2. a person who reports and analyzes news, sports, etc. as on radio or TV

4. **com·merce**   *n.* transactions

5. **com·mer·cial**   *adj.* of or connected with commerce or trade   –*n.* (*Radio & TV)* a paid advertisement   —**com·mer·cial·ly** *adv.*

6. **com·mute**   *v.* –**mut·ed, –mut·ing** 1. to change (an obligation, punishment, etc.) to one that is less severe   2. to travel as a commuter, a person who travels regularly between two points at some distance   —**com·mut·a·ble** *adj.*

7. **com·pe·ti·tion**   *n.* 1. a competing; rivalry   2. a contest, or match

8. **com·pro·mise**   *n.* a settlement in which each side gives up part of what it wants   –*v.* –**mised,   –mis·ing** to settle by a compromise

9. **com·put·er**   *n.* an electronic machine used as a calculator or to store data

10. **con·gress**   *n.* 1. the social act of assembling for some common purpose   2. a meeting of elected or appointed represenetatives

11. **con·gres·sion·al**   *adj.* of a congress   —**con·gres·sion·al·ly** *adv.*

12. **con·no·ta·tion**   *n.* any idea suggested by or associated with a word, phrase, etc. in addition to its basic or literal meaning

13. **con·ser·va·tion**   *n.* 1. a protection from loss, waste, etc.   2. the official care and protection of natural resources, as forests   —**con·ser·va·tion·ist** *n.*

14. **con·ser·va·tive**   *adj.* tending to uphold established institems or methods and to resist or oppose any changes in these [*conservative* politics]   –*n.* a conservative person   —**con·ser·va·tive·ly** *adv.*

15. **con·serve**   *v.* –**served, –serv·ing** 1. keep in safety; protect from harm, loss, or destruction   2. use cautiously and frugally

16. **de·po·sit**   *v.* –**sit·ed, –sit·ing** to place or entrust, as for safekeeping   –*n.* 1. something placed for safekeeping; specif. money in a bank   2. a pledge or part payment

17. **ea·ger**   *adj.* impatient or anxious to do or get

18. **fidg·et·y**   *adj.* nervous, uneasy

19. **fraud**   *n.* a person who is not what he pretends to be

20. **fret·ful**   *adj.* irritated, worried

21. **im·bed**   *v.* –**bed·ded, –bed·ding** 1. to set or fix firmly in a surrounding mass [to imbed tiles in cement]   2. to fix in the mind

22. **im·me·di·ate·ly**   *adv.* without delay; at once [go home *immediately*]

23. **im·mor·tal**   *adj.* 1. not mortal; living or lasting forever   2. having lasting fame [an *immortal* poet]   —**im·mor·tal·i·ty** *n.*   —**im·mor·tal·ly** *adv.*

24. **im·mor·tal·i·ty**   *n.* the quality of being immortal

25. **im·mu·ni·ty**   *n., pl.* –**ties** resistance to or protection from disease

191

26.**im·pa·tient** *adj.* feeling or showing restless eagerness or annoyanc because of delay, opposition, etc.

27.**im·peach** *v.* --**peached, –peach·ing** to challenge the practices or honesty of; esp. to bring (a public official) to trial on a charge or wrongdoing

28.**im·pet·u·ous** *adj.* acting with little thought

29.**im·pose** *v.* –**posed, –pos·ing** 1. compel to behave a certain way 2. inflict something unpleasant

30.**im·po·si·tion** *n.* a taking advantage of friendship, courtesy, etc. [staying for a meal when you are not invited is an *imposition*]

31.**im·pos·tor** *n.* a person who cheats or deceives others, esp. by pretending to be someone or something that he or she is not

32.**in·no·cent** *n.* free from sin, evil or guilt   —**in·no·cent·ly** *adv.*

33.**in·su·late** *v.* –**lat·ed, –lat·ing** 1. place or set apart 2. protect from heat, cold, or noise by surrounding with insulating material

34.**in·su·la·tion** *n.* any material used to insulate, to prevent the passage or leakage of electricity, heat, sound, etc.

35.**in·tu·i·tion** *n.* the direct knowing or learning of something without conscious use of reasoning; instant understanding [to sense danger by a flash of *intuition*]

36.**men·tion** *n.* 1. a remark that calls attention 2. official recognition of merit –*v.* –**tioned, –tion·ing** 1. make reference to 2.commend

37.**mi·mic** *n.* a person or thing that imitates

38.**mor·tal** *adj.* 1. one that must eventually die [all *mortal* beings] 2. causing death; fatal [a *mortal* wound]   —**mor·tal·ly** *adv.*

39.**mor·tal·i·ty** *n.* the condition of being mortal or sure to die

40.**no·ta·tion** *n.* a written record of something

41.**op·pose** *v.* –**posed, –pos·ing** 1. fight against; resist strongly 2. set against

42.**op·po·si·tion** *n.* 1. resistance or struggle against [his plan met *opposition*] 2. anything that opposes

43.**pre·ser·va·tion** *n.* 1. the activity of protecting something from loss or danger; saving 2. a process that saves organic matter from decay

44.**pre·serve** *n.* a place where game, fish, etc. are protected or kept for controlled hunting and fishing   –*v.* –**served, –serv·ing** 1. protect, save [preserve our natural forests] 2. prepare (food), as by canning, salting, etc. for future use

45.[40]**quack**[1] *n.* the noise made by a duck

46.**quack**[2] *n.* a person without proper training who pretends to be a doctor

47.**res·er·va·tion** *n.* a reserving or the thing reserved; specifi., *a)* public land set aside for special use [an Indian *reservation*] *b)* an arrangement by which a hotel room theater ticket, etc. is set aside for use at a certain time

48.**re·serve** *n.* 1. formality and propriety of manner [behaved with *reserve*] 2. something kept back or saved for future use [crude oil *reserves*] 3. armed forces that are not on active duty but can be called on in an emergency   –*v.* 1. hold back or set

---

[40] Words that have entirely different meanings, but are still spelled the same are called homographs. The dictionary lists them as separate entries, and differentiates between them with a small elevated number immediately after the entry word (superscript).

aside, esp. for future use [*reserve* the extra broth]   2. give or assign a resource for a particular person or cause [*reserve* me a seat]   3. arrange in advance [*reserve* a flight]

49. **serve**   *v.* 1. fulfill a function; perform a role [serves as secretary]   2. help with food or drink   3. put the ball into play

50. **ser·vice**   *n.* 1. work done or duty performed for others [repair *service*]   2. a religious ceremony [*services* begin at 8:00]   –*v.* **–viced, –vic·ing** 1. to furnish with a service   2. to make or keep fit for service, as by adjusting, repairing, etc. [we *service* kosher phones]

51. **tu·i·tion**   *n.* 1. teaching pupils individually   2. a fee paid for instruction

Practicing the words

A. First find and circle a form of the prefix **com** or **in** which is not scrambled. Then unscramble the rest of the letters to correctly spell one of the spelling words and write it on the line. Then mark which part of speech it is with the abbreviation.

1. sporimot   _____

2. upcomret   _____

3. comumet   _____

4. niotintiu   _____

5. subcomnoti   _____

6. nnoincet   _____

7. verseconivat   _____

8. dddeimbe   _____

9. lateiymedim   _____

10. cheapimde   _____

11. camecomril   _____

12. semporcomi   _____

13. talusinino   _____

14. saloniconserg   _____

15. nutimimy   _____

16. notitepicom   _____

17. tapimniet   _____

18. ononconitat   _____

19. taromimlyit   _____

20. tentramcomo   _____

B. Proofreading

A **padded sentence** has useless words and phrases. The main idea is buried by unnecessary words. A sentence can be improved by eliminating the unnecessary words.

What I think is that houses should have proper insulation.
The reason why I can't attend is because I have to babysit that night.
What Carol wants is for you to write the song.

Cross out the unnecessary words in each padded sentence. Then rewrite it on your looseleaf paper by omitting the unnecessary words.

1. What I mean is that the computer is a valuable machine.

_____

2. Carlo will be the commentator and the reason is because he is a clever speaker.

_____

3. War was avoided because of the fact that both countries agreed to compromise.

_____

4. What I think is that the senator should not be impeached.

_____

5. The thing is, this vaccine provides immunity from polio.

_____

6. What I went to the doctor for was to have this imbedded splinter removed.

_____

7. The reason why Leah seems impatient is because she is nervous.

_____

C. Find and write the spelling word that is either a synonym or antonym for each word. Then write A or S to show if the spelling word is a synonym or antonym. Then write the abbreviation for the part of speech.

1. contest _____ ___ ___

2. liberal _____ ___ ___

3. unhurried _____ ___ ___

4. later _____ ___ ___

5. advertisement _____ ___ ___

6. fire _____ ___ ___

7. accused _____ ___ ___

8. eternity _____ ___ ___

9. insight _____ ___ ___

10. faker _____ ___ ___

11. guilty _____ ___ ___

12. resistance _____ ___ ___

D. Connotations

A connotation is a special shade of meaning associated with a word. Both skinny and slender mean "thin," but slender has a more complimentary connotation. Skinny is less respectable.

The words spreading out from the spelling word are synonyms for the spelling word at the base. They have the same general meaning, but different connotations or shades of meaning. Choose the synonym with the *best* connotation for each sentence. Carefully read the definition in your spelling dictionary for each word. The underlined word in each sentence is an association clue. Paying attention to the underlined word will assist you in choosing the best match.

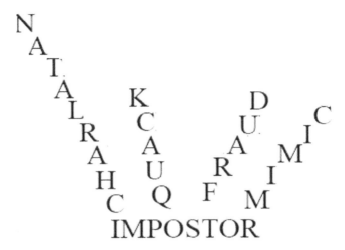

IMPOSTOR

1. The man <u>posing</u> as the king was a(n) _____.

2. The _____ claimed that his medicine <u>cured</u>

   everything.

3. The audience actually believed that the _____ was an

   <u>expert</u> on UFO's.

4. The _____ did an amazing <u>imitation</u> of the president.

5. After <u>cheating</u> people out of their money, the _____

   left town.

E. Do the same thing for this spelling word. The underlined words serve as clues to help you with the distinctions.

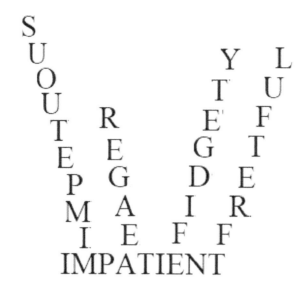

1. Benjy was _____ to leave for an <u>exciting</u> trip over the off-

   Shabbos.

2. The _____ child <u>burst into</u> the room without knocking.

3. <u>As soon as</u> the light turned green, the _____ driver blew

   his horn.

4. The _____ baby <u>cried</u> for its bottle.

5. The _____ diner <u>toyed with</u> the fork and <u>twisted</u> the

   napkin into knots.

F. Build a word pyramid by following the code. Use your spelling dictionary to find the four pyramid words that match the definitions.

The root **pos** means "to put or position."

1. one who put himself in another's place

_____

2. those who take the opposite position in an argument

_____

3. an idea put before others

_____

4. something that puts a burden on a person

_____

			P	O	S					
			P	O	S	11	12	10	3	
	4	6	P	O	S	11	8	10		
	2	3	P	O	S	4	11			
9	10	8	P	O	S	1	5			
	8	9	P	O	S	4	11	4	8	7
	4	6	P	O	S	4	11	4	8	7

A	D	E	I	L	M	N	O	P	R	T	U
1	2	3	4	5	6	7	8	9	10	11	12

G. Build another pyramid. Find the four pyramid words that match the definitions.

The root **serv** means "to help, keep."

1. one who keeps to established methods

_____

2. a program to keep natural resources safe

_____

3. that which can still help or be of use

_____

4. to keep safe or protected

_____

			S	E	R	V						
			S	E	R	V	5	3	4			
9	10	4	S	E	R	V	4					
	10	4	S	E	R	V	1	11	5	8	7	
3	8	7	S	E	R	V	1	11	5	12	4	
			S	E	R	V	5	3	4	1	2	6	4
3	8	7	S	E	R	V	1	11	5	8	7	

A	B	C	E	I	L	N	O	P	R	T	V
1	2	3	4	5	6	7	8	9	10	11	12

199

H. Fill in the blanks with the appropriate spelling words.

1. Silly Democrats __ __ __ __ __ __ __ __ __ President Trump - twice.

2. Make sure the tick's proboscis does not remain __ __ __ __ __ __ __ __ in the skin.

3. A __ __ __ __ __ __ __ __ __ __ __ Democrat is scarce.

4. A __ __ __ __ __ __ __ __ __ __ __ is a special shade of meaning associated with a word.

5. Most bochurim will not listen to a news __ __ __ __ __ __ __ __ __ __ .

6. Most of you __ __ __ __ __ __ __ to and from school on the bus.

7. The billboard shows __ __ __ __ __ __ __ __ __ __ announcements – a.k.a. advertisements.

8. The two parties made a __ __ __ __ __ __ __ __ __ __ to prevent a silly war.

9. The פורים שטיק created a __ __ __ __ __ __ __ __ __ __ in the בית מדרש.

10. צדיקים have great __ __ __ __ __ __ __ __ because they are close to Hashem.

11. The oldest __ __ __ __ __ __ __ __ __ __ __ __ committee is the Ways and Means committee.

12. The sturdy __ __ __ __ __ __ __ __ __ kept the temperature from changing too drastically.

13. The impeached official was found to be __ __ __ __ __ __ __ __ and was acquitted.

14. It took a long time to attain herd __ __ __ __ __ __ __ __ from COVID.

15. אמונה in the __ __ __ __ __ __ __ __ __ __ of our נפש is a basic requirement.

16. מצוות should be performed __ __ __ __ __ __ __ __ __ __ __, without delay.

17. I am __ __ __ __ __ __ __ __ for summer vacation to arrive.

18. שבתי צבי ימ"ש was an __ __ __ __ __ __ __ __, a false משיח.

19. There was class __ __ __ __ __ __ __ __ __ __ to write the best essay.

20. Having an unfiltered __ __ __ __ __ __ __ __ can be risky to your נשמה.

Key Concepts
- assimilated prefixes

Some more common prefixes and their assimilations. If they were always added directly to the base or root, some consonant combinations would be difficult to pronounce.

For example: a<u>d</u>ford   di<u>s</u>ficult   su<u>b</u>focate   co<u>n</u>respond   co<u>n</u>lapse

Instead, afford, difficult, suffocate, correspond, collapse.

They assimilate for purposes of easier pronunciation, but complicate the spelling because of the unexpected double consonants. It helps if you can remember the prefix and how it assimilated.

Lesson Spelling Rule: Assimilated prefixes solve pronunciation problems but cause spelling problems. Double consonants result when the last letter of the prefix changes to match the first letter of the root.

Prefixes used in this lesson:
- ad- motion towards; addition to; nearness to
- dis- away, apart; not; opposite of
- sub- under, beneath; lower in rank or position; to a lesser degree than; by or forming a division into smaller parts
- ob- to, toward, before; opposed to, against; completely, totally
- con- with or together; very or very much; all together
- in- no, not, without; in, into, within, on, toward

1	AD + FORD = AFFORD	11 COM+ RESPONDENT = CORRESPONDENT
2	AD + FLICTION = AFFLICTION	12 COM+ RUPT = CORRUPT
3	AD + FIRMATIVE = AFFIRMATIVE	13 IN + RESPONSIBLE = IRRESPONSIBLE
4	AD + FECTION = AFFECTION	14 IN + RIGATION = IRRIGATION
5	DIS + FICULT = DIFFICULT	15 IN + RESISTIBLE = IRRESISTIBLE
6	SUB + FERED = SUFFERED	16 COM+ LISION = COLLISION
7	SUB + FOCATE = SUFFOCATE	17 COM+ LAPSE = COLLAPSE
8	SUB + FICIENT = SUFFICIENT	18 IN + LUMINATE = ILLUMINATE
9	OB + FICIAL = OFFICIAL	19 IN + LEGIBLE = ILLEGIBLE
10	OB + FERED = OFFERED	20 IN + LITERATE = ILLITERATE

Pay attention to the spelling words.

1. When the prefixes in the first column are joined to roots that being with the letter **f**, how does the spelling of each prefix change? ____ becomes ____, ____ becomes ____, ____ becomes ____, and ____ becomes ____.

2. The roots in the second column begin with the letter **r** or **l**. When the prefixes **con** and **in** are joined to the letter **r**, **con** is spelled ____, and **in** is spelled ____.

3. When **con** and **in** are joined to the letter **l**, **con** is spelled ____, and **in** is spelled ____.

4. In all of the prefixes, which letter changes to match the first letter of the root? _____

5. **5.** What common spelling problem might occur in all of the list words because the prefixes are assimilated into the roots? _____

> Assimilated prefixes solve pronunciation problems but cause spelling problems. Double consonants result when the last letter of the prefix changes to match the first letter of the root.

1. **af·fec·tion**   *n.* fond or tender feeling
2. **af·firm·a·tive**   *adj.* answering "yes" [an *affirmative* reply]   *–n.* a word or expression indicating agreement   **—af·firm·a·tive·ly** *adv.*
3. **af·flic·tion**   *n.* anything causing pain or distress
4. **af·ford**   *v.* to have enough or the means for; bear the cost of
5. **as·sis·tant**   *adj.* assisting; helping [the store's *assistant* manager]   *–n.* a person who assists another or serves in a lower position; helper
6. **col·lapse**   *v.* **–lapsed, –lap·sing** 1. to fall down or cave in   2. to break down suddenly in health   *–n.* a failure or breakdown, as in business, health, etc.
7. **col·lide**   *v.* **–lid·ed, –lid·ing** to come into conflict; to crash together with violent impact
8. **col·li·sion**   *n.* a colliding, or coming together with sudden, violent force
9. **con·sis·ten·cy** *n., pl.* **–cies** 1. firmness or thickness, as of a liquid   2. a being consistent in practice or principle [he is unpredictable because he lacks *consistency*]
10. **con·sis·tent**   *adj.* 1. the same throughout in structure and composition   2. in agreement; in harmony [the testimony was *consistent* with the facts]
11. **cor·res·pon·dent**   *n.* a person hired by a newspaper to send news regularly from a distant city or country
12. **cor·rupt**   *adj.* changed from good to bad; having become dishonest [accepting bribes made him a *corrupt* official]   *–v.* to make or become corrupt **—cor·rupt·ness** *n.*
13. **de·sist**   *v.* **–sis·ted, –sis·ting** to stop doing something
14. **des·pon·dent**   *adj.* dejected, discouraged [he was *despondent* over the loss of his job]
15. **dif·fi·cult**   *adj.* 1. hard to do, make, understand, etc.   2. hard to satisfy, persuade, etc. [he was a *difficult* employer]
16. **il·leg·i·ble**   *adj.* difficult or impossible to read because badly written or printed, faded, etc.   **—il·leg·i·bil·i·ty** *n.*   **—il·leg·i·bly** *adv.*
17. **il·lit·er·ate**   *adj.* uneducated; esp., not knowing how to read or write   *–n.* an illiterate person; esp., one not knowing how to read or write
18. **il·lu·mi·nate**   *v.* **–nat·ed, –nat·ing** to give light to, to light up [candles *illuminated* the room]   **—il·lu·mi·na·tion** *n.*
19. **im·pos·si·ble**   *adj.* not possible; not capable of being or happening **—im·pos·si·bly** *adv.*
20. **in·ac·ces·si·ble**   *adj.* 1. that cannot be seen, talked to, etc. [an *inaccessible* public official] 2. not obtainable   **—in·ac·ces·si·bly** *adv*
21. **in·cred·i·ble**   *adj.* 1. not credible; unbelievable [an incredible story]   2. so great, unusual, etc. as to seem impossible [incredible speed]   **—in·cred·i·bil·i·ty** *n.* **—in·cred·i·bly** *adv.*
22. **in·ed·i·ble**   *adj.* not fit to be eaten
23. **in·ex·press·ible**   *adj.* that cannot be expressed or described [*inexpressible* sorrow]
24. **in·tan·gi·ble**   *adj.* not tangible; specif., a) that cannot be touched b) not material or physical; abstract c) hard to define or understand clearly [an *intangible* feeling of dread] **—in·tan·gi·bil·i·ty** *n.* **—in·tan·gi·bly** *adv.*
25. **in·vin·ci·ble**   *adj.* that cannot be defeated or overcome; unconquerable **—in·vin·ci·bil·i·ty** *n.* **—in·vin·ci·bly** *adv.*

26. **ir·re·sis·ti·ble** *adj.* that cannot be resisted [an *irresistible* force]
    —**ir·re·sis·ti·bil·i·ty** *n.*   —**ir·re·sis·ti·bly** *adv.*

27. **ir·res·pon·si·ble**   *adj.* lacking a sense of responsibility; unreliable, lazy, etc.
    —**ir·res·pon·si·bil·i·ty** *n.*   —**ir·res·pon·si·bly** *adv.*

28. **ir·re·vers·i·ble**   *adj.* that cannot be undone or annulled [an *irreversible* decision]

29. **ir·ri·gate**   *v.* –**gat·ed,** –**gat·ing** to supply (land) with water   —
    ir·ri·ga·tion *n.*

30. **of·fer**   *v.* –**fered** or –**ferred,** –**fer·ing** or –**fer·ring** to present for acceptance or
    consideration [to *offer* one's services]

31. **of·fi·cial**   *adj.* by, from, or with the proper authority [an *official* request]   –*n.* a
    person holding office   —**of·fi·cial·ly** *adv.*

32. **re·sist**   *v.* –**sist·ed,** –**sist·ing** oppose or withstand; refuse to comply

33. **re·sis·ti·ble**   *adj.* capable of being resisted, withstood, or frustrated

34. **res·pon·si·ble**   *adj.* 1. being the agent or cause of   2. held accountable   3. worthy of
    having trust   —**res·pon·si·bil·i·ty** *n.*   —**res·pon·si·bly** *adv.*

35. **res·pon·si·bi·li·ty**   *n., pl.* –**ties** 1. the condition of being responsible [he accepted
    responsibility for the error]   2. a person or thing that one is responsible for [arranging flights is
    your *responsibility*]

36. **spon·sor**   *n.* 1. a person or agency that agrees toi be responsible for, advise, or
    support a person, group, or activity   2. a business firm or other agency that pays for a radio or
    TV program on which it advertises something   –*v.* –**sor·ed,** –**sor·ing** to act as a sponsor
    for

37. **suf·fered**   *v.* –**fered** or –**ferred ,** –**fer·ing** or –**fer·ring** to undergo pain, harm, loss,
    a penalty, etc. [she *suffered* in the heat]   —**suf·fer·ing** *n.*

38. **suf·fi·cient**   *adj.* as much as is needed; enough [*sufficient* supplies to last through the
    month]   —**suf·fi·cien·tly** *adv.*

39. **suf·fo·cate**   *v.* –**cat·ed,** –**cat·ing** to die by cutting off the supply of oxygen to the
    lungs, gills, etc.   —**suf·fo·cat·ing** *n.*

Practicing the words
A. Find the fiften spelling words hidden in three directions in the puzzle → ↓ ↑ Write each word.

I	R	R	E	S	P	O	N	S	I	B	L	E	I
R	C	O	L	L	A	P	S	E	L	A	A	V	L
R	T	E	B	C	M	R	U	N	L	F	I	I	L
E	L	T	I	H	V	U	F	G	I	F	C	T	U
S	U	A	G	W	Z	S	F	O	T	E	I	A	M
I	C	C	E	M	J	K	E	Y	E	C	F	M	I
S	I	O	L	U	M	B	R	T	R	T	F	R	N
T	F	F	L	D	C	H	E	K	A	I	O	I	A
I	F	F	I	R	S	U	D	T	T	O	X	F	T
B	I	U	L	O	H	M	Y	B	E	N	D	F	E
L	D	S	U	F	F	I	C	I	E	N	T	A	O
E	O	F	F	E	R	E	D	A	F	F	O	R	D

1. _____

2. _____

3. _____

4. _____

5. _____

6. _____

7. _____

8. _____

9. _____

10. _____

11. _____

12. _____

13. _____

14. _____

15. _____

206

B. Proofreading

Find the misspelled word in each group and write the word correctly.

1. irrigation	2. suffocate	3.collapse
oficial	difficult	corupt
suffered	afliction	illuminate
correspondent	afford	suffocate

_____ _____ _____

4. colision	5. corrupted	6.correspondent
affliction	irigation	irresistible
illiterate	sufficient	illuminate
affection	offered	ilegible

_____ _____ _____

C. Rewrite each phrase by substituting a spelling word similar in meaning for each underlined word. Then expand each rewritten phrase into a sentence.

1. enough water

_____   _____

_____

_____

2. underwent a breakdown

_____   _____

_____

_____

3. presented sentiment

_____   _____

_____

_____

4. unreliable reporter

_____   _____

_____

_____

5. dishonest officeholder

_____   _____

_____

_____

6. elighten the uneducated

_____   _____

_____

_____

7. hard to buy

_____   _____

_____

_____

8. alluring assent

_____   _____

_____

_____

D. Add the suffix **ible** and the correct form of the negative prefix in to each word or root in the list below. Write each new word beside a synonym that is spelled with the **un** prefix and the **able** prefix. The first two words are on your spelling list.

access   reverse   vinc   express   poss   ed   leg   response   cred   tang

1. unreliable   _____

2. unreadable   _____

3. unbeatable   _____

4. unachievable   _____

5. unchewable   _____

6. unspeakable   _____

7. untouchable   _____

8. unbelievable   _____

9. unchangeable   _____

10. unattainable   _____

Mnemonic device: Think of the word **unable** to remind you that the prefix **un** and the suffix **able** frequently go together.

Now make up your own mnemonic device to help you remember that words that use a prefix beginning with the letter **i** often use a suffix that begins with the letter **i**.

_____

E. Build a word pyramid by following the code. Use your spelling dictionary to find the four pyramid words that match the definitions.

The root **spon** means "promise."

						S	P	O	N						
						S	P	O	N	11	9	10			
				10	5	S	P	O	N	11	6	13	5		
				4	5	S	P	O	N	4	5	8	12		
	6	10	10	5	S	P	O	N	11	6	2	7	5		
3	9	10	10	5	S	P	O	N	4	5	8	12			
			10	5	S	P	O	N	11	6	2	6	7	6	12	14

B	C	D	E	I	L	N	O	R	S	T	V	Y
2	3	4	5	6	7	8	9	10	11	12	13	14

1. not doing what is promised

   _____

2. one who promises to support or be responsible for another

   _____

3. a doing of what is promised

   _____

4. a feeling that there is no hope or promise

   _____

Build another pyramid. Find the four pyramid words that match the definitions.

The root **sist** means "to stand."

				S	I	S	T					
	6	8		S	I	S	T					
	4	5		S	I	S	T	5	4			
	1	12		S	I	S	T	1	8	13		
10	5	11		S	I	S	T	5	8	13		
3	9	8		S	I	S	T	5	8	3	14	
6	11	11	5	S	I	S	T	6	2	7	5	

A	B	C	D	E	I	L	N	O	P	R	S	T	Y
1	2	3	4	5	6	7	8	9	10	11	12	13	14

1. one who stands by to help

   _____

2. continuing to "stand through," refusing to give up

   _____

3. stood back from, stopped doing

   _____

4. can't be withstood

   _____

F. Fill in the blanks with the appropriate spelling word.

1. The economy's __ __ __ __ __ __ __ __ led to a terrible depression.

2. The U.S. claims to __ __ __ __ __ __ protection to people who suffer.

3. __ __ __ __ __ __ __ __ __ __ __ action means doing positively.

4. An __ __ __ __ __ __ __ __ __ person has not learned to read.

5. It is sometimes __ __ __ __ __ __ __ __ __ to come up with suitable sentences.

6. Yiddin are commanded to have __ __ __ __ __ __ __ __ __ for each other – ואהבת לרעך כמוך.

7. Some masks might cause one to __ __ __ __ __ __ __ __ __ and be uncomfortable.

8. Having disease is a great __ __ __ __ __ __ __ __ __ __.

9. The government __ __ __ __ __ __ __ __ refused to commit himself to provide assistance.

10. The invalid __ __ __ __ __ __ __ __ great pains.

11. Their news __ __ __ __ __ __ __ __ __ __ __ __ doesn't always state the entire truth.

12. The __ __ __ __ __ __ __ officials accepted bribes.

13. An __ __ __ __ __ __ __ __ __ __ __ __ __ government does not adequately support its military.

14. Class time is usually __ __ __ __ __ __ __ __ __ to complete the required work.

15. He was accustomed to the idea that his charm was __ __ __ __ __ __ __ __ __ __ __ __.

16. The driver avoided a __ __ __ __ __ __ __ __ __ by swiftly turning the wheel.

17. מצרים relied on the נילוס for __ __ __ __ __ __ __ __ __ of their fields.

18. Many people use a flashlight to __ __ __ __ __ __ __ __ __ __ the rooms during בדיקת חמץ.

19. Some students still turn in __ __ __ __ __ __ __ __ papers.

20. They __ __ __ __ __ __ __ him sufficient reasons.

211

Spelling Lesson 21

Key Concepts

- Quirky **q**

The letter **q** is always followed by the letter **u** in the English language. This is because on its own, the letter would be pronounced like **k**, as in Iraq. The u tells you to add either the sound of **w** and does not function as a vowel. To make it more confusing, there are some words in which the **qu** is still pronounced as **k**. As an extra confusing twist, at the end of a word it is always pronounced **k**, but it is even spelled with an extra (useless) silent vowel – **e**.

The pronunciation of **q** is usually **kw**, but never at the end of a word.
At the end of a word, it is always spelled **que** and always pronounced **k** (plaque).
At the beginning of a word it is always pronounced **kw** (quarrel).
In the middle of a word, it can be pronounced as **k** (conquer) or **kw** (equator).

In other words, at the end of a word, it is never pronounced **kw**. At the beginning of a word it is always pronounced **kw**.

Lesson Spelling Rule: The letter **q** is always followed by **u** in the English language, but is sometimes pronounced **k**, usually **kw**. At the end of a word (it is always pronounced **k** and) it is always spelled **que**.

1. UNIQUE
2. ACQUIRE
3. QUIZZICAL
4. CLIQUE
5. ACQUAINTED
6. QUIVER
7. PLAQUE
8. ADEQUATELY
9. QUESTIONNAIRE
10. COLLOQUIAL
11. QUARANTINE
12. MASQUERADE
13. INQUISITIVE
14. QUENCH
15. CONQUER
16. BANQUET
17. QUAINT
18. LACQUER
19. SEQUEL
20. QUINTUPLET

Pay attention to the spelling words.

1. Look at the underlined letters in each word. What letter always follows the letter q? _____

2. Say the first three words to yourself. What two letters make the single sound of the letter k? ___

3. What silent letter follows these letters? ___

4. In the next three words in the first column, what two letters make the sound of k? ___

5. In the remaining words on the spelling list, what two letters make the sound of kw? ___

> The letter **q** is always followed by **u** in the English language, but is sometimes pronounced **k**, usually **kw**. At the end of a word (it is always pronounced **k** and) it is always spelled **que**.

Spelling Dictionary

1. **ac·quaint**   *v.* **–quaint·ed, –quaint·ing** to make thouroughly familiar with

2. **ac·quire**   *v.* **–quired, –quir·ing** to come to have as one's own [to *acquire* knowledge]

3. **ac·qui·si·tion**   *n.* something acquired

4. **ad·e·quate**   *adj.* 1. enough or good enough; sufficient   2. barely satisfactory   **—ad·e·quate·ly** *adv.*

5. **ban·quet**   *n.* an elaborate meal; feast

6. **clique**   *n.* a small, exclusive circle of people

7. **col·lo·qui·al**   *adj.* being or containing the words, phrases, and idioms that are commonly used in informal speech and writing; informal   **—col·lo·qui·al·ly** *adv.*

8. **con·quer**   *v.* **–quered, –quer·ing** to overcome by physical, mental, or moral force; defeat   **—con·quer·or** *n.*

9. **cri·tique**   *n.* a critical analysis or evaluation of a subject, situation, book, etc.   *–v.* **–qued** appraise critically

10. **e·qui·nox**   *n.* 1. the time when the sun crosses the equator, making night and day of equal length in all parts of the earth: the **vernal equinox** occurs about March 21, the **autumnal equinox** about September 22   2. either of the two points on the celestial equator where the sun crosses it on these dates

11. **gro·tesque**   *adj.* having a twisted, strange, unreal appearance, shape, etc.; bisarre   **—gro·tesque·ly** *adv.* **—gro·tesque·ness** *n.*

12. **in·qui·ry**   *n. pl.,* **–ries** 1. an investigation or examination   2. a question; query

13. **in·qui·si·tive**   *adj.* 1. inclined to ask many questions or seek information 2. asking more questions than is necessary or proper; prying   **—in·qui·si·tive·ly** *adv.*   **—in·qui·si·tive·ness** *n.*

14. **jon·quil**   *n.* a narcissus having relatively small yellow flowers and long, slender leaves

15. **lac·quer**   *n.* a resin varnish obtained from certain trees, used to give a hard, smooth, highly polished finish to wood   *–v.* **–quered, –quer·ing** to coat with or as with lacquer

16. **man·ne·quin**   *n.* a model of the human body, used by window dressers artists, etc.

17. **mas·quer·ade** *n.* a ball or party at which masks and fancy costumes are worn   *–v.* **–ad·ed, –ad·ing** to take part in a masquerade

18. **pic·tur·esque**   *adj.* 1. having a wild or natural beauty, as mountain scenery 2. suggesting a mental picture; vivid [a *picturesque* description]

19. **plaque**   *n.* 1. any thin, flat piece of metal, wood, etc. used as a decoration or to commemorate or identify something   2. (pathology) a small abnormal patch on or in the body

20. **quaint**   *adj.* 1. unusual or old-fashioned in a pleasing way 2. unusual; curious; odd   —**quaint·ly** *adv.*   —**quaint·ness** *n.*

21. **quar·an·tine**   *n.* isolation or restriction on travel to keep contagious diseases, insect pests, etc. from spreading   *–v.* **–tined, –tin·ing** to place under quarantine

22. **quar·ry**   *n. pl.,* **–ries** a place where building stone, marble, or slate is excavated   *–v.* **–ried, –ry·ing** to excavate from a quarry

23. **quench**   *v.* **–quired, –quir·ing** 1. to extinguish, put out [water *quenched* the fire] 2. to satisfy; slake [he *quenched* his thirst]   — **quench·a·ble** *adj.*   —**quench·less** *adj.*

24. **ques·tion·naire**   *n.* a written or printed list of questions used in gathering information from one or more persons

25. **quin·tup·let**   *n.* 1. any of five offspring born at a single birth 2. a group of five, usually or one kind

26. **qui·ver**   *v.* **–vered, –ver·ing** to shake with a tremulous motion; tremble   —**qui·ver·y** *adj.*

27. **quiz·zi·cal**   *adj.* 1. gently mocking or teasing [a quizzical smile] 2. perplexed; questioning [a quizzical look on his face]   —**quiz·zi·cal·ly** *adv.*

28. **se·quel**   *n.* something that follows; continuation

29. **u·nique**   *adj.* having no like or equal; unparalleled   —**u·nique·ly** *adv.*   —**u·nique·ness** *n.*

Practicing the words
A. Write in alphabetical order the spelling words in which **qu** has the sound of **k** in the left column. Then write in alphabetial order the spelling words that begin with the sound of **kw** in the right column.

_____   _____

_____   _____

_____   _____

_____   _____

_____   _____

_____   _____

    _____

B. The words in each group are related in some way. Find the spelling word that fits each group. Then indicate what part of speech it is.

1. twin   triplet   quadruplet   _____ ____

2. sole   exclusive   only   _____ ____

3. get   obtain   procure   _____ ____

4. sufficiently suitable   satisfactorily _____ ____

5. shake   tremble   shiver   _____ ____

6. idiomatic   slang   informal   _____ ____

7. feast   dinner   meal   _____ ____

8. party   festival   gala   _____ ____

9. group   association   club   _____ ____

10. strange   unusual   eccentric   _____ ____

11. defeat   overcome   subdue   _____ ____

12. curious   quizzical   prying   _____ ____

13. extinguish   satisfy   appease   _____ ____

14. detention   isolation   restriction   _____ ____

15. continuation follow-up   installment   _____ ____

C. Complete this story with spelling words.

Moishy adjusted his costume as he arrived at the Purim __1__ party. He began to __2__ with excitement. He was well __3__ with everyone, but he couldn't recognize anyone. One person had measle spots painted on his face. A sign around his neck said, "Don't talk to me: I'm in __4__." Moishy saw an Egyptian king who had Paraoh II painted on his cloak. Behind him walked Paraoh III, his __5__. Moishy edged closer to the long __6__ table, which was covered with food. He helped himself to a glass of lemonade to __7__ his thirst. As he looked around, he saw no one else dressed like him and was certain that his costume was __8__. It might even win the __9__ that was being awarded as first prize. Just then he glanced at tho door. There he saw not two, not three, but four other people dressed as the same Rubik's Cube. Instead of being original, he was one in five. Maybe he could say that he had come as a __10__.

1. _____   10. _____

2. _____

3. _____

4. _____

5. _____

6. _____

7. _____

8. _____

9. _____

D. Find nine new **que/qu** words. Begin with the word **quiz** and find your way out of the

maze. Write each new word.

quiz

1. _____

2. _____

3. _____

4. _____

5. _____

6. _____

7. _____

8. _____

9. _____

```
L  Q  U  A  R  R  Y
I  N  Q  U  I  R  Y  E  Q
U  I  Q  U  E  G  R  O  U
Q  N  S  I  T  I  Q  T  I
N  I  E  R  Q→U  U  E  N
O  U  R  C  Z←I  E  S  O
J  Q  U  T  C  I  P  Q  X
N  E  N  N  A  M  E  U  A
O  I  T  I  S  I  U  Q  C
```

Unscramble the following sentences. Use one of your new words to complete each one.

You may add endings.

1. 21 is March the of date spring the _____ .

   _____

2. won grandmother prize her a for _____ .

   _____

3. is think I that odd statue _____ .

   _____

4. received play a the good _____ .

   _____

219

5. rock brother the works my at_____ .

_____

6. country drive a is the always in_____ .

_____

7. Mordechai a still stood as as_____ .

_____

8. when museum new exhibit will the its_____ .

_____

9. the your enclose receipt with _____ .

_____

E. Fill in the blanks with the appropriate spelling word.

1. פורים is really __ __ __ __ __ __ because there is a מצוה to drink much wine.

2. המן stood out from the rest of אחשורוש's __ __ __ __ __ __ __ of special advisors.

3. __ __ __ __ __ __ __ forms on teeth if you will not brush frequently.

4. Plenty of people will __ __ __ __ __ __ __ __ __ on פורים.

5. אחשורוש paid money so he did not need to __ __ __ __ __ __ __ in order to rule.

6. A shiny coating of __ __ __ __ __ __ __ helps the crumbs wash off the challah board.

7. המן offered money to __ __ __ __ __ __ __ the right to annihilate the אידין.

8. Over the vacation you might have become __ __ __ __ __ __ __ __ __ with some new friends.

9. I hope that you __ __ __ __ __ __ __ __ __ __ experienced the קדושה of יום טוב.

10. Slang is often used in __ __ __ __ __ __ __ __ correspondence.

11. We try to make children __ __ __ __ __ __ __ __ __ __ on the סדר night.

12. אחשורוש made a very long __ __ __ __ __ __ __ for 180 days.

13. The __ __ __ __ __ __ of the נס פורים was a second קבלת התורה באהבה.

14. אחשורוש likely wore a __ __ __ __ __ __ __ __ __ expression when he asked מי הוא זה ואי זה הוא?

15. A fancy word for a little shiver or tremble is __ __ __ __ __ __.

16. You often fill out a __ __ __ __ __ __ __ __ __ __ when submitting an application.

17. We were sick and tired of forced __ __ __ __ __ __ __ __ __ to try limiting

   COVID.

18. It is better to __ __ __ __ __ __ your thirst with water instead of soda.

19. On פסח many people still prepare food in __ __ __ __ __ __, old-fashioned ways.

20. A __ __ __ __ __ __ __ __ __ __ has 4 other siblings born with him.

Torahdike Authoring

The Young Ben Torah's Guide to Learning to Write

Lesson One

What is a sentence?

Key Concepts
- fragment
- sentence
- punctuation
- subject
- predicate

A **fragment** is a word or group of words that does not express a complete idea.

A **sentence** is a word or group of words that comprise a complete idea.

Punctuation is a system of signs placed throughout your writing that serve as map directions to enable your reader to navigate the ideas without confusion.

A **subject** is the noun that the sentence is about.

The **predicate** is what the sentence tells you about the subject.

When you write, you must make sure to sound intelligent and to be clear enough for your reader to follow along your ideas without too much confusion. The basic element of your writing will be the sentences that you use to form the content.

A **sentence** is a group of words that expresses a complete thought. It should be a clear and entire expression of whatever you want to say. A **fragment** does not express a complete thought, it is an incomplete idea.

By "complete thought" we mean the clear and entire expression of whatever you want to say. Which of the following groups of words expresses a complete thought:

1. Kayla
2. Found a kitten
3. Kayla found a kitten.

The third group of words expresses a complete thought. It is a complete sentence.

Sentence fragments do not express a complete thought. They are usually the result of carelessness. The writer's thoughts come faster than he or she can write them. The writer goes on to a new sentence without finishing the sentence he or she has started. The effect might be something like this:

1. Last night a funny thing   2. We were sitting around the dinner table
3. Suddenly, a loud bang

The first and third groups of words are sentence fragments. They do not express a complete thought.

For an idea to be expressed completely, it should be clear what the idea is about.

Incomplete Fragment
The mail in the box (*what about it?*)
Visited Hawaii during vacation (*who?*)
After our spelling test (*then what?*)

Complete Sentence
The mail in the box is for you.
Mr. Hooper visited Hawaii during vacation.
We'll have taffies after our spelling test.

If the group of words express a complete idea, they constitute a sentence and should have a punctuation mark to let the reader know where the end of the idea is. Otherwise, the reader becomes confused with the next idea, and instead of a single, complete idea it becomes a confusing mixture of ideas. If it does not contain a complete idea, then it is merely a fragment and needs more words to complete the idea.

The punctuation mark at the end of the idea lets the reader know if the idea is a statement or a question. If it is just a plain statement, the punctuation mark should be a period. If it is a question, you guessed it – the punctuation is a question mark. You can also let your reader know that it is an excited statement by replacing the period with an exclamation mark – that indicates to your reader that the idea should be received as if it was exclaimed, or shouted. You will learn more about punctuation marks later.

Fragments are also often the result of incorrect punctuation. Parts of sentences are written as if they were whole sentences:

1. About 3,300 feet down   2. In one of the world's deepest mines in
Idaho   3. In the warmth and dampness   4. The miners have grown a
lemon tree   5. About seven feet tall   6. Under light bulbs

Which of these six groups of words are sentences and which are fragments?

You can usually understand sentence fragments if they fit in with what a speaker has already said. You often use fragments in spoken conversation. You also use them in written conversation. In other writing, however, you should avoid sentence fragments.

Read each group of words carefully. If the words form a complete sentence, write the punctuation mark which should follow it. If the words form a fragment, write a short question about what is missing from the statement. Number one has already been filled out for you.

1. The furnace and the hot water heater _____*what about them?*_____

2. After school on Friday _____

3. The noise in the library_____

4. We put food in the cat's dish _____

5. The mail box on the corner _____

6. From the post office to the city hall _____

7. Everyone worked hard on the project _____

8. We always have pizza after Avos Uvanim _____

9. An announcement on Kol Beramah _____

10. Which color do you prefer _____

11. During the sale at Hat Box _____

12. The red or the blue _____

13. Whose bicycle is in the driveway _____

14. Why is everyone so late _____

15. Due to the heavy rains and flooding _____

16. With a special magnetic pencil _____

REMEMBER, TO BE A SENTENCE, THE GROUP OF WORDS MUST EXPRESS A COMPLETE IDEA. IF IT DOES NOT CONTAIN A COMPLETE IDEA, IT IS A FRAGMENT.

Every sentence contains two basic parts – a **subject** and a **predicate**. The subject tells whom or what the sentence is about. The predicate tells something about the subject.

SUBJECT (Who or what)	PREDICATE (What is said about the subject)
Hungry dogs	bark constantly.
A cold rain	fell all through the night.
My brother	laughed at his own mistake.

Each of the sentences expresses a complete thought. Each of them tells something (**predicate**) about a person, place, or thing (**subject**).

An easy way to understand the parts of a sentence is to think of the sentence as telling who did something, or what happened. The subject tells *who* or *what*. The predicate tells *did* or *happened*. You can divide sentences, then, in this way.

Who or what	Did or happened
The runner	crossed the finish line.
My parents	planted a garden.
The car	skidded on the wet pavement.
The bike	needs air in its tires.

The **subject** names someone or something about which a statement is to be made. It is always a noun, which is a person, place, or thing.

The **predicate** tells what is done or what happens. It is the information that the sentence wants to tell you about what the subject is doing or what happens to the subject. It always contains a verb. A verb is an action or a state of being.

If the sentence did not have a subject, the idea would not be clear because the reader would not know who it is about. Without a predicate, the reader does not know what the subject did or what happened to it. Together, the subject and predicate comprise a complete idea.

In each sentence below, find the subject and the predicate. Draw a vertical line between the subject and the predicate. Number one has already been filled out for you.

1. The book | fell off the pupil's desk.

2. Mr. Phillips handed out the test booklets.

3. All of my friends gave me mishloach manos.

4. Gamliel studies Spanish.

5. Ice hockey is my favorite winter sport.

6. The janitor found a wool cap in the locker room.

7. I ate a peanut butter and jelly sandwich for lunch.

8. Who remembers the correct answer?

9. My boots are waterproof.

10. The antique china teapot is from England.

11. Avrohom Fried sang a medley of songs.

12. The librarian showed us several new books.

13. Zelig played tennis with Meshullam.

14. My blue sweatpants are very comfortable.

15. Devorah babysits after school on Tuesdays.

16. The boy in the yellow T-shirt is my neighbor.

17. Everyone laughed.

18. The President held a news conference.

19. Each contestant chose a number from the jar.

20. The audience cheered enthusiastically.

21. Yoizel enjoyed his first piano lesson.

22. She listened to the news on the radio.

23. The council voted on the motion.

24. Brochoh and Binyomin cooked dinner.

25. Everyone in the world wants peace.

26. Several writers worked on the manuscript.

27. The diplomats discussed the treaty.

28. The predicate of a sentence tells something about the subject.

29. Shifra locked the garage door.

30. Each skier wore a jacket and a cap.

31. Benjy groped in the dark for the switch.

32. The dishwasher chugged noisily in the kitchen.

33. Leah's teacher agreed with the results.

34. I built these model cars.

35. Many walkers joined the hike.

36. The man with the clipboard asked some strange questions.

37. The team raised the money.

EVERY SENTENCE HAS A SUBJECT
AND A PREDICATE.
THE SUBJECT NAMES WHO OR
WHAT THE SENTENCE IS ABOUT.
THE PREDICATE TELLS WHAT
HAPPENED.

In most sentences, there are a few key words that are more important than the rest. These key words make the basic framework of the sentence.

Hungry **lions**	**roar** threateningly.
A large **truck**	**rumbled** down the street.
My **father**	**blew** the shofar well.

The subject of the first sentence is *Hungry lions*. The key word in this subject is *lions*. You can say *lions roar threateningly*. You cannot say *hungry roar threateningly*. The predicate in the first sentence is *roar threateningly*. The key word is *roar*. Without this word you would not have a sentence.

The key word of the subject is called the **simple subject**. It is the subject of the verb in the predicate. The key word of the predicate is called the **simple predicate**. It is the main verb of the predicate. We will generally use the word *verb* instead of the phrase *simple predicate*.

The verb and its subject are the basic framework of every sentence. All the rest of the sentence is built around them. To find this framework, first find the verb. Then ask yourself *who?* or *what?* before the verb. The answer to that is the simple subject.

My sister's cookies melt in your mouth.
Verb: melt
What melts? cookies
Simple subject: cookies

You will be able to tell a fragment from a sentence easily if you keep your eye on subjects and verbs.
A group of words without a subject makes you ask *Who did? What did? Who was? What was?*
A group of words without a verb makes you ask *What about it? What happened?*

Fragment	Ran up the avenue (Who ran up the avenue?)
Sentence	*The boy* ran up the avenue.
Fragment	A warm breeze (What about it? What happened?)
Sentence	A warm breeze *blew all afternoon*.

Asking yourself *who?* or *what?* before the verb will help you identify the subject of the sentence. This is especially helpful if there are a number of nouns in the subject. The noun which does the verb is the simple subject.

In the following sentences, the simple subject is in **bold** letters and the simple predicate is underlined.

Every young **child** <u>enjoys</u> a trip to the zoo.   {*Who* <u>enjoys</u>?}
A good **breakfast** <u>is</u> part of a healthful diet.   {*What* <u>is</u>?}
The red **sweater** in the drawer <u>needs</u> a button.   {*What* <u>needs</u>?}
A blue **Chevrolet** <u>sped</u> down the street.   {*What* <u>sped</u>?}

For each sentence below, first underline the verb and then circle its simple subject.

1. The people in our town act friendly.

2. A fierce storm blew across the Midwest.

3. Our school principal addressed the parents' meeting.

4. A branch caught in the blades of our lawnmower.

5. The answer to the question requires an explanation.

6. These magazines have good color photographs.

7. A good dictionary defines words simply.

8. The librarian helped me with my report.

9. The referee explained the rules of the game.

10. Peninah asked her brother for some help.

11. The phone rang several times.

12. Goldie's long, blond hair gleamed in the sunlight.

13. The huge gorilla frightened the children.

14. That program begins at 8:00 P.M.

15. The gardener prunes the hedges every spring.

16. The tall, lanky boy scored ten baskets during the game.

17. The English teacher explained the lesson simply.

THE SIMPLE PREDICATE IS THE MAIN VERB IN THE PREDICATE. THE SIMPLE SUBJECT IS THE NOUN WHICH DOES THE MAIN VERB.

18. My grandmother knits sweaters for us on Chanukah.

19. A quick dip in the pool improves your circulation.

20. The angry catcher shouted at the umpire.

Remember that it is easier to find the simple subject after you identify the main verb in the predicate. So first find the verb and underline it. Then ask yourself *who?* or *what?* before the verb to find its simple subject. There may be other nouns in the subject, so don't let that confuse you. The simple subject is the noun that does the verb.

21. The tiny, helpless infant cried for its mother.

1. Jeremy's new bike has a flat tire.

2. I need a pencil with an eraser.

3. Knee-deep snow awaited us outside the door.

4. My red and white apron is dirty.

5. The enthusiastic audience applauded the performers.

6. Temimah's team won the tournament.

7. Our neighbor brought a kugel for us.

8. The quilt on my bed keeps me warm.

9. Reporters from several newspapers called the school all afternoon.

10. The girl with the long hair fell down.

11. The dog barked loudly.

12. The train from Seattle arrived at 3:00.

13. Leslie hooked a rug.

14. Seashells littered the beach.

15. Gimpel entered the race.

16. Rain fell steadily all day long.

17. Azriel remembered his old friend.

18. That roan horse gallops with a limp.

19. George heard a funny story yesterday.

20. Stars twinkled brightly in the sky.

21. The pilot landed the plane with no difficulties.

22. The horse in that field leaped over the fence.

23. The kite lodged in the top of the tree.

24. Three wrapped packages lay on the front porch.

25. Our class discussed energy conservation.

26. Yoni's uncle explained his hobby.

27. Straight black lines mark the boundaries of the court.

28. I know a riddle.

29. The potter shapes the clay on the wheel.

30. The crowd roared its approval.

31. Kaila's routine on the balance beam was excellent.

32. The rug on the floor looked dirty.

33. Yaninah dances very well.

34. Dr. Sanders performed a delicate operation.

35. The party was a success.

36. Yirmiyahu made the placemats.

37. Magnets attract iron and steel particles.

38. All of the students played in the piano recital.

39. Eli Whitney invented the cotton gin.

40. We read the chapter.

41. Genendel buys all our supplies.

42. The parents enjoyed the performance.

43. The explorers discovered a lost city.

44. The announcer was nervous before the broadcast.

45. Yehudis has an older brother.

Lesson Two

Nouns and Subjects

Key Concepts
- nouns
- common noun
- proper noun
- subject
- pronoun

A **noun** names a person, place, or thing. A **common noun** refers to any of a whole class of things, or to the whole class, without referring to a specific one. When naming a specific person, place, or thing, that is called a **proper noun** and should be capitalized.

The **subject** of a sentence is the person, place, or thing that the sentence is telling you about.

A **pronoun** is a word that is not a noun, but takes the place of a noun in a sentence.

What are nouns?

A noun is a word used to name a person, place, thing, or idea. Things named by nouns may be things you can see (chair, tree, Crystal Lake, Mexico, light), things you cannot see (history, song, speech, patience, rules), or ideas (friendship, fairness, honesty, happiness, love).

Underline the nouns in each of the following sentences. There is more than one noun in each sentence.

1. Snow covered the mountains.

2. The water flowed gently down the hillside.

3. There was an old car in the garage.

4. Lightning told the boy that the storm was coming.

5. The chair my grandpa carved was a labor of love.

6. Horses, cows, and chickens are raised on that farm.

7. My favorite subjects in school are science and math.

238

8. The gymnasium was filled with anxious spectators.

9. Our family had a reunion last July in Michigan.

10. The green leaves turned golden in the autumn.

Remember that any person, place, or thing is a noun. It can be a thing that you can see, or that you cannot see. It can even be a thing that exists only in your mind, like an idea or a concept.

11. Chimpanzees are my favorite performers at the zoo.

12. The trees danced in the wind.

13. Grasshoppers have strong muscles in their legs.

14. Check the refrigerator and see if there's any mustard.

15. The lifeguard saved the lives of two children.

16. Two qualities a babysitter needs are patience and firmness.

17. The class studied the history of Spain last semester.

18. Their dog has just had five puppies.

19. Does Meshullam live in a house or in an apartment?

20. Schools and businesses closed after the storm.

21. My uncle prefers Fords to all other cars.

22. The crown contains rubies, diamonds, and emeralds.

A **common noun** is the name of a whole class of persons, places, or things or any non-specific one of them. It is a general name and does not refer to a special person, place, or thing.

> goat, bird, stream

A **proper noun** is the name of a particular person, place, or thing. It always begins with a capital letter.

> Billy, Verrazano, Washington

A proper noun may also consist of more than one word.

> West Virginia, Verrazano Narrows, New Jersey

When a common noun is used as part of a proper noun as a title or part of the name it is also capitalized.

> Atlantic Ocean, Mediterranean Sea, Lake Carasaljo

Common noun	Proper noun	Common noun	Proper noun
man	George Washington	lake	Lake Carasaljo
rabbi	Rav Chaim Kanievsky	park	Yellowstone Park
woman	Sara Schenirer	day	Memorial Day
road	County Line Road	general	General Eisenhower
continent	North America, Africa	month	July, September

Potential error: When a proper noun is written next to a common noun, but they are not a single name or title, the common noun remains lowercase.

> Goldberg family

Circle the proper nouns which should have been capitalized in the following sentences.

1. The janitor went for vacation to miami.

2. Our house is on the corner of avers avenue and dempster street.

3. The watsons traveled to denver, colorado, and boise, idaho.

4. One of the difficult languages to learn how to spell is english.

5. The name of the ocean on the east of the united states is atlantic.

6. The people who used to live in north america before the english came are called indians.

7. The day that follows sunday night is monday.

8. A cheap hotel better than a motel is the holiday inn.

9. Next thursday is my birthday.

10. The cohen family lives on grove street.

11. One of the last two states to join this country is hawaii.

12. The city of lancaster is a popular summer destination.

13. Our teacher showed maps of the andes and other mountains.

14. His brother goes to school in massachusetts.

15. The parade moved down state street.

16. At the start of the race, shmuel led.

17. The air in colorado is clear and unpolluted.

18. Playwright william shakespeare put on his plays at the globe theater.

For each common noun that is given, write a proper noun that is a member of that common noun next to it. For example, next to **month** you might write Elul or August.

1. month   _____   7. country   _____

2. neighbor _____   8. cereal   _____

3. singer   _____   9. camp   _____

4. city   _____   10. holiday   _____

5. ocean   _____   11. vehicle   _____

6. continent _____   12. book   _____

NOUNS ARE PERSONS, PLACES, OR THINGS.
COMMON NOUNS REFER TO A WHOLE CLASS OF PEOPLE, PLACES, OR THINGS, OR TO ANY OF THEM, BUT NOT SPECIFICALLY NAMING ONE OF THEM.
A PROPER NOUN NAMES A SPECIFIC NOUN AND SHOULD BE CAPITALIZED.

While we are on the subject of nouns, remember last chapter we learned about subjects in a sentence.

The subject of a sentence tells who or what is being talked about. Nouns are most often used as subjects, but sometimes a pronoun is used instead. (A pronoun is a word that is not a noun, but stands in place of a noun. The same word might sometimes be a pronoun for one noun and sometimes a different noun. You will learn more about pronouns later.)

Sometimes the subject is not right next to the verb. Other words may separate them. The subject might even come after the verb.

- Devorah entered the room quietly.
- Devorah always entered the room quietly.

Both sentences contain the same subject (*Devorah*) and the same simple predicate (*entered*). However, the second sentence has an extra word that is part of the predicate.

- The snake slithered through the grass.
- Through the grass slithered the snake.

Both sentences contain the same words, but their arrangement is different. Both have the same subject and predicate, yet the second one is more complicating to the reader because the subject comes after the predicate.

When writing questions, this is more common and less confusing.

- Where are the records?
- The records are where?

Both sentences contain the same words, yet this time the sentence with the subject after the predicate is easier to understand.

Remember, there might be many nouns in the sentence, yet the subject is only the answer to *who?* or *what?* did the simple predicate. So first find the simple predicate (the main verb) and then ask yourself *who?* or *what?* the verb. That will help you find the simple subject.

Circle each of the nouns used as a subject in the following sentences.

1. Thousands filled the stadium.

2. Thousands of people wearing coats and scarves filled the stadium.

   Avrohom Fried is my favorite singer.

3. From behind the curtain stepped the dancer.

4. The pen with the felt tip wrote well.

5. Cinnamon is a spice.

6. Into the pond waddled the duck.

7. The practice game lasted one hour.

8. The members of the team were satisfied.

9. There were several players chosen for the racquetball tournament.

10. Sherlock Holmes followed the clues on the map.

11. That woman became the superintendent.

12. There was only one solution to the puzzle.

13. My cousin entered this year's Special Olympics.

14. Out of the tree flew a colorful bird.

15. Dr. Chong had his office on the third floor.

16. The bicycle in the garage has a flat tire.

17. There were many people at the meeting.

18. There goes my sister.

19. There was a moment of silence before the game.

20. There is a good reason for my decision.

21. There is your watch.

22. There might be an encore after the concert.

23. There will be ten people at our *siyum*.

24. Here are the potatoes.

25. Down the street rushed the ambulance.

26. Down came the loose shingles.

27. From the stadium came a thunderous roar.

28. Through the forest blazed the flames.

29. On the corner stands the new library.

30. Here is the change from your dollar.

31. Into the clouds soared the airplane.

32. Hundreds of people participated in the siyum.

33. *Esrogim* with *gartels* were preferred.

THE SUBJECT OF THE SENTENCE IS THE NOUN OR PRONOUN THAT ANSWERS "WHO?" OR "WHAT?" DID THE VERB. IT OFTEN COMES BEFORE THE VERB, BUT OCCASIONALLY AFTERWARDS.

Occasionally, a sentence will seem to be missing the subject when it is clear who the subject is. If the sentence is imperative (meaning it states a command or request), the subject is often left out. Since commands and requests are always given to the person spoken to, the subject is *you*. Since the *you* is not given, we say that it is *understood*.

(*You*) Bring me the coffee cup.
(*You*) Wipe your feet.   (*You*) Stand up.

In the following sentences, find the subject and the verb and write them on the spaces. If the subject is the understood *you*, write it in parentheses.

		Subject	Verb
1.	Hang on!		
2.	Are there two minutes left?		
3.	Did you read the article about bicycles?		
4.	Economy is one advantage of the bicycle.		
5.	Down came the rain.		
6.	There comes the bus.		
7.	On the porch hung several plants.		
8.	Have you heard the drashah?		
9.	Are these books due today?		
10.	Over the phone came the reply.		
11.	Don't just stand there.		
12.	Here comes the mail.		
13.	Do you like to learn Mishnayos?		
14.	Now open your eyes.		
15.	Give him a chance.		
16.	There is a good reason for my decision.		
17.	Don't forget your promise.		
18.	There is your watch.		
19.	Have some cake.		
20.	Hurry!		

Lesson Three

Joining Short Sentences

Key Concepts
- choppy sentences
- coordinate conjunctions
- independent or dependent phrase
- adding single words
- adding groups of words

A **choppy sentence** is one that is too short.

A **coordinate conjunction** is a word that is used to join two sentences together to form a longer sentence. Examples of coordinate conjunctions are: **for, and, not, but, or, yet, so**.

A phrase which could exist as a sentence on its own is an **independent phrase**. One that cannot be a sentence on its own is **dependent**. Sometimes you can combine sentences by selecting the main word from a smaller sentence and **adding that word** to the main sentence. You might have to change its form. Other times, you can select a **group of words** from the second sentence to add to the main one. Again, you might have to change the form of a word to make it fit.

When writing for people older than third grade, you need to avoid writing too many short sentences.

Small sentences are boring to read. Many of them strung together look bad. They appear simple. This can also make your thoughts look simple. It seems you cannot sustain an idea for more than a few words. You only think in trivial ways. Small thoughts seem to come from small minds. Your reader might think you are simpleminded. Is that what you want?

A sentence is a group of words that states a single main idea. However, some main ideas are made up of smaller ideas. If each smaller idea is stated in a sentence of its own, the result is often choppy. The writing may give the reader only a vague idea of how the smaller ideas are related.

Consider the following group of sentences:

Pinchos sat in the dining room. He shredded his tissue. He was apprehensive.

The ideas can be combined in one sentence.

247

Pinchos sat in the dining room, apprehensively shredding his tissue.

The new sentence has only one main idea, but that main idea has several parts. The new sentence flows smoothly and shows how the ideas are related. It is much more effective than the group of sentences.

Another problem with choppy sentences is that it can sound like it was written by a child or intended for a young child to read. Young adults do not appreciate reading on such a simple level. Intelligent people prefer exciting, complex sentences that pack in a lot of information or interesting details.

> I have a wish. I want to create. What is my invention? A fireproof drone. Imagine taking pictures inside a volcano. The drone would be controlled remotely. You would not get hurt. It would be terrific.

Sounds like it was written by a child or for children. It would be tedious and cumbersome to read a book written in such short sentences.

A simple tool to join sentences together and form longer sentences is to use a **coordinating conjunction.**
Conjunction means attachment, and a coordinating conjunction is a word that combines two individual word or ideas. This is a great way of joining two ideas, each of which could have been a sentence on its own. The seven most common coordinating conjunctions are: and, but, for, nor, or, so, yet. Together, they form an acronym FANBOYS, which is a great way to remember them – for, and, nor, but, or, yet, so.

When joining two sentences with a coordinating conjunction, the first sentence loses its punctuation mark. Instead, use a comma before the conjunction.

> Lazer fed the animals. Shmuel cleaned all the animals' cages.
> Lazer fed the animals, and Shmuel cleaned all the animals' cages.
>
> Rivka joined the newspaper staff. She was a great writer.
> Rivka joined the newspaper staff, for she was a great writer.

When two sentences state similar ideas that are equally important, use the conjunction *and*.

> The doors were locked. The windows were boarded shut.
> The doors were locked, *and* the windows were boarded shut.

When two sentences state contrasting ideas of equal importance, use the conjunction *but* or *yet*.

The sound on this computer is not working. The picture projection is clear.
The sound on this computer is not working, *but* the picture projection is clear.

Mordechai wants to be a baal-koyreh. He never practices.
Mordechai wants to be a baal-koyreh, *yet* he never practices.

If a pair of sentences express a choice between ideas of equal importance use the word *or*.

Should we go skating? Should we go for a bike ride?
Should we go skating, *or* should we go for a bike ride?

When two sentences express cause and effect, use the word *for* or *so*. But there is a difference between them. If the first sentence is the cause, use *so*. When the first sentence is the effect, use *for*.

We are out of plates. I have to go to the store.
We are out of plates, *so* I have to go to the store.

I have to go to the store. We are out of chips.
I have to go to the store, *for* we are out of chips.

The word nor can only be used as a pair with another "no".
neither/nor
not/nor
It cannot be used to simply combine two shorter
sentences.
You will either have to make some slight rewording
or repositioning of the words in the second sentence.

---

7 COORDINATING CONJUNCTIONS FORM THE ACRONYM FANBOYS
FOR, AND, NOR, BUT, OR, YET, SO

Use coordinating conjunctions to combine the following sentences. Rewrite the entire sentence.

1.Menachem is a math teacher. He is bad at division. _____

_____

2.Plenty of vegetables were ready to be picked in Miriam's garden. She didn't go to the farmers' market this week.

_____

_____

3.I wanted something to eat. I looked in the fridge._____

_____

4.The host borrowed dozens of folding chairs. There were not enough chairs for the guests.

_____

_____

5.You can have macaroni and cheese for lunch. You can have leftover tuna fish. _____

_____

_____

6.I sat my phone down on the desk. I cannot find it now. _____

_____

_____

7.I haven't been to the supermarket yet this week. I plan to go today. _____

_____

_____

8.He said he'd be on time. He is five minutes late. _____

9. He looked at his watch and noticed he was late. He began to hurry. _____

_____

_____

10. You knew she needed help. You did nothing. _____

_____

11. The drizzle began. They were enjoying their game too much to stop. _____

_____

_____

12. I love to dance. I do not love to sing. _____

_____

13. She was getting very drowsy. She did not slow down a bit._____

_____

_____

14. They are poor. They are happy._____

_____

15. She waved at her uncle. Her uncle waved back with a smile._____

_____

_____

16. She knew the answer. She didn't tell me. _____

_____

_____

17.He did not miss a single comma. He did not make any spelling errors._____

_____

_____

18.I'm usually allergic to nuts. I did not have a reaction to your almond cake. _____

_____

_____

19.She closed her book with a bang and stood up. The noises in the room were not allowing her to concentrate.

_____

_____

YOU CAN USE A COORDINATING CONJUNCTION TO JOIN TWO SHORT SENTENCES.
DROP THE PUNCTUATION MARK FROM THE FIRST SENTENCE, AND INSERT A COMMA BEFORE THE CONJUNCTION.

A comma is only required before the coordinating conjunction when the second sentence is being used in its entirety. In this case it is an **independent phrase** because it could be a sentence by itself. Remember, a sentence is a complete idea that has a subject and a predicate. If you remove the subject from the second sentence, it is no longer an independent phrase and you do not need to use a comma before the conjunction.

> I picked up my pen. I could not think of what to write.
> I picked up my pen, but I could not think of what to write. (comma needed)
> I picked up my pen but could not think of what to write. (comma unnecessary)

When the *I* was retained, a comma was needed because the conjunction was combining two independent phrases. But in the last sentence, the *I* was dropped and "could not think of what to write" is not a complete sentence because it does not have a subject, so the comma was not needed.

Usually, it will be sufficient for you to simply check if there is a subject after the conjunction. As soon as you ascertain that there is no subject, you can tell that it is a dependent phrase and no comma is needed. If there is a subject, pay attention to the rest of the sentence to see if it is still independent and requires a comma.

In the following examples the conjunction has been bolded. Check whether it joins an independent phrase and requires a comma or a dependent phrase which does not require a comma.

1.   Peninah tried to fix the smudged paint **yet** the stain was still visible.

        Comma /No Comma

2.   You can tell me about your day now **or** wait till after supper.

        Comma /No Comma

3.   Shloimy ran as quickly as he could **but** he got drenched in the downpour.

        Comma /No Comma

4.   Moishy writes for the Mishpacha **and** submitted an article this week.

        Comma /No Comma

253

5.	Simcha was focusing his camera **and** did not notice the man behind him.

	Comma /No Comma

6.	You can choose to use the rowboat **or** go for a hike.	Comma /No Comma

7.	Dovid will build a table **but** he will not use any electric tools.

	Comma /No Comma

8.	Zalman tried to listen to the hesped **but** the wind made too much noise.

	Comma /No Comma

9.	Eliezer's bike chain fell off **so** he needed to walk his bike home.

	Comma /No Comma

10.	Tziporah lost her headband **for** the wind blew so strongly.	Comma /No Comma

A COMMA IS ONLY REQUIRED BEFORE THE CONJUNCTION IF BOTH PHRASES ARE INDEPENDENT. IF THE SECOND PHRASE IS MISSING THE SUBJECT, A COMMA IS UNNECESSARY.

Many times the ideas expressed by both sentences are so closely related that words are repeated in the sentences. You can combine the ideas of both sentences, using only the important parts of each sentence, eliminating the repeated words. You will not need a comma in this case because the phrase will be dependent on the other parts of the sentence.

When the sentence parts express similar ideas that are equally important, they can usually be joined by *and*.

> Channah designed the posters. She designed the banners.
> Channah designed the posters and the banners.

When the parts express contrasting ideas, they can usually be joined by *but* or *yet*.

> I burned the rolls. I made a delicious soup.
> I burned the rolls, but made a delicious soup.

> Shifra was busy. Shifrah was friendly, though.
> Shifra was busy, yet friendly.

When the parts express a choice between ideas they can usually be joined by *or*.

> Shall we rake the leaves today? Shall we rake the leaves next week?
> Shall we rake the leaves today or next week?

Combine the following sentences and sentence parts using a conjunction. Eliminate the *italicized words*.

1. Do you have a passport? *Do you have* any proof of citizenship?

_____

_____

2. Devorah bought boots. *She bought* an umbrella.

_____

_____

3. The wagon might have hit a rock. *The wagon might have* gotten stuck in a rut.

_____

_____

4. Goldy and Miriam do not have roller blades. *They do not have* skateboards.

_____

_____

5. Are you nearsighted? *Are you* farsighted?

_____

_____

6. Leah ate lunch. Yaninah *ate lunch*.

_____

_____

7. The mouse may have eaten the sandwich. The cat *may have eaten the sandwich*.

_____

_____

8. Aharon could do sit-ups. *He could* not *do* backbends.

_____

_____

9. The town had no sidewalks. *It had* few shade trees.

_____

_____

10. Dinosaurs are extinct. Wooly mammoths *are extinct*.[41]

_____

_____

11. Shimon lost the letter I sent him. *Shimon lost the* map *I sent him.*

_____

_____

12. The jam was made of raspberry. *The jam was* delicious.

_____

_____

13. The water was cold. *The water was* full of sharks.

_____

_____

> **YOU CAN OFTEN ELIMINATE UNNECESSARILY REPEATED WORDS WHEN COMBINING SMALLER SENTENCES WITH A CONJUNCTION.**

_____

[41] Maybe they perished in the mabul?

The ideas in a pair of sentences may not be equally important. Perhaps only one word in the second sentence is really important to the main idea expressed by the pair of sentences. The one important word can be added to the first sentence without the use of a conjunction. The new sentence will be a tighter and more effective way of expressing the idea.

> Gamliel is a photographer. *He's* good.
> Gamliel is a good photographer.

> Binyomin arranged the wrenches. *He did it* carefully.
> Binyomin arranged the wrenches carefully.

> We couldn't help admiring the team. *The team was* losing.
> We couldn't help admiring the losing team.

Sometimes, you may be able to add several single words to a sentence. This will allow you to combine more than two sentences. If one of the sentences expresses a main idea, and each of the others adds only one important detail to the main idea, you can combine them.

> A cat rested on the chair. The cat was large. The chair was wobbly.
> A large cat rested on the wobbly chair.

Be careful to choose the right location in the main sentence for each word that you add.

Sometimes you will need to use a comma when you add more than a single word to a sentence if they will be working together as an adjective[42]. You will learn more about this comma later.

> Sludge washed up on shore after the oil spill. *The sludge was* thick. *The sludge was* sticky.
> Thick, sticky sludge washed up on shore after the oil spill.

Sometimes you can use *and* to join the words that you add to the main sentence.

> Devorah received a message. The message was long. It was complicated.
> Devorah received a long and complicated message.

> [!NOTE]
> **YOU CAN COMBINE SENTENCES BY JUST ADDING SINGLE WORDS.**

---

[42] An adjective is a word that works to describe or limit a noun. When two words work independently of each other as adjectives before the same noun, it is called a coordinate adjective, and a comma is used to separate them.

Combine each of the following groups of sentences by adding the important words.
Eliminate the italicized words.

1. Yosef had a parrot *The parrot was* talkative.

    _____

    _____

2. Chantzy set the lamp on the desk. *The lamp was* polished. *It was* gleaming.

    _____

    _____

3. Miriam slipped into the room. *She came in* silently. *The room was* darkened.

    _____

    _____

4. Dov realized he was standing in cement. *The cement was* wet.

    _____

    _____

5. Rutie spread a glaze over the Yom Tov roast. *The glaze was* thick. *The glaze was made of* apricot.

    _____

    _____

6. The directory is in a drawer in the kitchen. *It is a* telephone directory. *It is* new.

_____

_____

7. The audience burst into applause after the play. *The audience was* delighted. *The applause was* enthusiastic. *The play was* inspiring.

_____

_____

8. The most popular performers were the two acrobats. Who were *they*? *They were* twins. *They were* from France.

_____

_____

9. Rocheli placed the coins in a box. *The coins were* shiny. *The box was* green.

_____

_____

10. The helicopter chugged through the storm. *The storm was* of hailstones. *The helicopter was* battered.

_____

_____

There is no hard and fast rule for this. Sometimes the same two sentences can be combined in different ways and the meanings will be different.

> Shimshon adjusted the sails. The sails were flapping.
> Coordinating conjunction: Shimshon adjusted the sails, for the sails were flapping.
> Adding single words: Shimshon adjusted the flapping sails.

As the writer you are in charge of what you want to say. Imagine that you are the reader, put yourself in his shoes, and pay attention to how it sounds to you. Is that what you meant to say? If not, try combining them a different way.

Combine the following sentences by adding important words to the main sentence. Sometimes it will be neater to use a coordinating conjunction, but other times it will be smoother to just add single words. Decide on your own how to combine the sentences.

1. Brochy cleared the table. Shifrah swept the floor.

    _____

    _____

2. The experiment was a success. The success was complete.

    _____

    _____

3. Meshulum is small. He is the star of the basketball team.

    _____

    _____

4. Eliyohu adjusted the gears. The wheels were slowing down.

    _____

    _____

5. Zevullun had paid his fare. The bus driver did not believe him.

_____

_____

6. The curtains faded in the sunlight. The sunlight was dazzling.

_____

_____

7. The rope was short. It was strong.

_____

_____

8. The babies crawled across the floor. The babies were muddy. The floor was shiny.

_____

_____

9. You must hurry. We will be late.

_____

_____

10. The cyclists displayed a map of their trip. The map was hand-made. They displayed it proudly.

_____

_____

11. The town Macomb has no airport. It has a train station.

_____

_____

> **THE METHOD YOU USE TO COMBINE SENTENCES MIGHT CHANGE THE MEANING SLIGHTLY. PAY ATTENTION TO HOW THE READER WILL PERCEIVE IT.**

Before you add an important word to a sentence, you might have to change the form of the word. There are numerous changes that might need to be made to accommodate the word.

You may have to add -*y*.

> Don't sit on that bench. *It* wobbles.
> Don't sit on that wobbly bench.

Sometimes you will have to add -ing or -ed.

> Nosson and Meir set up the chairs. They would fold.
> Nosson and Meir set up the folding chairs.

> Tuvyah smoothed the paper. It had a crease.
> Tuvyah smoothed the creased paper.

At other times, you will have to add -ly.

> Alizah solved our designing problems. She was quick.
> Alizah quickly solved our designing problems.

Often, the word ending in -ly can be placed in any of several positions in the sentence.
> Mazal remarked that she had not seen Temimah in years. Mazal was sad.
> Mazal sadly remarked that she had not seen Temimah in years.
> Mazal remarked sadly that she had not seen Temimah in years.
> Sadly, Mazal remarked that she had not seen Temimah in years.

Combine each pair of sentences by adding the important word and changing its form appropriately. Omit the italicized words.

1. Chaim backed away from the snake. *The snake* hissed.

2. I cleaned the shelves. *They were covered in* dust.

3. We arranged the roast on a platter. *The roast was in* slices.

4. Alexander whistled to tell us that he'd spotted the eagle. *His whistling was* soft.

5. The cat stalked the chipmunk. *The cat's movements were* slow.

For the next sentences, you choose the important word from the second sentence in each pair, and add it to the first sentence, changing it appropriately.

6. That stack of dishes may fall. The stack leans.

7. Ahuva scrubbed the tub. The tub had dirt in it.

_____

_____

8. Chevy made a banner. The banner had stripes.

_____

_____

9. Michael called my name. His voice was loud.

_____

_____

10. They had to wash the rags. The rags had oil on them.

_____

_____

WHEN ADDING WORDS, YOU SOMETIMES HAVE TO CHANGE THE FORM OF THE WORD. SOME COMMON CHANGES ARE ADDING -Y, -ING, -ED, -LY.
SOMETIMES, WHERE YOU ADD THE WORD TO THE SENTENCE DEPENDS ON HOW YOU CHANGED IT.

You might find that one sentence contains a group of words that can add important information to another sentence.

> Mommy is fixing supper. Mommy is in the kitchen.
> Not so clear[43]: Mommy is in the kitchen fixing supper.
> Very clear: Mommy is fixing supper in the kitchen.

You will have to use your common sense about where to add the group of words in the sentence. Sometimes it makes no difference, but at other times the sentence will be ludicrous if not added correctly. Here are some guidelines to help your writing be clear.

When the group of words give more information about someone or something, add it near the words that name the person or thing.

> The noise was startling. The noise was in the basement.
> The noise in the basement was startling.

When the group of words describes an action, add it near the words that name the action.

> Daniel was waiting. He was at the door.
> Daniel was waiting at the door.

If the group of words adds more information to the entire main idea of your sentence, you might add it at the beginning or the end of the sentence.

> Mr. Yankelowitz always sends his mother flowers. He sends them on his birthday.
> Mr. Yankelowitz always sends his mother flowers on his birthday.
> On his birthday, Mr. Yankelowitz always sends his mother flowers.

Combine each of the following pairs of sentences by adding a group of words to the first sentence. Eliminate the italicized words.

1. You will be sleeping in a bed. *The bed is one* with a canopy.

_____

_____

---

[43]   By adding a comma, it could be made clearer: Mommy is in the kitchen, fixing supper.

2. The blue coat is mine. *The coat is* in the lost-and-found.

_____

_____

3. The pastries look delicious. *The pastries were* at Heimishe Bakery.

_____

_____

4. Shimshy will be showing a blue sukkah. *It will be* at the sukkah display.

_____

_____

5. My brother loves to talk. *He talks* about the kuntres he is publishing.

_____

_____

Combine each of the following pairs of sentences.

6. Mount Fiji is a volcano. The volcano is in Japan.

_____

_____

7. The blister began to hurt. The blister was on my heel.

_____

_____

8. Moishy and Motty stood balancing. They were on the tightrope.

_____

_____

9. Faiga will mail the package. She'll mail it at noon.

_____

_____

10. Toiviya stood. He was at the center of the stage.

_____

_____

YOU CAN COMBINE
SENTENCES BY ADDING A
GROUP OF WORDS FROM A
SMALLER SENTENCE TO THE
SENTENCE WITH THE MAIN
IDEA. MAKE SURE TO INJECT
THE WORDS AT THE RIGHT
PART OF THE SENTENCE.

In some cases, when you add a group of words to a sentence, you will have to separate it from the rest of the sentence with a comma or a pair of commas. The comma is a punctuation mark that indicates to the reader that he should make a slight pause when reading the sentence because the next word(s) is slightly disconnected from the previous words. When the middle words are slightly disconnected from the words on both sides, a pair of commas indicate to slightly pause before and after the words.

My favorite bread is challah. *Challah is* a soft yeast bread.
My favorite bread is challah, a soft yeast bread.

"Tziyon Haloi Sishali" was written by Rabbi Yehudah Halevi. *"Tziyon Haloi Sishali" is* a poignant Tisha B'av kinnah.
"Tziyon Haloi Sishali," a poignant Tisha B'av kinnah, was written by Rabbi Yehudah Halevi.

Combine each of the following pairs of sentences by adding a group of words to the first sentence. Eliminate the italicized words. Decide whether to use one comma or a pair of commas.

1.   Mark's dog is the world's worst watchdog. *Mark's dog is* a dachshund[44].

_____

_____

2.   The man in the gorilla costume is Gavriel Applebaum. *He is* our neighbor.

_____

_____

3.   Shulamis's alarm clock is loud enough to wake the whole household. *Shulamis's alarm clock is* a small portable one.

_____

_____

4.   Neighbors of ours celebrate the Fourth of July. *They are* the Modernishers.

_____

_____

---

[44]   A dachshund is a species of dog.

5. Gimpel Katznellenbogenstien is the only bochur I know who has made a parachute jump. *He is* my cousin's roommate.

_____

_____

Combine each of the following pairs of sentences.

6. On the table lay my grandfather's most recent patented invention. It was a new method for refining gold.

_____

_____

7. Ruchamah was unable to open the register. Ruchamah was the substitute cashier.

_____

_____

8. We had cannoli for dessert on Hoshana Rabbah. Cannoli is an Italian pastry.

_____

_____

9. Rabbi Moskowberg organized our school's first Chol Hamoed Greater Adventure learning program. He is a famous Pirchei coordinator.

_____

_____

10. I participated in the 50th Yahrtzeit memorial for Rabbi Aharon Kotler in 2012. Rabbi Aharon Kotler was the first Rosh Yeshivah of Beth Medrash Govoha.

_____

_____

WHEN ADDING A GROUP OF WORDS TO A SENTENCE, YOU SOMETIMES NEED TO SEPARATE THEM FROM THE MAIN WORDS OF THE SENTENCE BY A COMMA OR PAIR OF COMMAS.
A COMMA INDICATES TO THE READER THAT THERE IS A SLIGHT PAUSE AND THE NEXT WORDS ARE SLIGHTLY DISCONNECTED FROM WHAT CAME BEFORE.

Remember to be sure to place the added information next to the words naming the person or thing. Sometimes you will need to change the form of one of the words to place the group of words in the right part of the sentence. The new form will usually en with *-ing* or *-ed*.

The man must have been a spy. *The man* stood under the street lamp.
The man standing under the street lamp must have been a spy.

They keep the octopus in a tank. *They* fill *the tank* with salt water.
They keep the octopus in a tank filled with salt water.

If you are not careful to place the new words at the right location, the meaning of the sentence might change from the way you intend. Try placing yourself in the reader's shoes and imagine how he will perceive the new sentence. Remember that the new words should go near the part of the sentence to which they are adding information and you can change the form of a word if necessary.

The crow must have been injured. *The crow was* dragging its left wing.
Wrong: The crow must have been injured dragging its left wing[45].
Right: The crow dragging its left wing must have been injured.

The fish was great. *The fish was* flown in from Maine.
Wrong: The fish was great, flown in from Maine.
Right: The fish flown in from Maine was great.

---

[45] This sounds like the injury happened when it was dragging it wing.

271

Inspector Watson stared at the mattress. *The mattress was* filled with money.
Wrong: Inspector Watson, filled with money, stared at the mattress.
Also Wrong: Filled with money, Inspector Watson stared at the mattress.
Right: Inspector Watson stared at the mattress filled with money.

The following two examples (both combined sentences contain the same words in different order) highlight how much of a difference is made by where you insert the added words.

Avrohom thought he saw his missing neighbor. *Avrohom was* peering through the bookstore window.
Peering through the bookstore window, Avrohom thought he saw his missing neighbor.

Avrohom thought he saw his missing neighbor. *His missing neighbor was* peering through the bookstore window.
Avrohom thought he saw his missing neighbor peering through the bookstore window.

Combine each pair of sentences by adding a group of words to the first sentence. Eliminate the italicized words.

1. The woman is Ruth's aunt. The woman is weaving a rug.

_____

_____

2. A man has left a large donation for Oorah. The man calls himself "a friend."

_____

_____

3. The singers were nervous. They were going on stage.

_____

_____

4. Rafaellah gives her baby a vitamin supplement. She dissolves it in orange juice.

_____

_____

5. Shmeeli Ungar was surprised to see hundreds of people. They were waiting outside the concert hall.

_____

_____

Combine each pair of sentences by adding an important group of words to the first sentence. Decide how the sentence should be combined and what changes may have to be made.

6. The people could hardly breathe. The people were packed into the tiny elevator.

_____

_____

7. Chavah searched through the pictures. The pictures were spread out on the table.

_____

_____

8. The library doesn't have the book. The book was reviewed in last week's circle.

_____

_____

9. The library will hold an exhibit of pottery. People make the pottery in the local day camps.

_____

_____

10. The snow squeaked under our boots. The snow had just fallen. {change *had* to *having*}

_____

_____

11. The faucet annoyed Zanvil. It dripped.

_____

_____

12. You can buy egg creams at the station. Egg creams are a New York specialty.

_____

_____

13. Hillel snuggled into the featherbead. It was warm. It was soft.

_____

_____

14. Do you have a passport? Do you have any proof of citizenship?

_____

_____

15. The crane lifted the beams. It lifted them from the stack.

_____

WHERE YOU ADD THE GROUP OF WORDS TO THE MAIN SENTENCE MAKES A DIFFERENCE . MAKE SURE TO ADD IT NEXT TO THE WORDS TO WHICH IT ADDS INFORMATION. YOU MIGHT NEED TO CHANGE THE FORM OF A WORD TO BE ABLE TO INSERT IT IN THE RIGHT PLACE.

Another way of combining sentences is substituting the entire idea of one sentence for a vague word in the main sentence. The words *something* and *that* are vague and might be able to be substituted with the entire idea of another sentence. But you might have to change the form of one of the words to make the substitution fit.

> *Something* improved my grade in spelling. *I* memorized the word list.
> Memorizing the word list improved my grade in spelling.

The idea of the second sentence explains the word something in the first. The form of the word *memorized* was changed to *memorizing*, so the entire idea could be substituted for the word *something*.

> *We* pounded the clay on the table. *That* helped us soften it.
> Pounding the clay on the table helped us soften it.

The word *pounded* was changed to *pounding*. Then the entire idea of the first sentence was substituted for *That* in the second sentence.

Combine each of the following pairs of sentences by substituting the entire idea of one sentence for a vague word in the other sentence.

1. People water cactus plants too much. That can harm them.

    _____

    _____

2. Baila has always enjoyed something. She exercises as soon as she gets up.

    _____

    _____

3. Penina waits in line for lunch. That makes her impatient.

    _____

    _____

4. Perel started a quilting business. That was Perel's best idea.

    _____

    _____

5. Tziporah practices the piano. That is Tziporah's favorite after-school activity.

_____

_____

In the next group of sentences, decide on your own what changes may have to be made.

6. Devorah and Dovid'l began something. They mixed the pancake batter.

_____

_____

7. I wrote a report about the Middle East. That took a lot of work.

_____

_____

8. Shprintza ran for president of the high school student council. That was not as easy as Shprintza had thought it would be.

_____

_____

9. Pinny planned on something. He would join us after mishmor.

_____

_____

10. I said goodbye to Shaul. That made me sad.

_____

_____

```
YOU CAN SUBSTITUTE THE IDEA OF AN
ENTIRE SENTENCE FOR A VAGUE WORD IN
THE MAIN SENTENCE LIKE SOMETHING OR
THAT.
REMEMBER TO CHANGE THE FORM OF A
WORD IF NECESSARY TO MAKE THE
SUBSTITUTION.
```

When adding information about a person, you can sometimes add it to a sentence by using the word *who* and inserting a group of words.

> The people are organizing another trip for next year. *The people* organized
the trip to Berditchev.
> The people who organized the trip to Berditchev are planning another trip
for next year.

In the example above, the group of words added to the first sentence is necessary to make it clear which people are meant. When that is the case, no comma is needed before the word *who*.

In some sentences, the added group of words is not absolutely necessary. The words merely add additional information. In such a case, insert a comma before the word *who* and another comma after the added words. This comma indicates to the reader to pause slightly because the words are not so directly related to the words next to them.

> Mr. Buchenwald and Rabbi Krohn are planning another trip for next year.
Mr. Buchenwald and Rabbi Krohn organized the trip to
Berdichev.
> Mr. Buchenwald and Rabbi Krohn, who organized the trip to Berditchev,
are planning another trip for next year.

Combine each of the following pairs of sentences by following the directions in the braces. Eliminate the italicized words.

1. Simcha Shtark hit the only home run. Simcha came into the game as a pinch-hitter. {use commas}

_____

_____

2. Duvvy entertained my parents for hours. Duvvy really knows how to tell a story. {use commas}

_____

_____

3. Boruch Perlowsky directed that video. Boruch Perlowsky is a talented director. {use commas}

_____

_____

4. Mr. Goodwin has a huge collection of campaign buttons. Mr. Goodwin enjoys politics. {use commas}

_____

_____

5. The bochur is Shmeeli Fixmacher. The bochur offered to repair your bike.

_____

_____

For the next set of sentences, decide on your own whether you need to use commas to combine the sentences.

6. Ezzie couldn't remember where he had put the permanent markers. Ezzie likes to have a place for everything and everything in its place.

_____

_____

7. I called Feivy. Feivy is at home with a cold.

_____

_____

8. Sendy Miller does volunteer work at the mezuzah gemach. Sendy wants to become a soyfer. _

_____

_____

9. The boy is visiting from Mexico. The boy is standing near the entrance.

_____

_____

10. People should sign up before the end of the day. They want to try out for the boys' choir.

_____

_____

> YOU CAN ADD A GROUP OF WORDS THAT ADD INFORMATION ABOUT A PERSON USING THE WORD *WHO*.
> IF THE INFORMATION IS NOT SO NECESSARY SEPARATE IT FROM THE REST OF THE SENTENCE WITH A PAIR OF COMMAS.

At times, the information added to a sentence is joined to it by the word *which* or *that*. Surprising as it may seem to you, there is a difference between them. *That* is used when the information is vital to the meaning of the sentence, but *which* is used when merely adding information that is not absolutely necessary. When you add information to a sentence that is not necessary, separate it from the rest of the sentence with a pair of commas.

If the information is necessary to make the meaning of the sentence clear, combine with **that**.

> This is the recording. I wanted you to listen to the recording.
> This is the recording that I wanted you to listen to.

However, when the group of words is not necessary, but just adds additional information, use the word **which** and separate it from the rest of the sentence with commas.

> Pea soup is not difficult to make. Pea soup is high in fiber and protein.
> Pea soup, which is high in fiber and protein, is not difficult to make.

You can sometimes omit the word that without changing the meaning of the sentence. It is usually preferable to omit unnecessary words.

> This is the recording I wanted you to listen to.

Combine each of the following pairs of sentences by using the word in the braces. Eliminate the italicized words.

1. These bricks came from the old city hall. The city plans to recycle these bricks. {which}

_____

_____

2. The repairman fixed Zelig's pocket watch. It was given to him by his grandfather. {which}

_____

_____

280

3. Goldie was upset because she had lost the new scarf. She had crocheted it herself. {that}

_____

_____

4. The repairman fixed the mp3 player. I found it in the attic. {that}

_____

_____

5. The children's book has just won a Pulitzer Prize. I read that book. {that}

_____

_____

For the next set of exercises, decide on your own whether to combine with *that* or *which*.

6. The map helped us find the campgrounds. Tzvi drew the map.

_____

_____

7. The computers were donated by local businesses. We use the computers for the class weekly.

_____

_____

8. The shoes turned my feet red. I bought the shoes on sale.

_____

_____

9. Yedidyah's bicycle helmet fits me perfectly. It no longer fits him.

_____

_____

10. Have you ever eaten in the pizza shop? Your sister recommended the pizza shop.

_____

_____

WHEN ADDING INFORMATION NECESSARY TO THE SENTENCE USE *THAT*. IF THE INFORMATION IS NOT NECESSARY, USE *WHICH* AND SEPARATE IT FROM THE REST OF THE SENTENCE WITH COMMAS.

You will often want to explain to your readers that something happened because of something else. If you do not make it clear that one thing caused another, your reader might not realize that one event was a cause and the other, an effect.

One way to explain to your readers the cause and effect is to clearly express the cause by using the word *because, since,* or *for*.

      We moved closer to BMG. I can walk to the Yeshiva for Yomim Noraim now.

      I can walk to the Yeshiva for Yomim Noraim now because we moved closer to   BMG.

      Since we moved closer to BMG, I can walk to the Yeshivah for Yomim Noraim   now.

Both words can be used (with the cause) either at the beginning of the sentence or at the beginning of the second half. However, if you begin the sentence with the cause, using *because* or *since*, you will need to use a comma to separate the effect from the cause. If you begin your sentence with the effect, no comma is needed at the beginning of the second half of the sentence. The word *because* or *since* serves as sufficient separation.

With comma

Since we moved closer to BMG, I can walk to the Yeshivah for Yomim Noraim now.

Because we moved closer to BMG, I can walk to the Yeshivah for Yomim Noraim now.

Since the stove is broken, we'll be having sandwiches for supper.

No comma

I can walk to the Yeshivah for Yomim Noraim now because we moved closer to BMG.

I can walk to the Yeshivah for Yomim Noraim now since we moved closer to BMG.

We'll be having sandwiches for supper for the stove is broken.

> YOU CAN SHOW CAUSE AND EFFECT BY USING A WORD THAT POINTS TO THE CAUSE.
> IF YOU POINT TO THE CAUSE AT THE BEGINNING OF A SENTENCE, USE A COMMA BEFORE THE EFFECT.
> IF YOU POINT TO THE CAUSE AT THE END OF THE SENTENCE, NO COMMA IS NEEDED.

The other way to show cause and effect is to point out the effect or result. With this method, you will usually also have to use a semicolon (;) before the word showing the effect[46]. Use words such as: *as a result, therefore, thus*, and *consequently* (but you might also need to use a comma after the word[47]).

> We moved closer to BMG; as a result, I can walk to the Yeshivah for Yomim Noraim now.
> The stove is broken; consequently, we'll be having sandwiches for supper.
> Pesach kept disturbing the class; therefore he got detention.
> He worked a long day; thus he slept well.

ANOTHER WAY TO SHOW CAUSE AND EFFECT IS TO HIGHLIGHT THE EFFECT OR RESULT BY USING WORDS THAT POINT IT OUT.
YOU WILL USUALLY NEED TO USE A SEMICOLON (;) BEFORE POINTING OUT THE RESULT.

---

[46] Using the coordinate conjunction *so* is an exception. It can be used without a semicolon, and it only needs a comma if the following phrase is independent.
[47] More on commas later.

Combine each of the following pairs of sentences by using the words in the braces. First decide which sentence states the cause, and which states the effect.

1. These shoes hurt my feet. {since} I don't wear them.

_____

_____

2. These shoes hurt my feet. {consequently,} I don't wear them.

_____

_____

3. Yossele has a wonderful voice. {because} He won the lead role in the choir.

_____

_____

4. Yossele has a wonderful voice. {therefore} He won the lead role in the choir.

_____

_____

5. Ezriel lost his watch. {because} He has been asking me for the time all day.

_____

_____

6. Pessie had a toothache. {as a result} She went to the dentist.

_____

_____

7. This schach mat is lighter. {since} It has fewer thick poles.

_____

_____

8. We were late for shacharis. {therefore} The alarm was not set.

_____

_____

9. I had to get the mop. {as a result} I spilled my coffee.

_____

_____

10. He got a speeding ticket. {consequently} Feivish was driving 75 m.p.h. in a 35 m.p.h. zone.

_____

_____

> *SINCE* AND *BECAUSE* POINT TO THE CAUSE. *CONSEQUENTLY, THEREFORE, AS A RESULT,* AND *THUS* POINT TO THE EFFECT.

Combine the sentences in each of the following groups into a single sentence.

1. Mark was sitting in a room.
   Mark was sitting alone.
   The room was dimly lit.
   Mark was listening to the news.
   The news was on the radio.

   _____

   _____

   _____

2. The newscaster was talking about a gorilla.
   The newscaster was Yaakov M.
   The gorilla was huge.
   The gorilla was kept at the zoo.
   The zoo was nearby.

   _____

   _____

   _____

3. The gorilla weighed four hundred pounds.
   The gorilla was so strong.
   It could pick up a car.

   _____

   _____

   _____

   _____

4. The zoo-keepers were worried.
   The gorilla could rip open its cage.
   The gorilla could escape.
   The escape would be easy.

   _____

   _____

5. Mark turned suddenly.
   Mark saw a hand.
   The hand was reaching through a window.
   The hand was large.
   The window was open.
   The hand was hairy.

   _____

   _____

   _____

Finish the story in your own words.

_____

_____

_____

_____

_____

_____

Review

Join the following pairs of sentences **by using a comma with a coordinating conjunction.**

1. Yesterday Dovid flew in a plane. He saw five states in an hour.

    _____

    _____

2. The tickets went on sale this morning. By the time we got to the show, they were all gone.

    _____

    _____

3. Pets can be fun. They require care and attention.

    _____

    _____

Join the following pairs of sentences **by using a coordinating conjunction without a comma.**

4. The Greek soldier buckled his armor. He rode after the elephant.

    _____

    _____

5. Next summer, Zecharyah might get a job as a sign poster. He might be a counselor.

    _____

    _____

6. I saw Shimon standing at the end of the hall. I saw Shifrah standing at the end of the hall.

_____

_____

Combine each group of sentences **by adding important words.** Eliminate the italicized words.

7. Robert looked for the election results in the paper. *He was* anxious.

_____

_____

8. My sweater shrank in the dryer. *My sweater was* wool.

_____

_____

9. A rainbow arched across the bay. *The rainbow was* pale. *The rainbow was* shimmering.

_____

_____

Combine the following sets of sentences **by adding an important group of words to the first sentence.** Eliminate the italicized words.

10. A local Hatzoloh member taught the first-aid course. *The member was* Mr. Yankel Tutzich.

_____

_____

11. Two statues guarded the entrance. *The statues were* of monkeys. *It was the entrance* to the zoo.

_____

_____

12. Did you see the recipe for chocolate latkes? *The recipe was* in this week's Treo.

_____

_____

Combine each of the following pairs of sentences **by substituting for the italicized word and changing the form of one of the words.**

13. Dr. Hendricks is very good at *something*. He puts his patients at ease.

_____

_____

14. Zeldy combs her pet goat's long fur. *That* can be tedious.

_____

_____

15. *Something* became Yehudis's passion. She practiced tennis.

_____

_____

16. People parachute from planes. *That* requires training.

_____

_____

Combine each pair of sentences **with the word *who*** and eliminate the italicized words.

17. Mr. Bellow has now joined a troupe of jugglers. *He* used to be very clumsy.

_____

_____

18. The boy saved four families. *The boy* spotted the smoke.

_____

_____

19. Students limit their career choices. *Students* don't explore many areas of study.

_____

_____

Combine each of the following pairs of sentences **with *that* or *which*** and eliminate the italicized words.

20. I can fix the lamp. *It* fell off the table.

_____

_____

21. I wanted someone to invent a pen. I would never be able to lose *it*.

_____

_____

22. This building was once a rich man's mansion. *The building* is now a museum.

_____

_____

Combine the following pairs of sentences **showing cause and effect by using the words in the braces.**

23. Chelly overslept. {as a result} She missed the bus for the class picnic.

_____

_____

24. Avigdor's car ran out of gas. {because} We missed the first half of the Adireinu event.

_____

_____

25. Avigdor's car ran out of gas. {so} We missed the first half of the Adireinu event.

_____

_____

26. The doctor put his arm in a cast. {therefore} He broke his arm.

_____

_____

27. Shmelke never brushes his teeth. {since} He has five cavities.

_____

_____

28. Mr. Kranker has lung cancer. {as a result} He's smoked cigarettes daily for twenty years.

_____

_____

29. The underpass was flooded. {consequently} We received seven inches of rain in four hours.

_____

_____

30. Cars needed more time to stop. {therefore} The streets were snow packed and icy.

_____

_____

31. Her secretary took a message. {so} The boss was busy.

_____

_____

32. The referee called a penalty. {because} A basketball player was traveling.

_____

_____

33. I flipped a light switch. {since} The light came on.

_____

_____

34. The child is obese. {consequently} A child eats only junk food and never does anything active.

_____

_____

35. Many plants and animals in the water died. {as a result} An oil spill caused crude oil to spill into the water.

_____

_____

36. Many buffalo were killed. {because} Buffalo almost became extinct.

_____

_____

37. The cake did not come out as planned. {so} Mimi didn't follow the recipe correctly.

_____

_____

Lesson Four

Paragraphs

Key Concepts
- paragraph
- topic sentence
- unity

A **paragraph** is a group of sentences that work together to support one main idea.
A **topic sentence** is usually the first sentence of a paragraph that tells you what the paragraph is about.
When all the sentences in the paragraph work together, that is called **unity**.

A paragraph is a group of sentences that work together to explain one main idea. That idea is usually stated in the first sentence. The rest of the sentences develop the main idea more fully. Following is an example of a well-written paragraph.

> *Elchonon slept more soundly that night than he had in a long time.* His dreams were of the new friend he had made that day in camp. He dreamed of Meshulam and himself swimming laps together in the pristine blue water of the Olympic-sized pool. He dreamed of running races together and winning points for their color-war team. He dreamed pleasant dreams like this until the morning when the sun came through the window and woke him.

The first sentence tells you that the paragraph is going to be about Elchonon's sound sleep. This is the one main idea of the paragraph The rest of the sentences develop that idea. They give you a sense Elchonon's long and peaceful rest.

When all of the sentences in a paragraph relate to one main idea, the paragraph has unity. Sometimes a paragraph contains sentences that stray from the main idea. These "extra" sentences can be removed easily to create a unified paragraph.

Other paragraphs, like this one, have more serious problems.

> Practical writing should be a required course in every high school in the United States. To write practically, one must be able to organize his ideas and express them in a coherent manner. Many people do not know how to string two sentences together to express an intelligent thought and write letters and emails that make them look foolish. There is no reason that a person should leave his teenage years writing like an ignoramus. If a young person starts his life knowing how to write well because he learned in a practical course, he will be equipped for success.

The first sentence in this paragraph is about the need for a practical writing course in every high school. Each of the next three sentences introduces a different idea. The second sentence defines practical writing. The third sentence makes a statement about poor writers. The fourth sentence criticizes unskilled writers. Only the last sentence relates directly to the opening sentence in the paragraph. It begins to explain why a writing course is useful.

The sentences in this paragraph do not develop one main idea. They are, therefore, a series of unrelated sentences, not a unified paragraph.

A PARAGRAPH IS A GROUP OF SENTENCES THAT WORK TOGETHER TO SUPPORT A SINGLE MAIN IDEA.
THE MAIN IDEA IS EXPRESSED IN THE TOPIC SENTENCE.
WHEN ALL THE SENTENCES PERTAIN TO THE MAIN IDEA THE PARAGRAPH HAS UNITY.
WITHOUT UNITY, THE SENTENCES DO NOT FORM A PARAGRAPH.

"How long does a paragraph have to be?" is a question asked by most young writers. Surprisingly, the answer is easier than you might suppose: *Your paragraph should be long enough to develop your main idea.* For example, the following paragraph is too short to explain the topic sentence clearly:

> Almost all of us agreed that Shmerel was the most greased-out boy we knew. To us regular people, he seemed to be a malach.

How was Shmerel so greased-out? What did he do? The question can only be answered by adding more sentences.

> Almost all of us agreed that Shmerel was the most machmir boy we knew. His Yarmulka was bigger than the largest Gerrer cholent bowl any of us ever saw; it reached from ear to ear. His brisker payos popped out from underneath the Yarmulka and stuck out at least a tefach on each side of his head. The sounds he made during keriyas shema were puzzling to make out as he repeated most words six time. His shemoneh esrei took 8 minutes longer than chazaras hashatz. Birchas Hamazon took fourteen minutes after each meal, and even his al hamichya took a good four minutes. He never ate any candy or sweets, and by the time he finished his beracha rishona on a bag of chips, most of us were already done. To us regular children, he seemed to be a malach.

The detailed information in the longer paragraph explains clearly and completely why Shmerel was considered a greased-out boy.

> # THE RIGHT LENGTH FOR A PARAGRAPH IS AS LONG AS IT TAKES TO DEVELOP THE MAIN IDEA.

In the following groups of sentences, there is one which would not fit with the unity of the others. Cross out that sentence. Then decide whether the remaining sentences give enough information about the main idea to make a fully developed paragraph.

1. Ecology poster   Paragraph/No Paragraph
    a) My friend and I made a poster on ecology.
    b) We put pictures of endangered animals on the poster.
    c) My brother and I have a club.

2. Underwater band   Paragraph/No Paragraph
    a) People laugh when they hear about a band that plays underwater.
    b) Richard Bailey, an inventor, organized such a band in 1974.
    c) Sound waves travel more slowly underwater.
    d) Musicians dress in diving gear and play instruments they make themselves.

3. Lonely deserts   Paragraph/No Paragraph
    a) Deserts can be so quiet they can seem spooky.
    b) I had an uncle who went to the Sahara Desert.
    c) However, the next morning you may find dozens of tracks around your camp.
    d) You can ride across a desert all day without seeing or hearing any living creatures.

4. Rope tricks   Paragraph/No Paragraph
    a) Do you know anyone who spins three ropes at one time?
    b) I do.
    c) Her name is Becky Claussen, and she puts on trick-roping shows.
    d) Maybe I would try the trampoline

5. Baby kangaroos   Paragraph/No Paragraph
    a) A young kangaroo, called a joey, lives in its mother's pouch.
    b) The pouch is on the front of its mother's body.
    c) Baby opossums ride on their mothers' backs.
    d) The joey moves in just after birth.

6. Dad's job   Paragraph/No Paragraph
    a) My father's job is a very important one.
    b) He is in charge of repairing broken traffic signals.
    c) It is his responsibility to make sure that traffic is properly regulated at all times.
    d) We learned about traffic safety in our gym class.
    e) If my father didn't do his job every day, many delays and serious traffic accidents might occur.

7. An important scientist   Paragraph/No Paragraph
    a) Dr. J Allen Hynek is a recognized authority on unidentified flying objects.
    b) He has written several books on the subject.
    c) Dr. Hynek is the director of the Center for UFO Studies at Northwestern University.
    d) He served as technical consultant on the movie *Close Encounters of the Third Kind*.
    e) The number of people who report seeing UFO's has increased recently.

8. The Tea Party   Paragraph/No Paragraph
    a) The Boston Tea Party of 1773 put the American Revolution on the road of no return.
    b) Before the tea party, problems between Great Britain and the colonies could have been settled peacefully.
    c) George III was the King of England in 1773.
    d) When Great Britain punished Boston for dumping the tea into the harbor, people throughout America began to think of independence.
    e) Two years later, the colonies decided to revolt.

9. South Bend   Paragraph/No Paragraph
    a) South Bend is a city in north-central Indiana.
    b) It is situated on the St. Joseph River, eighty miles southeast of Chicago.
    c) The name of the city is derived from its location on the south bend of the river.
    d) My uncle lives in South Bend.
    e) South Bend was first settled by fur traders in about 1820.
    f) Now South Bend is a bustling center of industry with a population of about 130,000.

10.   Stars   Paragraph/No Paragraph
    a) Stars are hot, luminous, celestial bodies.
    b) Stars vary in size, temperature, and brightness.
    c) The sun, a star, is about average in all respects.
    d) The sun appears to be larger and brighter than other stars because it is by far the closest to the earth.
    e) Even though the earth is surrounded by stars the sun appears so much brighter that its light obscures the light from other stars during daylight hours.
    f) A planetarium is a place to study stars.
    g) Thus, the other stars can be seen and studies only during darkness.

> **EXTRA SENTENCES THAT DO NOT HAVE TO DO WITH THE MAIN IDEA DISTURB THE UNITY OF THE PARAGRAPH AND SHOULD BE REMOVED.**

In the next few "paragraphs," one or more sentences do not relate to the man idea of the paragraph. Cross out the "extra" sentences. Then decide whether the remaining sentences give enough information about the main idea to make a fully developed paragraph.

1. Deep-sea diving requires more than putting on a wet suit and an iron mask. Treasures lie buried at the bottom of the sea. Jacques Cousteau has spent most of his life filming undersea life. Divers must be knowledgeable about their equipment.

Paragraph/No Paragraph

2. All animals have senses, but not all animals use them in the same way. Man people have lost their sense of hearing. A frog, for instance, does not see a fly as we see it – in terms of legs, shape of wings, and number of eyes. In fact, a frog won't spot a fly at all unless the fly moves. Frogs are amphibious animals. Put a frog into a cage with freshly killed insects, and it will starve.

Paragraph/No Paragraph

3. My cousin and I learned most of our family's history by playing in Grandmother's attic. Grandmother lived in a little town in Ohio. In one corner stood a brass-bound trunk, filled with forgotten dolls once treasured by aunts and mothers. Grandfather's World War I uniform hung proudly on a metal rack, along with once-stylish dresses. The clothing now is much more comfortable than it was thirty years ago. When we dressed up in the old-fashioned clothes, we felt that the past was truly part of our lives.

Paragraph/No Paragraph

4. Jeff Daniels is deaf, yet he knows when his telephone rings or his alarm clock goes off. His "hearing ear" dog, Rags, tells him. Rags, who was trained by the American Humane Association, alerts his master whenever there is a knock on the door or a phone call and leads Jeff to the source of the sound. Seeing-eye dogs are used by blind people.

Paragraph/No Paragraph

A PARAGRAPH MUST CONTAIN ENOUGH SENTENCES TO PROVIDE SUFFICIENT DETAILS TO SUPPORT THE MAIN IDEA.

The topic sentence is usually the first sentence in a paragraph. It tells what the rest of the paragraph is going to be about. The topic sentence is key to paragraph unity. It states the one main idea that must be developed by the other sentences. If a sentence relates directly to the topic sentence, it belongs to the paragraph. If it relates only indirectly or not at all, it does not fit and should be removed.

The topic sentence is important from the point of view of both the writer and the reader. It helps the writer to focus on the one idea that gives direction to the paragraph. It helps the writer to stay on the track so that he or she does not bring in ideas that are unrelated to the main idea. For the reader, the topic sentence acts as a guide by letting him or her know immediately what the entire paragraph is going to be about.

Let's look at another paragraph to better understand what the topic sentence does.

> Police in Arizona are after a different kind of thief. They're chasing people who steal cactus plants and sell them to gardeners. The thieves' favorite cactus is the saguaro. Some gardeners pay high prices for these large, slow-growing plants. Thieves are taking so many plants that some people fear some kinds may disappear from the desert.

The topic sentence of the paragraph is a general statement. It presents the idea of a different type of thief without giving any specific information about it. The other sentences in the paragraph explain what they steal and who they sell it to. The same arrangement can be found in most paragraphs. The topic sentence gives an idea that pertains to the specific ideas in the rest of the paragraph.

In each group of sentences, choose the sentence that works best as the topic sentence and circle its letter.

1. Toy safety

    a) Toys with sharp edges can cause cuts or puncture wounds.

    b) Buttons on stuffed animals and dolls can be swallowed and cause choking.

    c) Toys must be carefully examined to avoid safety hazards.

    d) Toys that propel objects can cause serious eye injuries.

    e) Toys that are meant to be used by older children should be kept out of reach of younger

       children.

2. Family exercises

    a) Dad jogs every morning.

    b) Everyone in our family has taken up exercising.

    c) Billy plays handball and tennis.

    d) Mom swims twice a week.

    e) Even Grandma has started taking long walks after dinner.

    f) I have joined the track team at school.

3. Cholesterol-ly foods

    a) Egg yolks are also high sources of cholesterol.

    b) Liver and other organ meats are high in cholesterol.

    c) Nuts and peanut butter have a high cholesterol content.

    d) Cholesterol, a crystalline fatty alcohol, is present in high concentration in many foods.

    e) Some dairy products are said to contain high amounts of cholesterol.

THE TOPIC SENTENCE HELPS BOTH THE WRITER AND THE READER.

4. Smile

    a) Start a smile (right now!) with your eyes crinkling the wrinkles around them and bringing up the muscles of your cheeks.

    b) Did you know that?

    c) Nobody can resist you when you smile like that.

    d) You are beautiful when you smile naturally.

    e) It makes others feel pleasant, too.

    f) Isn't it a pleasant feeling?

5. Barbara's appetite

    a) When Barbara gets out of bed in the morning, her first words are, "Is breakfast ready?"

    b) You're likely to find her in the hallway between classes eating a sandwich.

    c) Barbara is an avid food junkie.

    d) Orange juice two bowls of cereal, several pieces of toast with jam, two glasses of milk – such a breakfast is standard for Barbara.

    e) And what do you suppose she says when she rushes into the house after school?

    f) At school she can hardly wait for lunch.

    g) "Anything in the refrigerator?"

THE TOPIC SENTENCE HELPS THE WRITER FOCUS ON THE MAIN IDEA OF THE PARAGRAPH. IT HELPS HIM OR HER STAY ON TOPIC AND AVOID BRINGING IN IDEAS THAT ARE UNRELATED TO THE MAIN IDEA.

6. Introductions

   a) Then look at the new person's face, smile, and say, "How do you do?"

   b) Give the person a good, firm handshake as you speak.

   c) You will enjoy being introduced to others if you know how to behave.

   d) Say his or her name.

   e) Look at the person who is doing the introducing until he or she says the name of the person to whom you are being introduced.

   f) With its help, you will find that you can start a conversation quite easily.

   g) If your introducer has given you a conversation clue, follow it up.

7. Matter

   a) Things that were never alive, such as minerals and glass, are inorganic matter.

   b) Living things are organic matter.

   c) Lumber, wood, and cotton were once alive, so they are organic matter.

   d) Anything that takes up space is called "matter."

   e) Matter can't be destroyed, but it can be changed into energy.

8. Jack's eating

   a) Jack drinks so much milk that Father jokes about buying a cow.

   b) Jack's standard question after school is, "What's for dinner?"

   c) When Jack packs his school lunch, it looks like a grocery bag.

   d) My brother Jack claims that his hobby is eating.

   e) Mother is threatening to put a padlock on the refrigerator.

> THE TOPIC SENTENCE ACTS AS A GUIDE TO HELP THE READER IMMEDIATELY KNOW WHAT THE ENTIRE PARAGRAPH WILL BE ABOUT.

9. Snow Transformations

   a) The bare branches of the maple trees were outlined in shimmering white.

   b) Our yard looked magically different after the heavy winter snow.

   c) The bushes in front of the garage drooped, heavy with snow blossoms.

   d) The old garage wore a fresh white coat of snow-paint.

   e) The bird bath near the house had become a frosty snow-cone.

10.   Giraffes' height

   a) Sometimes a giraffe's height can lead to its death.

   b) Every time a giraffe takes a drink of water, it is in danger.

   c) A giraffe takes a long time to bend its legs apart.

   d) A giraffe can't drink easily because it can't kneel down.

   e) While a giraffe is drinking, it is helpless if a lion or tiger attacks.

11. Mrs. Paulson

   a) When my little brother had the measles, Mrs. Paulson played checkers with him every day.

   b) Mrs. Paulson often bakes cookies for us.

   c) Mrs. Paulson bandages our scraped knees without scolding us for being careless.

   d) I guess every child on the block has had her for a babysitter at one time or another.

   e) Bespectacled Mrs. Paulson is like a grandmother to everyone in the neighborhood.

Now go back and reread each group of sentences. Form a paragraph from each group by rearranging the sentences. Write a number next to the letter of the sentence to indicate its order.

The topic sentence of a paragraph has two main jobs:

1. It must state the main idea of the paragraph, which is the idea developed by the rest of the sentences.
2. It must capture the reader's attention so that he or she wants to find out more about the main idea.

When formulating the paragraph, a writer might express an idea that is too general to be developed in a single paragraph. Following is an example of such a sentence:

There are many kinds of cats.

This subject is so broad that about all the writer could do is list the different cat breeds. The paragraph would probably be as dull to write as it would be to read.

Suppose the topic sentence were revised like this:

The Siamese cat has earned itself a prominent place in feline history.

The main idea has now been narrowed so it could be developed in one paragraph.

Too broad: Boats have been involved in wars throughout history.
Narrowed: The submarine revolutionizes warfare during World War I.

Below are poorly written topic sentences that are too broad. Rewrite each sentence so that it becomes sufficiently narrow to be covered in a paragraph.

1. Exercise is important. _____

_____

2. Americans love to eat good food. _____

_____

3. America's history is filled with heroes. _____

_____

4. There is too much pollution near cities. _____

_____

5. Renewable sources of energy can help the planet. _____

_____

Any writer who puts time and effort into a paragraph wants it to be read. If the topic sentence is dull and uninteresting, however, the reader may not read the entire paragraph:

Look at the following topic sentence:

> I'd like to tell you about the use of teaching machines in the schools of the future.

This sentence makes clear what the rest of the paragraph is going to be about. It is a general statement that is narrow enough to be developed in one paragraph. The sentence, though, is flat and unimaginative.

Now look at this topic sentence:

> In the world of tomorrow, teaching machines will take into account different learning rates, working as fast (or as slowly) as the students using them.

Your response to this sentence might be, "Hmm, sounds interesting. Tell me about it." It catches your attention and engages your interest.

> Uninteresting: I am going to tell you about the basic equipment required for skiing.
> Better: Give careful thought to the equipment you will need to make your downhill skiing venture safe yet fun.

Below are poorly written topic sentences that are too uninteresting. Rewrite each sentence so that it becomes interesting enough to catch a reader's attention.

1. Hockey is a very dangerous game. _____

_____

_____

2. Street crime has increased during the past decade. _____

_____

_____

3. Our family traveled to Canada last summer. _____

_____

_____

A TOPIC SENTENCE SHOULD BE NARROW ENOUGH TO BE ABLE TO BE COVERED IN A SINGLE PARAGRAPH.

4. In this paragraph I am going to explain several ways of conserving energy. _____

_____

_____

5. Summer is the best time of the year. _____

_____

_____

6. This story about a blind deer made me very sad. _____

_____

_____

7. There are many ways to raise money when you need it. _____

_____

_____

8. Younger brothers take advantage of their sisters. _____

_____

_____

9. I like all kinds of music. _____

_____

_____

10. My favorite sports are basketball and football. _____

_____

_____

YOUR TOPIC SENTENCE
SHOULD BE INTERESTING
ENOUGH TO ENGAGE YOUR
READER'S ATTENTION.

In the following paragraphs, the topic sentence has been removed. For each paragraph, write a good topic sentence. You will need to read the paragraph carefully, making sure you understand its main idea. Be sure that your topic sentence is not too broad. Write a sentence that is sure to interest your reader.

1. First, I overslept. Then, I was in such a hurry that I ripped my shirt when I put it on. I rushed so during breakfast that I burned my tongue on my hot chocolate. Of course, I missed my bus so I had to run nine blocks to school. I stepped in every puddle on the street. When I arrived at school, hot, sweaty, muddy, and tired, the building was deserted. It was the first day of spring vacation!

_____

_____

2. In cities, all deliveries were by horse and wagon. Horses moved urban local passengers by carriage, omnibus, and horse-drawn streetcars. Stagecoaches bore passengers, mail, and baggage across rough and dusty Western roads, negotiating steep grades and fording unbridged streams. After 1840, teams of fast trotting horses for light coaches became popular in the East.

_____

_____

3. The dynamite had been frozen and thawed many times. Its paper covering had absorbed the nitroglycerine, making it dangerous no matter how carefully it was handled. In fact, dynamite like that sometimes explodes when two sticks of it are pulled apart, as the ghosts of a good many miners could tell you.

_____

_____

4. Children are cared for by pediatricians. Cardiologist handle heart problems. Radiologists take and interpret x-rays. Ophthalmologists are eye specialists. Orthopedic specialists deal with back and other bone problems. For ear, nose, and throat disorders, otolaryngologists abound. It's hard to find a regular, all-around doctor these days.

_____

_____

5. They took him into a room where there were only some boxes and three bananas hanging from the ceiling. They wanted to see how long it would take the chimp to pile up the boxes and climb on them. The chimp did not touch the boxes. He pushed one of the men under the bananas, crawled up on his back, and brought the bananas down in two minutes.

_____

_____

6. The slender frill shark is very suggestive of a marine shark or monster. The sand tiger shark is characterized by numerous sharp, wicked-looking teeth protruding from its mouth. The whale shark, the largest species of shark, is the only spotted shark that has the mouth at the tip of the head. Some of the most beautiful sharks in the word are found among the small catsharks.

_____

_____

7. He was a husky, long-legged chap, to me a perfect physical specimen. I asked him where he'd been, and he replied that he had been climbing the foothills north of town. I asked why he did it. He told me that his doctor had advised it; that he was trying to correct certain difficulties following an illness. He was climbing the foothills every day to develop his lungs and legs.

_____

_____

8. Stroll back through time down the cobblestone streets. Watch a blacksmith pounding red hot metal into door hinges, locks, keys, even street lamps. In the Gallegos House, sniff the huge black cauldron bubbling with garden fresh onions, peppers, garlic, and fennel spicing up a meat and rice recipe gleaned from eighteenth century Spanish records. Carpenters, silversmiths, cigar makers, people weaving fine threads into delicate lace – craftspeople of all description gather in colorful St. Augustine. St. Augustine offers you a rare chance to breathe in the mood of yesteryear.

_____

_____

9. Like a bicycle, it can be pedaled. Like a motorcycle, it is equipped with a gasoline-powered engine. Like both the bicycle and the motorcycle, the moped must be handled carefully in automobile traffic. It is a small machine that can help you quickly and easily get around town.

_____

_____

10. Beneath the desert sands and rocks lie the largest deposits of crude oil in the world. Two-thirds of all the known oil reserves in the world are in the Middle East. It is known that there are over 100 million barrels of oil under the deserts and hills of Saudi Arabia, Iran, Yemen, and Iraq.

_____

_____

THE TOPIC SENTENCE IS REALLY USEFUL TO THE READER BY HELPING HIM QUICKLY GRASP THE MAIN IDEA OF YOUR PARAGRAPH. WITHOUT A TOPIC SENTENCE, IT CAN BE DIFFICULT TO FOLLOW THE THOUGHTS OF THE PARAGRAPH. MAKE SURE YOUR TOPIC SENTENCE IS NARROW ENOUGH TO BE FULLY COVERED IN THE PARAGRAPH. MAKE SURE TO WRITE AN INTERESTING TOPIC SENTENCE TO ENGAGE YOUR READER.

Lesson Five

Developing a paragraph

Key Concepts
- developing a paragraph
- sense words
- prewriting
- definition sentence
- topic sentence
- unity

Developing a paragraph means taking the idea of your topic sentence and expanding it with the following sentences to fully explain your idea.
Sense words are words that are vividly descriptive with regards to the five senses.
Prewriting is an easy system of organizing your thoughts on paper in preparation of your writing.
A **definition sentence** contains the word or term that will be defined, states the broader category under which it falls, and lists specific details that set it apart from the rest of the category.
A **topic sentence** is usually the first sentence of a paragraph that tells you what the paragraph is about.
When all the sentences in the paragraph work together, that is called **unity**.

When writing a paragraph, there are specific tools that can help you expand the idea in your topic sentence into a fully developed paragraph.

One way to write a good paragraph is to use specific details. Details are items of information that work together to create an impression in a reader's mind. Using many descriptive details will help your reader form an image in his mind's eye of what you are writing about.

A great example of descriptive words in early English writing is:

His beard was broader than a shovel, and red
As a fat sow or fox. A wart stood clear
Atop his nose, and red as a pig's ear
A tuft of bristles on it. Black and wide
His nostrils were.

Many visual details are given that appeal to the reader's sense of sight, with phrases such as these:

broader than a shovel   red as a pig's ear
red as a fat sow or fox   tuft of bristles
atop his nose   black and wide

In just a few lines the poet succeeds in communicating a clear picture of a person's appearance by choosing such vivid details.

Visual details can be used to build a paragraph that describes a place or a thing. In the following example, the topic sentence is a general statement about where they camped. The rest of the sentences expand that idea with clear and bright descriptive details about it.

That summer we camped along the railroad tracks on the outskirts of the village. Our tent was next to the last in a row of several others just like it – a square of brown canvas curtains with a roof sloped like a pyramid, held up by a poled that peeped through a vent at the top. The plank floor of the tent was set up on bricks, the ends of the timbers sticking out in front, making a shelf that we used for a porch. The roof was held down by ropes staked down at the four corners and along the sides. Between the tents there were lean-to's where the women cooked and washed clothes in iron tubs, heating the water over stone fire pits. The swamp came up close in back, and in front spilled into a ditch, making a moat that separated the camp from the tracks just beyond. Over this ditch there was a catwalk of planks leading to the tracks, the main street of the neighborhood.

The details that follow the topic sentence tell the reader about the location of the tent, its appearance, about the way it was constructed, about the lean-to's between the tents, about the swamp behind and in front of the campsite, and about the tracks beyond the ditch. Each detail is carefully selected and described to give the reader a good idea of what the camp looked like.

DEVELOP YOUR PARAGRAPH BY WRITING SENTENCES FOLLOWING YOUR TOPIC SENTENCE TO EXPAND AND EXPLAIN THE IDEA THERE ARE MANY WAYS OF DEVELOPING YOUR PARAGRAPH.

There are many types of descriptive details that you can use to develop your sentence. By far, the most common and easiest are those that have to do with the five senses. The five senses are sight (vision), sound (hearing), touch (feeling), odor (smelling), and flavor (tasting). Expanding your vocabulary with sense words will enhance your ability to develop your paragraph with many details. Sense words are those that have to do with any of the five senses. There are many shades of meaning that can be conveyed with different words, and the better you are acquainted with them, the clearer your writing will be.

The Sense of Sight

You can see everything around you, but do you ever stop to examine something carefully enough so that you can describe it precisely?

Here are two examples of the same scene. Which one helps the reader "see" better?

> The man stood in the forest. He was looking for something. He saw nothing.

> The wiry young man stood in the midst of lush greenery, looking intently for a flash of color among the trees. All he saw was green.

The one with more "sight words" is able to convey a much more vivid picture to the reader.

Here are some "sight words" you might use:

COLOR	MOVEMENT	SHAPE	APPEARANCE
scarlet	scamper	crinkled	glimmering
emerald	dash	chunky	freckled
coral	crawl	wiry	cluttered
plum	tumble	square	muddy
silver	shiver	thin	crooked
sapphire	hustle	lank	splotchy
crimson	scurry	flat	mottled
gold	flit	spherical	tattered
tan	snake	beveled	sparkling

Now try your hand at coming up with more sight words.

_____   _____   _____

_____   _____   _____

_____   _____   _____

"SIGHT WORDS" ARE WORDS THAT DESCRIBE VISUAL EFFECTS AND HELP YOU CONVEY A WORD PICTURE TO YOUR READER.

The Sense of Hearing

Most of us hear well enough, but we often do not really listen. Can you hear all the sounds that surround you? Can you hear silence? Think about each sound separately.

There are many words that describe the sounds you hear.

LOUD SOUNDS	SOFT SOUNDS	SPEECH SOUNDS
Crash	sigh	yell
thunder	snap	screech
piercing	patter	scream
racket	swish	whisper
clap	crunch	murmur
bang	crinkle	whimper
uproar	hiss	giggle
blare	click	sing
boom	squeak	snort
explosion	squeal	chatter
blast	scratch	drawl
deafening	scrape	hum
earsplitting	tap	shout

Now try your hand at coming up with a few sound words for each category.

_____   _____   _____

_____   _____   _____

_____   _____   _____

"SOUND WORDS" HELP YOUR READER EXPERIENCE THE WORLD AS YOU WANT TO DESCRIBE IT. THEY VIVIDLY PORTRAY THE EXPERIENCE OF WHAT IS TAKING PLACE AND HOW THE CHARACTERS INTERACT.

The Sense of Touch

We are so familiar with our fingers at the tips of our hands, but do we pay attention to the way we experience the textures of the world around us? The sense of touch is so integral to our experience of the world around us and helps us connect with what we see, hear, and smell in an interactive way.

Some word for touch:

SOFT/SMOOTH	ROUGH	WET/DRY	SHARP	TEMPERATURE
bald	jagged	damp	barbed	hot
downy	grooved	oily	serrated	cold
inflated	abrasive	drenched	wiry	dry
feathery	blunt	sopping	jagged	icy
tiled	chapped	spongy	angular	fiery
varnished	sandy	soggy	crenelated	frigid
yielding	rusty	dusty	spiny	freezing
slick	stubbly	sweaty	spiky	cool

Try coming up with your own words for touch:

_____   _____   _____

_____   _____   _____

_____   _____   _____

SENSE WORDS THAT HAVE TO DO WITH THE SENSE OF TOUCH CONVEY TO YOUR READER THE SUBSTANCE OF WHAT YOU ARE WRITING ABOUT. IT INVOLVES SO MANY DETAILS ABOUT TEXTURES, EDGES, AND SHAPES.

Other Senses

Some words for smell:

PLEASANT ODOR	UNPLEASANT ODOR	FAINT/STRONG ODOR	ODORS THAT RESEMBLE
bouquet	stench	pungent	earthy
savory	stink	heady	floral
fragrant	putrid	piquant	minty
aromatic	cloying	odorous	smoky
balm	reek	rank	woody
aroma	fetid	whiff	fruity
perfumed	malodorous	scent	fishy

Try to come up with at least three more of your own:

_____   _____   _____

Some words for taste:

SWEET	SPICY	SOUR	SALTY
mild	hot	tart	unsalty
robust	sharp	bitter	brackish
syrupy	seasoned	acidic	savory

Try to come up with at least two more of your own:

_____   _____   _____

USE AS MANY SENSE WORDS AS YOU CAN TO HELP YOUR READER EXPERIENCE AS MUCH AS HE CAN OF YOUR WRITING.

Suppose you want to describe a person. Everybody has some special distinction – something in the way he or she looks, or dresses, or act – which makes that person an individual. There are the specific details you would include in your description of that person. Some of the details would be visual details about the person's appearance. Others might be details about the person's behavior, moods, and outlook on life.

In the following paragraph, notice how different kinds of details are combined to give a great description of the person.

> He was a colored child, with huge blue eyes that seemed to glow in the dark. From the age of four on he had a look of being full-grown. The look was in his muscular, well-defined limbs that seemed as though they could do a man's work and in his way of seeing everything around him. Most times he was alive and happy. The only thing wrong with him was that he got hurt so easily. The slightest rebuke sent him crying; the least hint of disapproval left him moody and depressed for hours. But the other side of it was that he had a way of springing back from pain. No matter how hurt he had been, he would be his old self by the next day.

The paragraph begins with a physical description, giving specific details about the child's outward appearance; for example, "a colored child," "huge blue eyes," and "muscular, well-defined limbs." It goes on to describe the child's general mood. Next, it mentions his sensitivity and resilience. The details help the reader form an image of a unique individual.

It is just as important to amass a vocabulary for words that describe character details as it is to compile a vocabulary of sense words.

Some examples of character words are:

ATTITUDES	BEHAVIOR	CHARACTER	APPEARANCE
happy	awkward	brave	handsome
angry	graceful	adventurous	messy
moody	busy	loyal	neat
sad	slothful	generous	prom
cheerful	clever	appreciative	ugly
cautious	tough	humble	tall
silly	rude	arrogant	serious

Now come up with some of your own:

_____   _____   _____

_____   _____   _____

_____   _____   _____

The success of a piece of writing often depends on the time you spend before you ever begin to write. This time is needed for prewriting, which is the planning stage for your writing. You will use a system of organizing your thoughts to be able to write smoothly. It involves gathering your thoughts and committing them to paper in a very tentative manner, without regard for grammar or spelling. Then it involves thinking over what you wrote down, removing ideas which don't belong, and possibly rearranging what you have written. You will be doing two basic things:

1. Deciding exactly what you will be writing about
2. Finding the best way to present your ideas

Begin by choosing and limiting a topic. After you choose the topic that interests you, make sure that you narrow it down to a manageable size. If you are writing a paragraph, make sure that you don't choose a topic that needs an entire essay. If you are writing an essay, make sure not to limit your topic to something that can be covered in a single paragraph.

Next, decide on your purpose. Ask yourself, *What do I want to say about my topic?* Do you want to describe it, criticize it, or explain it? Decide what effect you want to have on your reader. You can entertain, inform, explain, or persuade. Knowing what you want to say will help you decide which details you select. Knowing what you want to accomplish with your writing is important for the style that you use.

Gather the information that you will use for your writing. Make a list of specific details that you might use for developing your topic. Sometimes the details will be from your knowledge, memory, or experiences. At other times you will need to gather information from reference sources. List as many details or pieces of information as you can think of.

Look over your list of specific details and ask yourself these questions:
Are all of the details related to my topic and purpose?
Can any details be added that would make my purpose clearer or my writing more interesting?
Adjust your list as necessary. You may change one idea or several. You might even revise or change your topic.

Once you have completed your list, try putting the details into a logical order. If you are telling a story, you would probably want to present your details in the order they occurred. If you are describing a scene or an object, you might want to arrange your details in the order in which a viewer would noticed them. If you are presenting an argument, you might decide to organize your facts from least important to most important.

PREWRITING STEPS:
1. CHOOSE A TOPIC AND LIMIT IT.
2. DECIDE ON THE PURPOSE OF YOUR WRITING.
3. GATHER YOUR INFORMATION AND LIST AS MANY DETAILS AS POSSIBLE.
4. ORGANIZE THE INFORMATION LOGICALLY.

Focusing on the sense of sight, choose one of the following situations to write a paragraph about. Begin by writing it down. Then decide on the purpose of your writing. Gather as many details about it as you can and list them on the lines. Use as many words of color, movement, shape, and appearance as you can.

- a park in summer
- a family simcha celebration
- your favorite animal
- a family trip
- kashering for Pesach
- biur chometz
- hadlakas ner Chanukah
- Hoshana Rabba Hakafos

Topic:

_____

Purpose:

    I want to (describe, explain, criticize, etc.)_____

    I want to (entertain, inform, explain, etc.)_____

_____	_____
_____	_____
_____	_____
_____	_____
_____	_____
_____	_____
_____	_____
_____	_____
_____	_____
_____	_____

Next, review your list of details, and ask yourself whether they are all relevant to your topic and purpose. Cross out any that are irrelevant.

Ask yourself if any details can be added to make the topic clearer or more relevant. List any such details here.

_____   _____

_____   _____

_____   _____

Thinking about a logical order for your paragraph, try numbering your ideas in the approximate order that they would appear in the paragraph. This does not need to be specifically precise. It is sufficient to gain a relative idea of how to arrange the details.

Now write a topic sentence for your paragraph, making sure that it is interesting enough to engage your reader.

_____

_____

Develop the topic sentence into the body of the paragraph. Remember your purpose and try to write in a manner that will best achieve it.

_____

_____

_____

_____

_____

_____

_____

_____

_____

Focusing on the sense of sound, choose one of the following situations to write a paragraph about. Begin by writing it down. Then decide on the purpose of your writing. Gather as many details about it as you can and list them on the lines. Use as many words of sound as you can and try your best to describe it vividly.

- pastrami frying in a skillet
- the noise at a game in the park
- a carnival
- a fire
- a baby crying
- a storm
- a group at lunch
- a jet taking off
- an excited puppy
- a deserted classroom
- chazaras hashatz
- a crowded bagel store
- hachnasas Sefer Torah
- dancing at a school Bar Mitzvah
- tekias shofar
- a chazzan chanting Keil Molei Rachamim
- singing at a chupa
- selichos
- waves at the beach
- a traffic jam

Topic:

_____

Purpose:

      I want to (describe, explain, criticize, etc.)_____

      I want to (entertain, inform, explain, etc.)_____

_____   _____

_____   _____

_____   _____

_____   _____

_____   _____

_____   _____

_____   _____

_____   _____

_____   _____

_____   _____

_____   _____

_____   _____

_____   _____

_____   _____

Next, review your list of details, and ask yourself whether they are all relevant to your topic and purpose. Cross out any that are irrelevant.

Ask yourself if any details can be added to make the topic clearer or more relevant. List any such details here.

_____   _____

_____   _____

_____   _____

Thinking about a logical order for your paragraph, try numbering your ideas in the approximate order that they would appear in the paragraph. This does not need to be specifically precise. It is sufficient to gain a relative idea of how to arrange the details.

Now write a topic sentence for your paragraph, making sure that it is interesting enough to engage your reader.

_____

_____

Develop the topic sentence into the body of the paragraph. Remember your purpose and try to write in a manner that will best achieve it.

_____

_____

_____

_____

_____

_____

_____

_____

_____

Sometimes the best way to develop a topic sentence is by using facts or figures. Facts are items of information known to be true. Figures are numbers, dates, and statistics about something. Following is an example of this method of developing a paragraph. Notice that the writer used a few figures along with many facts.

> A most enchanting part of Puerto Rico is El Yunque Rain Forest, named after the 3496-foot-high mountain El Yunque. This 28,000-acre stretch of jungles, hills, streams, and waterfalls, a bare hour's drive from San Juan, is the only rain forest in the West Indies and the only tropical preserve of the United States National Park Service. Here, giant ferns unfurl feathery branches up to 30 feet. Orchids in pastel shades cling to their host trees. Among the 200 species of trees are hardwoods which, elsewhere, were cut down centuries before to build Spanish cathedrals, forts, monasteries, and homes. One of these is the mighty *ausubo*, called the bullet wood tree because of the toughness of its wood.

In the opening sentence, the author introduced the subject of the paragraph – the El Yunque Rain Forest. Then followed with facts and figures about the forest.

It is a 28,000-acre stretch of jungles, hills, streams, and waterfalls.
It is an hour's drive from San Juan.
It is the only rain forest in the West Indies.
It is the only tropical preserve of the United States National Park Service.
Giant ferns there grow up to 30 feet.
Orchids grow there also.
In the forest are 200 species of trees.
Some of the forest's trees are hardwoods.
The *ausubo* is called the bullet wood tree because of its hard wood.

Together, these facts and figures develop the idea that the El Yunque Rain Forest is an enchanting part of Puerto Rico.

In the following paragraph, figures are used to give weight to the main idea.

> Until the 1930's, many Americans believed that anyone who couldn't find work was lazy and shouldn't be helped by the government. The experience of the Great Depression (1929-1939) changed that. From 1931 to 1940, the unemployment rate was never less than 14 percent of the total work force. In 1993, gthe worst year of the Depression, 25 percent (one out of every four persons) couldn't find a job – any job.

The topic sentence tells us that "Until the 1930's many Americans believed that anyone who couldn't find work was lazy…." The paragraph explains that the Great Depression changed that idea and presents dates and unemployment statistics. The figures in this paragraph emphasize the idea that there can be reasons other than laziness for a person's not working (presumably because so many people who could not find work couldn't all be lazy).

A topic sentence might express an idea that is best developed through the use of examples. Following is such a sentence.

Poverty can be measured by more than income.

The writer could have supported this idea with facts and figures like the following:

- The percentage of American families whose income falls below the official poverty line
- The percentage of American families that do not have indoor plumbing
- The number of complaints received each winter from tenants who do not have sufficient heat in their apartments
- The number of rat bites treated each year at one hospital

Instead, the writer gave several examples from the experience of one family. The facts and figures in the paragraph relate to that family rather than to poor people in general.

> Poverty can be measured by more than income. There are five people in Charlie Thompson's family. They live in a one-bedroom apartment. The building they live in violates at least fifteen city building-code regulations. It has exposed electrical wiring. The plumbing does not work properly. In December, during 8 days of subfreezing weather, the heat did not go above forty-eight degrees. Charlie wakes up each night to make sure that his brothers and sisters are not bothered by rats. Mr. Thompson's take-home pay from a part job is $3,170 per month. The rent is $1745 per month.

In this paragraph, the idea that "Poverty can be measured by more than income" becomes drastically clear through a series of examples. By focusing on the living conditions of one poor family, the examples make a stronger emotional impact on the reader than impersonal facts and figures could ever have done.

> Dogs often sense when they are needed. Dobby, a dachshund[48], sensed that his old friend, a Chihuahua, was having trouble finding his way. Dobby trained himself to become a seeing-eye dog. He began to lead his blind companion up and down stairs and to food. Dobby held doors open and even took his friend for walks in the park. The dachshund would gently hold the Chihuahua's ear in his mouth to guide the other dog along. Dobby was truly a best friend.

This specific example of one dog caring for another gets the author's point across in a dramatic way.

YOU CAN DRAMATICALLY DEVELOP A PARAGRAPH BY USING AN EXAMPLE TO SUPPORT YOUR TOPIC SENTENCE.

---

[48]   A dachshund and a chihuahua are species of dog.

Choose one of the following sentences to write a paragraph about, developing it by using an example. Begin by writing it down. Then decide on the purpose of your writing. Gather as many details about it as you can and list them on the lines.

- Music can soothe the most savage beast.
- Never trust a computer.
- Violence in the news can lead to nightmares.
- Some people get too attached to their pets.
- Many American Presidents have served only one term.
- Violence has increased both on and off the playing field.
- You can add just about anything to a basic hot dog.

- Not everything that glitters is as valuable as gold.
- Clothing that looks stylish may feel far from comfortable.
- Some healing drugs come from unlikely sources.
- Young animals play in ways similar to human children.
- Philadelphia has interesting museums.
- Life in the wilderness was hard for the pioneers.
- Some animals make better pets than others.

Topic:

_____

Purpose:

    I want to (describe, explain, criticize, etc.)_____

    I want to (entertain, inform, explain, etc.)_____

_____   _____

_____   _____

_____   _____

_____   _____

_____   _____

_____   _____

_____   _____

_____   _____

_____   _____

_____   _____

Next, review your list of details, and ask yourself whether they are all relevant to your topic and purpose. Cross out any that are irrelevant.

Ask yourself if any details can be added to make the topic clearer or more relevant. List any such details here.

_____   _____

_____   _____

_____   _____

Thinking about a logical order for your paragraph, try numbering your ideas in the approximate order that they would appear in the paragraph. This does not need to be specifically precise. It is sufficient to gain a relative idea of how to arrange the details.

Now write a topic sentence for your paragraph, making sure that it is interesting enough to engage your reader. You should improve the original sentence from the list.

_____

_____

Develop the topic sentence into the body of the paragraph. Remember your purpose and try to write in a manner that will best achieve it.

_____

_____

_____

_____

_____

_____

_____

_____

_____

Another way to develop a paragraph is with an incident. Following is an example of such a sentence:

> Life in this electronic age is tough on kids.

The writer could have supported this topic sentence with several examples of how the electronic age is "tough on kids." Instead, he related an incident that illustrates the main idea.

> Life in this electronic age is tough on kids. Two sixth-graders felt the call of the fish pole one afternoon and took along their walkie-talkies. Word of this got to the teacher, who borrowed a walkie-talkie from another student. The teacher tuned in and, sure enough, heard the truants. He promptly cut in to suggest that they appear in the classroom post-haste. They did.

An incident, like the one in this paragraph, can be drawn from personal experience or from a writer's imagination. Whatever its source, though, the characteristics and function of an incident remain the same. It is a brief "story" that illustrates the general idea in the topic sentence.

Choose one of the following sentences to write a paragraph about, developing it by using an incident – either from your experience or your imagination. Begin by writing it down. Then decide on the purpose of your writing. Gather as many details about it as you can and list them on the lines.

- A practical joke can backfire.
- You're never too old to learn to ride a bike.
- I never believed in ghosts.
- My dog taught me the meaning of loyalty.

- One today is worth two tomorrows.
- You're never too old to cry.
- Running away never solved a problem.
- Old Rob was certainly an unusual dog.

Topic:

_____

Purpose:

    I want to (describe, explain, criticize, etc.)_____

    I want to (entertain, inform, explain, etc.)_____

_____   _____

_____   _____

_____   _____

_____   _____

_____   _____

_____   _____

_____   _____

_____   _____

Next, review your list of details, and ask yourself whether they are all relevant to your topic and purpose. Cross out any that are irrelevant.

Ask yourself if any details can be added to make the topic clearer or more relevant. List any such details here.

_____   _____

_____   _____

_____   _____

Thinking about a logical order for your paragraph, try numbering your ideas in the approximate order that they would appear in the paragraph. This does not need to be specifically precise. It is sufficient to gain a relative idea of how to arrange the details.

Now write a topic sentence for your paragraph, making sure that it is interesting enough to engage your reader. You should improve the original sentence from the list.

_____

_____

Develop the topic sentence into the body of the paragraph. Remember your purpose and try to write in a manner that will best achieve it.

_____

_____

_____

_____

_____

_____

_____

_____

_____

_____

_____

At times, a writer will want to use a word or a phrase in a very specific way or to introduce a term that the reader might be unfamiliar with. To make certain that the term will not be misunderstood, the writer will provide a definition.

Every good definition has three parts:

1. The term or word to be defined
2. The general class to which the term belongs
3. The particular characteristic that sets the term apart from the other members of the general class

Study the following examples:

TERM TO BE DEFINED	GENERAL CLASS	PARTICULAR CHARACTERISTIC
Leukemia is	a disease	affecting the blood-forming organs.
Hypnotism is	a kind of sleep	induced by motions of the hands or other suggestions.
Fear is	a feeling	of nervous excitement when facing danger.
A tariff is	a tax	placed on certain goods brought into a country.
A radio is	an electronic device	used to listen to broadcasted shows.
A pilgrim is	a person	who travels to a sacred place.
Hyperventilation is	a condition of the body	when breathing too fast and deeply than the body needs.
A quarterback is	a football player	who directs the team.
A zebra is	an animal like a horse	with wide black-and-white stripes.
A hurricane is	a strong, swirling storm	that usually measures several hundred miles in diameter.
A snorkel is	a breathing tube	that can be used only on the surface of the water.
Sorrow is	a feeling of grief	that comes from suffering, loss, or regret.
Geography is	a science	dealing with the earth and its life.
A granary is	a building	in which grain is stored.

Notice that each example contains all three components. The term, word, or idea to be defined is first mentioned. Then the sentence mentions the general class to which it belongs, along with defining characteristic(s) that set it apart from the rest of the general class.

A GOOD DEFINITION HAS THREE PARTS: 1) THE IDEA TO BE DEFINED, 2) THE GENERAL CLASS TO WHICH THE IDEA BELONGS, 3) THE PARTICULAR CHARACTERISTIC THAT SETS THE IDEA APART FROM THE OTHER MEMBERS OF THE GENERAL CLASS.

Avoid these common errors when making a definition.

1. Defining the word or phrase by using *where* or *when*.
   Sorrow is when a person feels grief. – Sorrow is not a "when"; it is a feeling.
   A granary is where grain is stored. – A granary is not a "where"; it is a building.
2. Defining the term with the same word or a variation of the same word.
   Hypnotism is the process of hypnotizing.
   Hyperventilation is the condition caused by hyperventilating.
3. Putting the term into too large a general class.
   A granary is a place where grain is stored. – "Place" is way too vague.
   A radio is something to listen to. – "Something" is too vague.

Choose 5 of the following words for which to write a three part definition.

Air	Cotton candy	Hang-glider	Minnow	Summer
Airplane	Courage	Hat	Motorcycle	Table
Apple	Cube	Helicopter	Mug	Tadpole
Aspirin	Cucumber	Hieroglyphics	Notebook	Taffy
Autumn	Cup	Honor	Pants	Taxi
Bathtub	Desk	Horse	Pen	Tea
Battery	Dog	House	Pencil	Teacher
Bed	Doughnut	Ice cream cone	Penny	Tefillin bag
Bike	Drill	Igloo	Pineapple	Tie
Binder	Duck	Jacket	Plate	Tiger
Book	E-scooter	Jump	Popularity	Tornado
Bottle	Egg	Ketchup	Purse	Tree
Building	Electric car	Klaf	Ocean	Tuna
Bus	Elevator	Knife	Sausage	Umbrella
Calculator	Energy	Lemonade	Scissors	Wallet
Camera	Folder	Looseleaf	Shirt	Watch
Candle	Friend	Love	Shoe	Water
Cantaloupe	Friendship	Loyalty	Shopping bag	Watermelon
Car	Gemara	Magnetism	Skyscraper	Whiteboard
Card	Giraffe	Map	Snob	Winter
Cat	Glasses	Meat	Soda	Yarmulka
Chumash	Gossip	Mezuzah	Spring	Zebra
Coffee	Hamburger	Milk	Suit	Ziploc bag

1.

_____

_____

2.

_____

_____

3.

_____

_____

A basic definition can be accompanied by an explanation, an illustration, or both. The definition can thus be developed into a paragraph.

Water that is fit to drink is called *potable water*[49]. It must be clear and colorless, pleasant-tasting, free of harmful bacteria, and fairly free of dissolved solids. Although distilled water is pure, it does not make the best drinking water. Small amounts of mineral matter and air in the water make it taste better, unlike distilled water which has a "flat" taste.

Empathy is a feeling of positive regard for others – being able to sense how the other person is feeling and the emotion taking place. It also takes in the ability to communicate the feeling back to that person in the receiver's own words. It means "the ability to walk in another person's moccasins."

A pueblo was a type of village built by the Indians of the Southwest. Its buildings were placed in a receding terrace formation and each one housed a number of families. The houses were flat-roofed and built of stone or clay. They were America's first apartment houses. Some of the houses were four stories high, and some had over five hundred rooms. The people reached their homes by climbing up ladders placed on the outside of the larger buildings. When other tribes raided a village, the Pueblo Indians pulled up the ladders and the enemy had a hard time getting in. A room below the ground was special. It was called a kiva and was used for ceremonies and social meetings.

In these three paragraphs, the basic definitions function as topic sentences. Each sentence contains the three necessary parts of a definition.

TERM TO BE DEFINED	GENERAL CLASS	PARTICULAR CHARACTERISTIC
Potable water is	water	that is fit to drink.
Empathy is	a feeling	of positive regard for others.
A pueblo was	a village	built by the Indians of the Southwest.

The other sentences in each paragraph give additional details about the word or phrase being defined. The reader comes away with a clear understanding of what the term means.

---

[49] Reversing the order of the three components of the definition is fine, so long as all three components are in the sentence.

Each of the following sentences presents a faulty definition. A part of the definition may be missing. The general class may be too large. The term may have been defined with the same word. Rewrite the definition correctly in the boxes alongside.

FAULTY DEFINITION	TERM TO BE DEFINED	GENERAL CLASS	PARTICULAR CHARACTERISTIC
A good friend is a special person.			_____
Play is activity.			
A novel is written in prose.			_____
Studying is when you read and think.			_____
A dog is a kind of animal.			
A fly has two wings.			
A bicycle is a machine with two wheels.			_____
Quarantine is when you're isolated because you're sick.			_____ _____
The sun is something that gives off light and heat.			_____
Anthropology is all about people.			_____
A lyric is a song.			

Graduation is the act of being graduated.			_____
R.S.V.P. is when you must answer someone's invitation.			_____ _____
A hat is a thing people wear on their heads.			_____
Passing a course is when you get above a certain grade.			_____

Choose one of the earlier terms to write a paragraph about, developing it by use of a definition. The definition sentence will be your topic sentence. Begin by writing down the word you will define. Then decide on the purpose of your writing. Gather as many details about it as you can and list them on the lines.

Topic:

_____

Purpose:

       I want to (describe, explain, criticize, etc.)_____

       I want to (entertain, inform, explain, etc.)_____

_____   _____

_____   _____

_____   _____

_____   _____

_____   _____

_____   _____

_____   _____

_____   _____

_____   _____

_____   _____

Next, review your list of details, and ask yourself whether they are all relevant to your topic and purpose. Cross out any that are irrelevant.

Ask yourself if any details can be added to make the topic clearer or more relevant. List any such details here.

_____   _____

_____   _____

_____   _____

Thinking about a logical order for your paragraph, try numbering your ideas in the approximate order that they would appear in the paragraph. This does not need to be specifically precise. It is sufficient to gain a relative idea of how to arrange the details.

Now write the definition sentence for your paragraph, making sure that it contains all three components of a proper definition. Try to make it as interesting for your reader as you can.

_____

_____

Develop the topic sentence into the body of the paragraph. Remember your purpose and try to write in a manner that will best achieve it.

_____

_____

_____

_____

_____

_____

_____

_____

_____

_____

A PARAGRAPH CAN BE DEVELOPED BY EXPANDING A GOOD DEFINITION SENTENCE. YOU CAN ADD EXPLANATIONS, EXAMPLES, OR AN INCIDENT TO ADD INFORMATION TO YOUR DEFINITION FOR A GOOD PARAGRAPH.

Lesson Six

A Bit More Grammar

Key Concepts
- singular and plural
- noun
- pronoun
- possessive
- apostrophe
- verb
- helping verb
- vowel
- consonant
- object
- direct object
- indirect object

Singular means one, and **plural** means more than one. Most nouns have one form for singular and a different form for plural.

A **noun** is a word that names a person, place, or thing.

A **pronoun** is a word that stands in place of a noun.

Possessive is the form of a noun or pronoun that is used to show that the noun or pronoun owns something.

An **apostrophe** is a mark that looks like a floating comma.

A **vowel** is a sound that is made with the open mouth or throat,

A **consonant** it any letter sound that is not a vowel.

A **verb** is a word that tells an action or state of being,

An **object** is a word in a sentence that has an action done to or on it.

A **direct object** is a noun that has the verb performed on it.

An **indirect object** is a noun that receives the direct object.

When referring to a single noun, it is called (surprisingly enough) **singular**. The word *shoe* is singular. It stands for only one shoe. The word *shoes* is plural. It stands for more than one shoe. When a noun stands for more than one person, place, or thing, it is **plural**. Most nouns have two forms: a singular form and a plural form.

Most English nouns become plural according to the first two of the following rules.
1. To most singular nouns, add **s** to the end of the word to form the plural.

    ropes   boots   books   desks

2. When the singular form ends in **s**, **sh**, **ch**, **x**, or **z**, add **es** to the end of the word.

    glasses   bushes   coaches   boxes   buzzes

3. When a singular noun ends in **o**, usually add **s** to the end of the word.

    rodeos   studios   photos   Eskimos   solos   pianos

    But sometimes, if the **o** is preceded by a consonant, add **es** to the end of the word.

    Potatoes   heroes   cargoes   echoes   tomatoes

4. When the singular noun ends in **y** with a consonant before it, change the **y** to **i** and add **es**.

    city-cities   lady-ladies   country-countries

    If the **y** is preceded by a vowel (*a, e, i, o, u*) do not change the **y**. Simply add **s**.

    toy-toys   play-plays   day-days

5. Some nouns ending in **f** simply add **s**.

    beliefs   chiefs   dwarfs   handkerchiefs

    Many words ending in **f** or **fe** change the **f** to **v** and add **es** or **s**. Since there is no rule to follow, these words have to be memorized. Here are some examples of such words:

    thief-thieves   leaf-leaves   life-lives

    shelf-shelves   half-halves   calf-calves

    loaf-loaves   wife-wives   knife-knives

6. Some nouns have the same form for both the singular and plural. They need to be memorized.

    deer   salmon   trout   sheep   moose

    elk   tuna   cod   pike   bass

7. Some nouns form their plurals in special ways:

    child-children   goose-geese   man-men

    mouse-mice   ox-oxen   woman-women

Write the plural form beside each noun.

1. rodeo _____   2. fox _____

3. gravy _____   4. root _____

5. six _____   6. hero _____

7. valley _____   8. solo _____

9. crate _____   10. lady _____

11. kiss _____   12. coach _____

13. boy _____   14. potato _____

15. play _____   16. auto _____

17. pen _____   18. flash _____

19. grape _____   20. stone _____

21. boat _____   22. diary _____

23. wish _____   24. switch _____

25. echo _____   26. wife _____

27. tomato _____   28. chief _____

29. monkey _____   30. roof _____

31. story _____   32. puff _____

33. city _____   34. calf _____

35. piano _____   36. loaf _____

37. baby _____   38. dwarf _____

39. loss _____   40. bluff _____

41. sheep _____   42. wolf _____

43. elf _____   44. radio _____

45. belief _____   46. company _____

47. thief _____   48. serf _____

49. house _____   50. box _____

51. leaf _____   52. wharf _____

53. shelf _____   54. bush _____

Even if you are referring to a large group of things or people, if you are treating them as a whole group it is a singular noun. When referring to more than one noun, and not treating them as a collective unit, you need to change to the **plural** form.

55. scarf _____   56. cargo _____

57. loaf _____   58. country _____

59. knife _____   60. photo _____

61. life _____   62. toy _____

63. couch _____   64. child _____

65. axe _____   66. glass _____

67. ox _____   68. book _____

69. deer _____   70. bookshelf _____

71. valley _____   72. witch _____

343

73. flash _____ 74. chimney _____

75. donkey _____ 76. trout _____

77. day _____ 78. roof _____

79. studio _____ 80. boot _____

81. buzz _____ 82. belief _____

83. desk _____ 84. mouse _____

85. rope _____ 86. louse _____

87. tooth _____ 88. goose _____

89. watch _____ 90. trio _____

91. splash _____ 92. track _____

93. half _____ 94. perch _____

95. ditch _____ 96. cry _____

97. horse _____ 98. peach _____

99. tree _____ 100. party _____

MOST NOUNS BECOME PLURAL BY MERELY
ADDING S TO THE END OF THE WORD,
UNLESS IT ENDS WITH AN "S" SOUND (S, CH,
SH, X, Z) WHEN ES IS ADDED.
SOME TIMES THE PLURAL FORM IS
IRREGULAR. USUALLY, NO CHANGE NEEDS
TO BE MADE TO THE NOUN, BUT THERE ARE
SOME EXCEPTIONS. WHEN THE LAST LETTER
OF THE NOUN IS Y, AND THE LETTER BEFORE
THE Y WAS A CONSONANT, THE Y GETS
CHANGED TO IE.
WHEN THE LAST LETTER IS F OR FE,
SOMETIMES CHANGE THE F TO V AND THEN
ADD S OR ES.

Notice that no form of plural makes use of an apostrophe. The apostrophe is a
punctuation mark that looks like a floating comma (') and is used to indicate that some
letters were removed from a word to form a contraction. It is also used to indicated the
possessive form of a noun – to show that the noun owns something. The only time an
apostrophe is used for plural is when using the plural form of letters, numbers, or words
in foreign characters.

> 3 f's = fff
> five 3's = 33333
> 2 יתד's = יתד יתד

Find as many errors as you can in the following sentences. Cross them out and rewrite them correctly.

1. We placed all of the dishs on the benchs in the hallway.

    _____

2. Several different companys make CB radioes.

    _____

3. The thiefs took several loafs of bread.

    _____

4. The babys were getting new tooths.

    _____

5. Several companys sell frozen mashed potatos.

    _____

6. First cut the tomatos in halfs.

    _____

7. The deers were eating the green shootes and leafs on the bushs.

    _____

    _____

8. Use these brushs to paint the bookshelfs.

    _____

9. The larger boxs had scratchs on them.

    _____

10. My blue Purim pantes are covered with patchs.

    _____

11. Both of those churchs will have rummage sale's._

_____

12. The kitchen shelfs were filled with dishs and glasss.

_____

_____

13. We sliced the potatos in quarteres.

_____

14. Bunchs of graps were heaped on the cartes.

_____

15. Echos of the music could be heard in all the roomes._

_____

16. These are photoes of horss, cowes, oxes, and sheeps.

_____

_____

17. The leafs on the treees were turning brown.

_____

18. Those dictionarys are found in most librarys.

_____

19. What qualitys must heros have?

_____

20. The fire chieves met to discuss meanes of fire prevention in our citys.

_____

_____

21. We used two loafs of bread to make the sandwichs._

_____

22. My brother and cousin are freshmans in high school._

_____

23. The elfs granted the childs three wishs.

_____

24. Our heros stand up for their beliefes.

_____

25. We caught several trouts and basses for supper._

_____

26. The tribes mourned the losss of their chieves.

_____

27. Sheeps crossed the valleies in large herdes.

_____

28. We photographed several meese and gooses in Canada._

_____

29. My earmuffes and glovs were taken by thiefs.

_____

30. Boruch spotted three field mouses in the garden._

_____

31. I heard the babie's crying at night.

_____

32. I asked my bosse's to give me permission to leave early._

_____

33. The womens in the Ezras Noshim were unable to hear the Megillah because of the

noise's.

_____

_____

34. The partys on Purim are so much fun.

_____

35. The crowdes fill the streetes on Purim.

_____

36. Some boyes rent horss and ride on the street's.

_____

MOST SINGULAR NOUNS DO NOT HAVE ANY
CHANGES MADE TO THE NOUN WHEN MADE
PLURAL. JUST ADD *S* OR *ES* TO THE END OF
THE SINGULAR FORM.

When the last letter of a singular noun is **y**, sometimes a slight change needs to be made to the base word. If the letter right before the **y** is a vowel, no change is needed and simply add the **s**. If the letter preceding the **y** is a consonant, then the **y** must be changed to an **i** and **es** must be added.

This pattern is used whenever adding a suffix that begins with a vowel[50] to a word ending in **y**. If the letter preceding the **y** is a vowel, change nothing. But if a consonant precedes the **y**, change the **y** to **i** before adding the suffix. When changing a verb from present tense to past tense (**-ed**) make sure to follow this pattern with verbs that end in **y**.

Rewrite the following sentences changing the underlined singular noun to plural and the present tense of the verb to past tense.

1. The insurance <u>agency</u> <u>employs</u> many people.

   _____

   _____

2. Mr. Shaw's <u>decoy</u> <u>sways</u> gently on the pond.

   _____

   _____

3. The <u>penalty</u> <u>dismays</u> the hockey player.

   _____

   _____

4. Our art <u>gallery</u> <u>defrays</u> the cost of the exhibit.

   _____

   _____

5. The <u>subway</u> <u>conveys</u> thousands of commuters.

   _____

   _____

---

[50]   The suffix **ing** is an exception. No change is made to the **y** even if the preceding letter is a consonant.

6. Which <u>century</u> in the past <u>defies</u> understanding?

_____

_____

7. The <u>pulley</u> <u>modifies</u> the distribution of weight.

_____

_____

8. The other <u>celebrity</u> <u>envies</u> the star of the show.

_____

_____

9. The singers of the <u>medley</u> <u>apply</u> new words to old tunes.

_____

_____

10. Which firm's <u>attorney</u> <u>tallies</u> the results?

_____

_____

WHEN YOU ADD A SUFFIX THAT BEGINS WITH A VOWEL TO A WORD ENDING IN *Y*, YOU NEED TO CHECK THE LETTER PRECEDING THE *Y*.
IF IT IS A VOWEL, NO CHANGE IS MADE.
BUT IF THE LETTER PRECEDING *Y* IS A CONSONANT, CHANGE THE *Y* TO *I* BEFORE ADDING THE SUFFIX.
THIS SAME PATTERN IS USED WHEN CHANGING A SINGULAR NOUN THAT ENDS IN *Y* TO ITS PLURAL FORM.
IF THE LETTER PRECEDING *Y* IS A VOWEL, MERELY ADD *S* AFTER THE SINGULAR.
BUT IF THE LETTER PRECEDING *Y* IS A CONSONANT, CHANGE THE *Y* TO *I*, AND ADD *ES*.

Some words that end with **f** or **fe** form the plural by changing **f** to **v** and adding **es**. Expand each phrase into a complete sentence using the plural form of the underlined word, which will need to be made plural in this manner.

1. gently swaying <u>leaf</u>_____

_____

2. defrayed the cost of new library <u>shelf</u>_____

_____

3. penalties in both <u>half</u>_____

_____

4. envied the exciting <u>life</u> of hatzoloh members _____

_____

5. traveled on the subway by <u>themself</u>_____

_____

6. attorneys who prosecuted the two <u>thief</u>_____

_____

RARELY, WHEN MAKING A NOUN PLURAL, YOU NEED TO ALSO CHANGE THE SINGULAR FORM IN ADDITION TO ADDING *S* TO THE END.

MOST NOUNS THAT END IN *F* PRECEDED BY A VOWEL JUST NEED TO ADD *S* TO BECOME PLURAL. IF IT ENDS IN *F* PRECEDED BY A CONSONANT OR IN *FE*, THEN YOU MIGHT NEED TO CHANGE THE *F* TO *V* BEFORE ADDING *S* OR *ES* TO FORM THE PLURAL ENDING *VES*.

Possessive is the form of a noun or pronoun that is used to show ownership – that the noun or pronoun owns something. We use this to show that a thing belongs to a person.

Yehudah's coat   the doctor's bag   Devorah's car

We also use this to show that something is a part of a person or related to him.

Zalmy's nose   Bentzy's fears   Gamliel's posture

Occasionally, we even speak of things in a possessive way.

the city's problem   the year's end   a stone's throw

The symbol used to form the possessive form of a noun is called an apostrophe ('). It looks like a floating comma.

If the noun is singular, the way to make it possessive is to add **'s** after the noun.

Pinchos's hat   Mother's apron   Charles's food

If the noun is plural, and ends in any letter other than **s**, add **'s** after the noun.

children's toys   men's sweaters   geese's noises

But if the noun is plural and ends in **s**, simply add an apostrophe after the **s**.

students' project   babies' bottles   the Goodmans' van

Write the possessive form of these nouns.

1. bee   _____   2. watchman   _____

3. carpenter   _____   4. waitress   _____

5. child   _____   6. Thomas   _____

7. princess   _____   8. conductor   _____

9. mouse   _____   10. winner   _____

11. mirror   _____   12. ladies   _____

13. winner   _____   14. women   _____

15. Max   _____   16. People   _____

17. Alex   _____   18. Luis   _____

19. singer   _____   20. dresses   _____

21. lake   _____   22. Osnas   _____

23. vase   _____   24. ducks   _____

25. countries   _____   26. socks   _____

27. stereos   _____   28. benches   _____

29. foxes   _____   30. sheep   _____

31. statues   _____   32. birds   _____

33. dogs   _____   34. Miriam   _____

THE POSSESSIVE FORM OF A NOUN SHOWS THAT IT OWNS SOMETHING.

THE POSSESSIVE FORM OF A SINGULAR NOUN IS MADE BY ADDING 'S AFTER THE NOUN.
THE SAME IS FOR A PLURAL NOUN THAT ENDS IN ANY LETTER EXCEPT S.
IF A PLURAL NOUN ENDS IN S, SIMPLY ADD AN APOSTROPHE AFTER THE S.

Rewrite each phrase to show the possessive form of the underlined word.

1. the tricks of the <u>magician</u>

   _____

2. the ingredients of the <u>cereal</u>

   _____

3. the guarantee of the <u>saleswoman</u>

   _____

4. the gymnasium of the <u>home team</u>

   _____

5. the rights of the <u>citizens</u>

   _____

6. the calendar of the <u>secretary</u>

   _____

7. the uniform of the <u>guards</u>

   _____

8. the beginning of the <u>custom</u>

   _____

9. the category of the <u>children</u>

   _____

10. the license of the <u>driver</u>

   _____

Notice that the possessive form of the noun does not depend on the amount of its belongings. A singular noun may possess numerous items and a plural noun might possess a single item. Deal with each noun on its own. First, identify the owning noun which needs to be changed into possessive form. If it is singular, add 's. Do the same if it is plural and ends in any letter other than s. If it is plural and ends in s, just add an apostrophe. Then identify the noun(s) belonging to it and determine if it is singular or plural and write it in its proper form regardless of how many nouns are in possession of it/them.

Fill the blanks with the correct possessive and plural noun.

	One person/object possessing one item		Two people/objects possessing two items	
		_____	The boy jacket	_____
1	The boy jacket			
2	My parent car	_____	My parent car	_____
3	My boss hat	_____	My boss hat	_____
4	The woman dress	_____	The woman dress	_____
5	The child toy	_____	The child toy	_____
6	The passerby glance	_____	The passerby glance	_____
7	One month vacation	_____	Two month vacation	_____
8	One dollar worth	_____	Two dollar worth	_____
9	The razor edge	_____	The razor edge	_____
10	The chair leg	_____	The chair leg	_____

JUST FOR FUN

If it's house – houses	Why is it mouse – mice
If it's hero – heroes	Why is it banjo – banjos
If it's cupful – cupfuls	Why is it passerby – passersby
If it's box – boxes	Why is it ox – oxen
If it's safe – safes	Why is it knife – knives
If it's goose – geese	Why not moose – meese
If it's die – dice	Why not pie – pice and lie – lice
If it's mouse – mice	Why not spouse – spice
If it's cherub – cherubim	Why not bathtub – bathtubim
If it's foot – feet	Why not root – reet and boot – beet
If it's man – men	Why not pan – pen and fan – fen and can – cen
If it's tooth – teeth	Why not booth – beeth

A word that tells an action or state of being is a **verb**. It is easy to understand what an action is because it usually involves motion and doing something.

walk　　　　cling　　　　dance　　　　ate　　　　throw

Sometimes it tells an action that is not possible to see.

thought　　　remembers　　liked　　　　assumed　　needs

A word that tells of an occurrence or change in state is also a verb. For example:

ignited　　　ended　　　　awoke　　　　died　　　　illuminated

But what is a state of being? Here are some examples:

is　　　　　　seems　　　　become　　　　sounds　　smells

These are called linking verbs because they connect the subject or noun to other words in the sentence.

Many linking verbs can also be used as action verbs.

LINKING VERB	ACTION VERB
The melon *looked* ripe.	Aliza *looked* at the melon.
The melon *felt* ripe.	Aliza *felt* the melon.
The night *grew* cold.	Aliza *grew* melons.

Find the verb in each sentence and circle it. Then write *action* or *linking* to show what kind it is.

1. That hamantash smells scrumptious.　　　　_____

2. These kreplach taste delicious.　　　　　　_____

3. The Baal Koyreh appeared for the Megillah with a chazzan hat.

    _____

4. Shulamis looked in the basement.　　　　　_____

5. Many visitors waited in line to give the Rov mishloach manos.

    _____

6. The children twirled their graggers.　　　　_____

7. Those grapes look luscious. _____

8. The clouds blocked the noon sun. _____

9. The sky looks ominous. _____

10. The recording sounds hazy. _____

11. The breeze smells clean and fresh after the storm. _____

12. The glorious sunset looked like a blaze of fire. _____

13. The speaker on Taanis Ester sounded interesting. _____

14. I finished my writing assignment in class. _____

15. Purim was fun. _____

SOME VERBS DO NOT TELL OF AN ACTION. THEY ONLY TELL THAT SOMETHING IS. THESE ARE CALLED LINKING VERBS.
MANY LINKING VERBS CAN ALSO BE USED AS ACTION VERBS.

Write two sentences for each of the following verbs. In one sentence, use the word as an action verb. In the other sentence, use the word as a linking verb.

tasted _____

_____

_____

smell _____

_____

_____

feel _____

_____

_____

looked _____

_____

_____

A verb may consist of one word or of several words. It may be made up of a **main verb** and **helping verbs**. **Helping verbs** are words that tell you about the state of a verb. Some examples of helping verbs are given here.

Helping Verb	+	Main Verb	=	Verb
might have	+	gone	=	might have gone
will	+	see	=	will see
are	+	driving	=	are driving
could	+	go	=	could go

Sometimes the parts of a verb are separated from each other by words that are not part of the verb. In each of the following sentences, the verb is bolded. The words in between are not part of the verb.

> I **have** never **been** to Disney World.
> We **did** not **see** the accident.
> The bus **has** often **been** late.

Some verbs are joined with other words to make contractions. The word *not* is an adverb – it modifies the verb. It is never part of a verb.

Contraction	**Verb**
hasn't (*has not*)	*Has*
weren't (*were not*)	*Were*
I've (*I have*)	*Have*
we'd (*we had* or *would*)	*had* or *would*

Remember that the **subject** of a sentence is the noun that the sentence tells you about. To find the subject, find the main verb of the sentence and ask yourself *who?* or *what?* did the verb.

> VERBS ARE ACTIONS, OCCURRENCES, OR STATES OF BEING.
> HELPING VERBS TELL YOU ABOUT THE STATE OF THE MAIN VERB.
> SOMETIMES OTHER WORDS GET IN BETWEEN HELPING VERBS AND THE MAIN VERB.

361

For the following sentences write the subject in the space before the sentence. (If the subject is the understood *you*, write it in parentheses.) Then find the verbs in each sentence. Write the verb in the space after the sentence and circle the main verb.

1. _____ We have not gone to the lake once this summer.

   _____

2. _____ This report has not been completed.

   _____

3. _____ Don't just stand there.

   _____

4. _____ The buses often arrive late.

   _____

5. _____ I have never been to Martha's Vineyard in Massachusetts.

   _____

6. _____ Gimpel did not watch any movies.

   _____

7. _____ The 747 will arrive at midnight.

   _____

8. _____ The hockey team is practicing on the ice until 6 P.M.

   _____

9. _____ Now open your eyes.

   _____

10. _____ Our class is going on a field trip at the end of the year.

   _____

11. _____ The package may have been delivered to the wrong house.

_____

12. _____ I am going to a ski lodge next weekend.

_____

13. _____ We aren't giving our panel discussion today.

_____

14. _____ Wipe your feet.

_____

15. _____ The ambulance had cautiously approached every intersection.

_____

16. _____ Jim and I will finish this job later.

_____

17. _____ It hasn't rained for a month.

_____

18. _____ Use some bright colors on the poster.

_____

19. _____ Our play rehearsal wasn't very successful.

_____

20. _____ Raul was carefully walking around the fountain.

_____

21. _____ We haven't planted a flower garden this year.

_____

22. _____ My sister and I have already made a rock garden, already.

_____

23. _____ The counselors had quickly collected the test booklets.

_____

24. _____ These books should have been moved.

_____

25. _____ We couldn't believe the noise in the lunchroom.

_____

26. _____ It has been raining steadily for three days.

_____

27. _____ The bus did not stop at our corner.

_____

28. _____ Give her a chance.

_____

29. _____ Ricky couldn't have known about the change in plans.

_____

30. _____ We don't watch television.

_____

31. _____ Who would have guessed the answer?

_____

32. _____ Drive carefully on the icy roads.

_____

33. _____ A raccoon was noisily rummaging through our garbage cans.

_____

34. _____ You've really done a good job on the project.

_____

35. _____ The boat has been cautiously circling the lake.

_____

36. _____ Barbara will probably be home on Monday.

_____

37. _____ Devorah is certainly eating a big dinner.

_____

38. _____ The spaghetti sauce hasn't simmered long enough.

_____

39. _____ The 8th Day will be performing here in a few months.

_____

40. _____ Most of us have already taken that test.

_____

41. _____ Hurry up!

_____

42. _____ Have some dessert.

_____

43. _____ Don't forget your promise.

_____

Many sentences begin with the word *there*. Sometimes *there* is used as an adverb modifying the verb to tell *where* something is or happens. An adverb is a word that describes or tells you about a verb. In that case, it is part of the predicate. The predicate is the part of the sentence that tells you about the subject.

> There stood the boy. (The boy stood *there*.)
> There is our bus. (Our bus is *there*.)
> There are the apples. (Our apples are *there*.)
> There is the restaurant. (The restaurant is *there*.)

In other sentences, *there* is only an introductory word to help get the sentence started.

> There is no candy in the machine. (No candy is in the machine.)
> There are some mistakes here. (Some mistakes are here.)
> There should be some food here. (Some food should be here.)
> There is no help in sight. (No help is in sight.)

In most sentences beginning with *there*, the subject comes after the verb.

In the following sentences, circle the subject and underline the entire verb, excluding other words that are in between. Then indicate whether *there* is used as an adverb or introductory word.

1. There were many people at the meeting.   _____

2. There goes my sister.   _____

3. There was a moment of silence before the game.

    _____

4. There is your watch.   _____

5. There is a good reason for my decision.   _____

6. There might be an encore after the concert.   _____

7. There will be ten people at our party.   _____

8. There he goes.   _____

9. There stood the trophy.   _____

10. There they are.   _____

11. There will be basketball practice tomorrow.   _____

12. There go the runners. _____

13. There I sat. _____

14. There I waited in line for over an hour. _____

15. There will be a picnic tomorrow. _____

16. There was a sudden pause. _____

17. There will be pony races. _____

18. There goes the bus. _____

19. There is cheesecake for dessert. _____

20. There will be no school on Erev Pesach. _____

21. There is the lock for your bicycle. _____

22. There are plenty of napkins. _____

23. There might be a thunderstorm on Friday. _____

24. There came a chilly wind. _____

25. There will be an assembly at noon. _____

26. There are several students in line. _____

IN MOST SENTENCES THAT BEGIN WITH *THERE*, THE ORDER OF SUBJECT AND PREDICATE IS REVERSED.

SOMETIMES, *THERE* TELLS YOU ABOUT THE VERB AND IS PART OF THE PREDICATE.
OTHER TIMES, *THERE* IS JUST AN INTRODUCTORY WORD TO HELP START THE SENTENCE.

Verbs are time-telling words. Not only do they tell of an action or a state of being, they also tell when the action takes place. They tell whether the action or state of being is past, present, or future. There are two ways verbs tell time:

1. By changing their spelling:
   walk—walked   sleep—slept

2. By using helping verbs:
   will sleep   has slept   had slept

Each different form of a verb that indicates a different time is called a **tense**. There are six possible tenses, but we will deal only with the three **simple tenses**. These are present, past, and future.

The **present tense** of a verb is the same as the name of the verb:

run   go   walk   sleep

The **past tense** of regular verbs is formed by adding **ed** to the present tense[51]:

walked   placed

The past tense of irregular verbs is usually shown by a change of spelling:

shine—shone   swing—swung

The **future tense** is formed by using shall or will with the present tense:

shall go   will run

The three tenses just described are called the simple tenses. They describe
What is happening now: *present tense*
What happened before: *past tense*
What will happen later: *future tense*

THERE ARE THREE SIMPLE TENSES OF VERBS.
PAST TENSE TELLS WHAT HAPPENED.
PRESENT TENSE TELLS WHAT IS HAPPENING.
FUTURE TENSE TELLS WHAT WILL HAPPEN.

---

[51]   Remember that if a word ends in a silent **e** and a suffix is added that begins with a vowel, the final **e** is dropped.

Just as there are singular and plural forms of nouns, there are some singular and plural forms of present tense verbs. The plural form of the present tense is the same as the name of the verb.

We run   They eat   Reuvein and Shimon learn

The singular form of the present tense adds an **s** to the end of the name of the verb.

Yehudah runs   Daniel eats   Yehoshua learns

The verb be is an irregular verb and its singular present tense is *is*, but its plural is *are*:

Zevulun is   Yissochor and Naftali are

Another irregularity of be is that it also has singular and plural forms of past tense:

Sholom was   Yitzchok and Rivka were

When writing, make sure that your subject and its verb agree. This means that if you use a singular subject, make sure that you use a singular tense of the verb. If your subject is plural, make sure that its verb is plural.

SINGULAR	PLURAL
was	were
is	are
has	have
earns	earn
lives	live
practices	practice
keeps	keep
eats	eat

THE SUBJECT AND VERB MUST BE IN AGREEMENT. IF THE SUBJECT IS SINGULAR, YOU MUST USE A SINGULAR VERB. IF THE SUBJECT IS PLURAL, YOU MUST USE A PLURAL VERB.

Some verbs complete the meaning of a sentence without the help of other words. The action that they describe is complete.

The boys came.   We are going.

Some verbs, however, do not express a complete meaning by themselves. They need other words to complete the meaning of a sentence.

> Sue hit ____. (Hit what? Sue hit the *ball*.)
> Jane raised _____. (Raised what? Jane raised the *window*.)

The word that receives the action of a verb is called the **direct object** of the verb. In the sentences above, *ball* receives the action of *hit*. *Window* receives the action of *raised*.

Sometimes the direct object tells the *result* of an action.

> We dug a hole.
> Edison invented electric lights.

To find the direct object, first find the verb. Then ask *whom?* or *what?* after it.

Carlos saw the President.	Maria bought six oranges
Verb: saw	*Verb*: bought
Saw whom? President	*Bought what?* oranges
Direct object: President	*Direct object*: oranges
Anne painted a picture.	The accountant called her secretary.
Verb: painted	*Verb*: called
Painted what? picture	*Called whom?* secretary
Direct object: picture	*Direct object*: secretary

A verb that has a direct object is called a transitive[52] verb. A verb that does not have an object is called an intransitive verb.

A verb may be intransitive in one sentence and transitive in another.

Intransitive: We were *watching*.	We are *eating*.
Transitive: We were *watching* the game.	We are *eating* hamburgers.

Many verbs used without objects are followed by adverbs[53] that tell *how, where, when,* or *to what extent*. These words are adverbs that go with or modify the verb. Do not confuse them with direct objects. The direct object tells *what* or *whom*.

---

[52]   Transitive means going out. The verb "goes out" on its direct object. In contrast, an intransitive verb, does not "go out" on anything – it remains on the subject.
[53]   An adverb is a word that is used to tell you about a verb – how much, when, where, or how.

To decide whether a word is a direct object or a modifier of the verb, decide first what it tells about the verb. If it tells *how, where, when,* or *to what extent,* it is an adverb. If it tells *what* or *whom,* it is a direct object.

> Don worked *quickly.* (*quickly* is an adverb telling *how.*)
> Sue worked the *problem.* (*problem* is a direct object.)
> Allison read *carefully.* (*carefully* is an adverb telling *how.*)
> Bernie read the *instructions.* (*instructions* is a direct object.)

In each sentence, circle the subject and underline the direct object (if there is one). In addition, decide whether the italicized word is an adverb or direct object – and indicate it by writing after the sentence.

1. Who want these old *posters?*   _____

2. Several guests left *early.*   _____

3. Someone left a red *sweater.*   _____

4. I carefully answered every *question* on the test.

    _____

5. The band plays *often.*   _____

6. The band plays good *music.*   _____

7. Our school sponsored a *carnival* last spring.

    _____

8. I enjoyed *that.*   _____

9. I enjoyed that delicious *pie.*   _____

10. We ordered *spaghetti* for dinner.   _____

11. Please return *soon.*   _____

12. Please return my *camera.*   _____

13. The salesclerk wrapped my *package* beautifully.

    _____

14. Michele tried *again*.   _____

15. Mark tried the *door* again.   _____

16. The flag hung *limply* from the pole.   _____

17. We hung a welcome *sign* on our door.   _____

18. Everyone sang our class *song*.   _____

19. We cheered the team's *victory*.   _____

20. We cheered *loudly*.   _____

21. Yvette bought a *magazine* after school. _____

22. The firefighters worked *hard*.   _____

23. I worked the *problem* easily.   _____

24. Both blankets slipped *off*.   _____

25. Dad slipped his *key* into the lock.   _____

THE NOUN THAT
RECEIVES THE VERB OR IS
THE RESULT OF THE VERB
IS ITS DIRECT OBJECT.
TO FIND THE DIRECT
OBJECT ASK WHOM OR
WHAT AFTER THE VERB.

Some words tell *to whom* or *for whom* something is done. Other words tell *to what* or *for what* something is done. These words are called the **indirect objects** of the verb.

It is only an indirect object if it appears in the sentence between the verb and the direct object. (If it comes after the direct object of the verb, it usually has a preposition[54] word which separates it from the verb and is no longer an indirect object of the verb – it is the object of the preposition.)

> Ann knitted **Kim** a *sweater*. (knitted *for* Kim)
> We gave the **boat** a *coat* of paint. (gave *to* the boat)
> I brought **Tina** some *seashells* from Florida. (brought *to* Tina)
> John made **me** a *key ring*. (made *for* me)
> Hope gave her **dog** a *bath*. (gave *to* her dog)

The words *to* and *for* are never used with the indirect object. The words to and for are **prepositions**. Any noun or pronoun following *to* or *for* is the object of the preposition.

> They baked **me** a cake. (*me* is the indirect object of *baked*)
> They baked a cake for me. (*me* is the object of the preposition *for*)

> Mom sent **us** some *cookies*. (*us* is indirect object of *sent*)
> Mom sent some *cookies* to us. (*us* is object of the preposition *to*)

Underline the verb(s) in the predicate. Circle the direct object. Draw a box or diamond around the indirect object.

1. Shifrah's mother bought her a necklace.

3. Zanvil told Peretz a story animatedly.

4. Help me!

5. Reuvein loves his Zaidy deeply.

6. The students eat cake hungrily.

7. The family hugged their uncle tightly.

8. Shmerel plays drums in the band.

---

[54] A preposition is a type of word that tells you the position or relationship of a noun in the sentence.

9. The basketball hit a car.

10. Don't forget the instructions.

11. My brother loaned me five dollar reluctantly.

12. I'll check my calendar.

13. Nobody expects the Spanish Inquisition.

14. Sing us a song.

15. Teach a man to fish.

16. Give yourself a break.

17. Miriam gave away a book.

18. Malkie gave Devorah a booklet.

19. Mark asked Carlos many questions.

20. Kevin ate meat, potatoes, peas, and bread for Sunday dinner.

21. The secretary told the members the sad news of the president's death.

22. Have you asked them their names?

23. Shalom invited me to his Bar Mitzvah.

24. The school offered me a job.

25. Rami gave his friends chocolate.

26. My grandfather used to tell me funny stories.

27. The artist designed the shul a new *paroiches*.

28. The students gave the teacher a card.

29. Berel's grandmother baked him a cake.

30. He gave them a bag full of coins.

31. Rush Limbaugh told Mother the news.

32. Hillary never sent Bill any emails.

33. Why did you give her that?

34. The professor assigned the students some homework.

35. Do you always tell your children a bedtime story?

36. The waiter was pouring one of the guests a glass of wine.

37. The huge gorilla frightened the children.

38. My grandmother knits sweaters for us for Chanukah.

39. The angry catcher shouted at the umpire.

40. Knee-deep snow awaited us outside the door.

41. Our neighbor brought a kugel for us.

42. The angry janitor shouted loudly at the bus driver.

43. The basketball rebounded off the rim.

44. Here is a letter for you.

45. The loose shingles came down.

46. Drive carefully on the icy roads.

47. The spaghetti sauce simmered long enough.

48. A raccoon was noisily rummaging through our garbage cans.

49. The enthusiastic audience applauded for the performers.

50. Straight white lines mark the boundaries of the court.

THE INDIRECT OBJECT OF A VERB IS THE NOUN THAT COMES IN BETWEEN THE VERB AND ITS DIRECT OBJECT. THE INDIRECT OBJECT IS THE RECIPIENT OF THE DIRECT OBJECT AND ANSWERS THE QUESTION *"TO WHOM/WHAT?"* OR *"FOR WHOM/WHAT?"*

Having to repeat every noun every time the noun was mentioned in a sentence would be very tedious and take a long time. Instead of repeating the noun each time, a **pronoun** can be used to replace it. A pronoun is a word that takes the place of a noun. Without pronouns, we would have to talk like this:

> Dovi found Dovi's notebook in Dovi's classroom.
> Dovi took Dovi's notebook to the Bais Medrash.

Fortunately, we can substitute pronouns for the noun, and we can talk like this:

> Dovi found his notebook in his classroom. He took it to the Bais Medrash.

The words *his* and *he* are pronouns that stand for the noun *Dovi* and are used in place of it. The word *it* is a pronoun that stands for the word *notebook* and is used in its place.

There are many different types of pronouns. Some replace male nouns, some female, and some are generic. Some refer to single nouns, some refer to plural nouns, and some can refer to unknown nouns.

Personal pronouns are used to take the place of nouns that name persons. They refer to persons in three ways:
1. When the pronoun refers to the person speaking, it is in the first person:
   I, me, my, mine, we, our, ours, us
2. When the pronoun refers to the person spoken to, it is in the second person:
   you, your, yours
3. When the pronoun refers to some other person or thing that is being spoken of, it is in the third person:
   he, his, him, she, her, hers, it[55], they, them, their, theirs

> Examples: The letter was addressed to *me*.
> (speaker—first person)
> The phone call is for *you*.
> (person spoken to—second person)
> The boys are looking for *him*.
> (person spoken of—third person)

Pronouns in the third person that refer to male persons are said to be in the **masculine gender**. Pronouns that refer to female persons are said to be in the **feminine gender**. Pronouns that refer to things are said to be in the **neuter gender**.

> Examples: Boruch bought *his* ticket yesterday.
> (*His* is masculine in gender.)
> Malkie says that bag is *hers*.
> (*Hers* is feminine in gender.)
> The janitor reached for the broom, but *it* fell out of reach.
> (*It* is neuter in gender.)

---

[55]   Although never used in place of a person's name, *it* is still called a personal pronoun.

Animals are often referred to by *it* or *its*. They may also be referred to by *he, him, his, she, her,* or *hers*.

Because pronouns don't tell us which noun they replace, they can become very confusing. The **antecedent** (what comes before) is the noun which the pronoun replaces. When you write, you should always make sure that it is clear which antecedent is being replaced by the pronoun. That means you should not use a pronoun before naming the antecedent. If you begin by using a pronoun, the reader does not know which noun it refers to.

Then, make sure it remains clear by not using a pronoun which could replace a different noun. In other words, if you are talking about a male, and mention a female pronoun, you can still use the male pronoun for the male until you mention a different male. Once you mention a different male, you should repeat the antecedent before using a pronoun because it could get confusing again.

Circle the pronoun(s) and draw an arrow connecting each pronoun to its antecedent (the noun it represents).

1. Gamliel read the book, and he reported on it.

2. The people on Oakdale St. keep their homes neat.

3. Water the aravos twice a week, and give them plenty of sun.

4. Osniel saw the bus coming, but he couldn't catch it.

5. Tuviyah wanted Shimshon to help him with the project.

6. After Perel wound the watch, she put it on.

7. The Smiths called Ovadiah, and they invited him to dinner.

8. Dan's cousin has three fish tanks in his room.

9. The sun rose and cast its beams on the still water.

10. Shmerel's family loves to ski; they go skiing often.

11. Sheftel lent Yocheved his bicycle because hers had a broken chain.

12. The doctor came out to greet his patients.

13. Gavriel will hand Sarah the book that belongs to her.

14. Naomi left her math book in her locker.

15. Snow was all over the field this morning but it melted.

16. Gavriel and Gedaliah visited their cousins in Minneapolis.

17. Kayla came by to pick up her jump rope before supper.

18. The store owner said that he would sponsor us in the bike-a-thon.

19. The Sierra Nevadas are mountains in California. They include Mount Whitney.

20. Devorah lost her mittens.

21. Lemmel and his best friend are going to Chicago and they will compete in a spelling be there.

22. Yeruchum opened the envelope, but he found nothing in it.

23. Joel and Jim Hertz raised tomatoes. They sold them to the neighbors and made money.

24. The Farechters parked their cars in the driveway while the workers repaired their garage roof.

25. Meilech, have you found your raincoat?

26. Bubby looked for her glasses, but she couldn't find them.

27. A seismograph records earthquakes. It indicates their intensity.

28. Totty and Mommy have their tickets for the school play.

29. Zeidy packed his suitcase, but forgot to put it in the trunk.

30. Did Penina and Malka find the packages they had wrapped?

There are two forms of personal pronouns: subject and object.

Subject forms

First person	Second person	Third person
I, we	You	he, she, it, they

Object forms

First person	Second person	Third person
me, us	You	him, her, it, them

When the pronoun is used as a subject, you must use its subject form. In addition, when it follows a linking verb in the predicate.

Subject: *I* agree with Shifra.
Subject: *She* is not happy.
After linking verb: This is *he*.
After linking verb: It was *I*.

When the pronoun is used as a direct object or an indirect object, you must use its object form. In addition, when the pronoun is the object of a preposition (short connecting words such as of, *for, to, with,* and *by*), it must be used in its object form.

Direct object: The horse kicked *him*.
Direct object: Yechezkel helped *them* with the shopping.
Indirect object: Zelig gave *him* a gift.
Prepositional object: The candy is for *us*.
Prepositional object: Write a letter to *them*.

Circle the correct pronoun(s).

1. (We, Us) hiked for three miles.

2. That much exercise tires (me, I) out.

3. Will (she, her) be at the awards assembly?

4. Tell (them, they) about your recent good fortune.

5. Is the gift for (we, us)?

6. My brother gave (me, I) his notebook.

7. (She, Her) enjoys decorating the sukkah.

8. This is a surprise to (me, I).

9. The waterfall drenched (I, me).

10. Dad called (us, we) to dinner.

11. We grilled hamburgers for (they, them).

12. The manager gave (he, him) a uniform.

13. Dan told (I, me) a bubbeh mayseh.

14. Each of (us, we) wants the window seat on the bus.

15. (Them, They) are the hardest workers.

16. That notebook must be (your, you, yours).

17. Both of (they, them) forgot about (we, us).

18. (Mine, My) is the oldest bike in the rack.

19. (We, Us) helped (they, them) with the clean-up.

20. Who borrowed (you, your, yours) hoverboard?

21. It was (she, her) on the phone.

22. The chicken farmer was (she, her).

23. The cashier handed (he, his, him) a receipt.

24. Binyomin and (she, her) went to the grocery.

25. The quickest shoppers were (us, we).

26. Zevulun and (he, him) hang up posters after Shabbos.

27. The real winner of the raffle was (she, her).

28. The skaters were Zangvil and (us, we).

29. Two of the biggest masmidim were (he, him) and (I, me).

30. The soldier saluted Zechariah and (he, him).

31. Miriam and (she, her) were good students.

32. The leaders will be (him, he) and (she, her).

33. When will you send (her, she) and (I, me) the report?

34. All the children followed (they, them) and (we, us) out to the kiddush.

35. Everyone likes (her, she).

36. (They, Them) plan to sell their car.

37. The shifting wind blew at (she, her) from all sides.

38. Pinchos showed Peninah and (us, we) the gartel esrog.

39. The archaeologist helped (they, them) at the dig.

40. Gavriel met Leah and (her, she) at the train station.

41. Please help the customers and (us, we) with (our, ours) shopping.

42. The contestant answered (they, them).

43. The host greeted (he, him) and (I, me).

44. The invalid thanked (she, her) for the help.

45. The best davener was (she, her).

46. (I, Me) strolled along the stream.

47. Rus and (I, me) drew the pictures.

48. Had anyone heard from (he, him)?

49. Dad gave Sariel and (he, him) a ride to the shuk.

50. The announcer awarded Berel and (me, I) the prize.

51. Everyone in the audience saw (us, we) and the rest of the singers.

52. The stranger asked (he, him) and (she, her) for directions.

53. Were you and (they, them) the winners?

54. The teacher called on Paltiel and (I, me).

55. The Goldenkarantzes and (we, us) have never met.

56. The principal reminded the staff and (us, we) about the new rules.

57. The cashier gave Malky and (he, him) too much change

PERSONAL PRONOUNS HAVE SUBJECT FORMS AND OBJECT FORMS.
THE SUBJECT FORMS ARE *I, WE, YOU, HE, SHE, IT, THEY*
THE OBJECT FORM ARE *ME, US, YOU, HIM, HER, IT THEY*

A compound pronoun is one that has more than one part. Usually it contains a form of the word *self* as part of it. For example, *myself, yourselves, itself, themselves.* It can only be used in a sentence after the antecedent is also mentioned in the sentence (either the noun itself or a personal pronoun).

In each sentence, insert the correct compound personal pronoun.

1. I bought _____ a new jacket.

2. The doctor _____ came out to greet her patients.

3. Terry, can you fix the flat tire _____

4. The singer accompanies _____ on the piano.

5. The children in the fifth grade wrote the songs _____.

6. An automatic sprinkler turns on and off by _____.

7. Brent, have you hurt _____

8. The babies in the nursery cried _____ to sleep.

9. Shprintza taught _____ how to play the guitar.

10. We were all angry at _____ for being so thoughtless.

11. The investment paid for _____ the first year.

12. I finished the painting _____.

13. Temima prepared the dinner _____.

14. Mom and I sanded the cabinets _____.

15. The story _____ was boring, but the cartoons were hilarious.

16. Can you three do the work _____ ?

A COMPOUND PRONOUN (HAS SELF ADDED TO IT) CAN ONLY BE USED AFTER THE NOUN OR REGULAR PRONOUN HAS ALREADY BEEN NAMED IN THE SENTENCE.

Pronouns are treated nearly identically to nouns, except in the matter of possessive form. Whereas nouns become possessive by adding an apostrophe, pronouns do not use an apostrophe. There is a unique form of possession for each pronoun. Actually, there are two possessive forms. One form is used when the pronoun is modifying another noun, and the other is when the pronoun is used alone.

Modifying another noun: my bag
your coat
their gloves
her hat
our boots

Used alone: (The bag is) mine
(The coat is) yours
(The gloves are) theirs
(The hat is) hers
(The boots are) ours

THERE ARE TWO FORMS OF POSSESSIVE PRONOUNS.

WHEN USED AS AN ADJECTIVE USE *MY, OUR, YOU, HER, HIS, ITS, THEIR*

WHEN USED ALONE, USE *MINE, OURS, YOURS, HERS, HIS, ITS, THEIRS*

Lesson Seven

Assorted Exercises

Key Concepts
- homonyms
- synonyms
- antonyms
- contraction
- apostrophe

A **homonym** is a word that sounds like another word that has a different meaning and spelling.

A **synonym** is a word that has a meaning similar to another word.

An **antonym** is a word that has a meaning nearly opposite to another word.

A contraction is a word that has been shortened by removing some of its letters, which is indicated by an apostrophe in their place.

An apostrohe is a symbol that looks like a floating comma.

Homonyms are words that sound alike but are spelled differently.

      sell and *cell*

A contraction is a word that has been shortened by removing some of letters and inserting an apostrophe in their place. Sometimes two words are combined in a single contraction. In this case, make sure to put the apostrophe in place of the missing letters, not necessarily between the original words.

      didn't = did not

Occasionally, a contraction is a homonym to a different word. You might be confused about how to spell the word you want to write. If you recall whether the word you want is really the two words shortened in the contraction or whether it is a single word, you can easily remember whether to use the apostrophe. Only the contraction gets an apostrophe, not the other word.

Complete the following sentences with the correct homonyms:

1. there/they're/their   _____ seems no reason _____ happy about _____ loss.

2. who's/whose   _____ going to the event, and _____ car will he use?

3. wear/where   _____ in the world can I _____ this silly sweater?

4. your/you're   _____ cousin is coming to the siyum _____ making tonight.

5. here/hear   If we _____ the shofar from their minyan, it disturbs our mitzvah over _____.

6. there/they're/their   _____ hats were left _____ in the car with the windows open – _____ going to get ruined in the rain.

7. who's/whose   _____ going to remove the stinky squash _____ smell really disturbs us?

8. wear/where   _____ the handsome sweater, and hang up the ugly one _____ I told you.

9. your/you're   _____ going to be in trouble if you don't put

_____ clothes away.

10. here/hear   If you _____ the radio over

_____, please let me know.

11. there/they're/their   _____ looking for _____ car

over _____.

12. who's/whose   _____ the person _____

portrait is on the wall?

13. wear/where   _____ is the shirt I wanted to

_____?

14. your/you're   _____ ruining _____

new shoes.

15. here/hear   Can you _____ the music over

_____?

USE YOUR UNDERSTANDING OF THE WORDS TO HELP YOU COMPLETE THESE SENTENCES WITH THE CORRECT HOMONYMS. IT CAN BE VERY HELPFUL TO TRY AND THINK WHETHER THE WORD IS REALLY A CONTRACTION OF TWO SHORTER WORDS. IF IT IS, YOU CAN REMEMBER TO USE THE APOSTROPHE IN PLACE OF THE MISSING LETTERS. IF IT IS NOT A CONTRACTION, CHANCES ARE THAT THERE IS NO NEED FOR AN APOSTROPHE TOGETHER WITH THE PRONOUN.

Words can "match" in several ways:

1. spelling – They can have the same spelling, but have different sounds and meanings.
    Bow and arrow   bow made of a ribbon
    Bow down
2. meaning – synonym – they can be entirely different words with similar meanings.
    Bow down
    bend down
3. sound – homonym – they can mean different things and spellings, but sound alike.
    Bow down
    bough of a tree (branch)
4. opposite – antonym – they can have meanings that are opposite to each other.
    Bow down
    straighten up
5. pair – they can be logical pairs regardless of their spelling, pronunciation, or meanings.
    Cereal and milk (they are served and eaten together)
    spaghetti and meatballs

A word might have several meanings that are different from each other.

Cordial –

MEANING	EXAMPLE	SYNONYM
showing natural kindness	a *cordial* hostess	hospitable
warm friendliness	*cordial* welcome	genial
deeply felt	*cordial* dislike	profound
Reviving	*cordial* waters	invigorating
Liqueur	rum *cordial*	cocktail, grog, spirits
stimulating medicine	cough *cordial*	cough drop

So how do you figure out?

    CONTEXT CLUES

"Context" means the words surrounding a word. Based on its context, or the words around it, you can often easily figure out the intended meaning of the word and understand the writing.

For the following words, a brief definition has been provided, often with a few meanings. Some of the words have homonyms next to them.

flair –   skill or instinctive ability
flare –   1) fire or blaze of light
              2) sudden outburst

3) to open or spread outward

vacant –   empty, blank

significant – 1) having meaning
2) important
3) numerous
4) having or likely to have influence or effect
5) probably caused other than by chance

evade –   1) escape - slip away
2) elude by strategy or skill
3) avoid facing up to or performing
4) avoid answering directly
5) baffle

rejoice –   1) gladden   synonyms gratify, please, satisfy
2) feel great delight   synonyms exult, gloat, glory, joy

assist –   1) to give supplementary aid   synonyms abet, prop, ease, benefit
2) to help
3) to be present as a spectator
4) an act that helps   synonyms lift, asset, support
5) the action that enables a teammate to score or putout

implore –   1) make an earnest request   synonyms appeal, beseech, entreat
2) to say a request in an urgent manner

prosperous – 1) favorable/auspicious
2) marked by success or economic well-being   synonyms wealthy, rich, affluent
3) flourishing   synonyms thriving, booming, vibrant

universal –   1) including all or the whole   synonyms total, entire, complete
2) present everywhere   synonyms all-over, ever-present, ubiquitous
3) existing under all conditions
4) embracing a major part or the greatest portion
5) comprehensively broad   synonyms general, manifest
6) applying to everyone/everything
7) adapted or adjustable for varied sizes/shapes/uses

absurd –   1) ridiculously unreasonable   synonyms foolish, unwise, silly
2) meaningless

modify –   1) make less extreme   synonyms lessen, lighten, mitigate, soften
2) limit the meaning
3) make minor changes   synonyms alter, substitute, switch
4) to make basic or fundamental changes

388

5) to undergo change

remote – 1) separated by space greater than usual ---- that armchair was remote from the dining room set   synonyms faraway, distant
2) far removed in space, time, or relation ---- remote history
3) out-of-the-way, secluded ---- remote mountain   synonyms cloistered, lonely, sheltered, hidden
4) doing something indirectly or from a distance ---- remote control
5) slight, small ---- remote possibility   synonyms frail, negligible, slim, tiny
6) distant in manner, aloof ---- administrator remained remote from the workers
synonym aloof, antisocial, detached

impede – interfere with

muffle – 1) wrap up, envelop
2) to wrap with something to dull the sound ---- muffle the oars
3) to deaden the sound of
4) to suppress ---- muffled her anger

invalidate – 1) to make invalid
2) logically inconsistent - self-contradicting ---- invalidate the accounts
3) being without truth – invalidated the arguments
4) being ineffective ----- invalidate the contract

demolish – 1) tear down ---- demolish the structure
2) break to pieces ---- demolish the car in an accident
3) destroy ---- demolish his career
4) strip of any pretense of merit or credit ---- demolish the claim

discard – 1) to get rid of ---- discard the bald tires
2) to remove from one's hand ---- discard 3 cards and choose another 3
3) to reject ---- discard that idea

delicate – 1) pleasing to the senses ----- delicate aroma or flavor
2) marked by daintiness or charm ----- delicate design
3) marked by fineness of workmanship ---- delicate lace
4) marked by keen sensitivity ---- delicate instincts
5) fastidious/squeamish ---- delicate tastes and likes
6) weak/sickly ---- delicate child
7) fragile ---- delicate crystal
8) requiring skill or tact ---- delicate negotiations
9) deeply personal ---- delicate matters
10) marked by great precision ---- delicate measuring tool

deliberately – 1) in a planned manner ---- he misbehaved deliberately
2) with full awareness ---- he testified deliberately

389

3) in a slow, unhurried way ---- he spoke deliberately

passionate –   1) easily aroused to anger ---- a passionate man
               2) filled with anger ---- the bear was passionate in defense of her cubs
               3) related to intense feeling ---- a passionate admirer
               4) enthusiastic ---- passionate about chazarah

astound –   to fill with wonder or bewilderment

diverse –   1) unlike, differing from one another ---- they had diverse interests
               2) composed of distinct elements ---- diverse crowd

USE THE FOREGOING DEFINITIONS,
EXAMPLES OF USAGE, AND SYNONYMS
TO ANSWER THE QUESTIONS ON THE
FOLLOWING PAGES.

Circle the letter of the word that best matches the word. Then write a sentence using that word.

1. A **cordial** friend
   a) aggressive   b) chummy   c) antagonistic   d) relative

2. a **flair** for quickly making friends
   a) talent   b) handicap   c) weakness   d) might

3. a **vacant** stare
   a) complete   b) overflowing   c) blank   d) rushing

4. a **significant** smile
   a) meaningful   b) worthless   c) unknown   d) minor

5. **evade** the penalty
   a) dodge   b) accept   c) catch   d) seek

6. an occasion to **rejoice**
   a) bemoan   b) weep   c) delight   d) lament

7. **assist** the congregation
   a) oppose   b) fail   c) harm   d) aid

8. **implore** the governor
   a) hint   b) comfort   c) quiet   d) beg

9. **prosperous** season
   a) declining   b) unsuccessful   c) affluent   d) bankrupt

10. **universal** concern
    a) general   b) component   c) individual   d) particular

11. **absurd** idea
    a) realistic   b) intelligent   c) unwise   d) earnest

12. **modify** an outfit
    a) broaden   b) stabilize   c) change   d) freeze

13. **remote** region
   a) large   b) distant   c) close   d) friendly

14. **impede** his way
   a) clear   b) untie   c) obstruct   d) assist

15. **muffle** the cries
   a) mute   b) amplify   c) magnify   d) expose

16. **prudent** manager
   a) careless   b) foolish   c) untimely   d) sensible

17. **invalidate** a sale
   a) dissolve   b) enact   c) permit   d) approve

18. **demolish** the church
   a) rebuild   b) destroy   c) fabricate   d) assemble

19. **discard** a suggestion
   a) adopt   b) utilize   c) forsake   d) keep

20. very **delicate** dessert
   a) rough   b) sturdy   c) numb   d) elegant

21. disobeyed the rule **deliberately**
   a) accidentally   b) impulsively   c) willingly   d) randomly

22. **passionate** interest
   a) detached   b) enthusiastic   c) cold   d) useful

23. **astound** the readers
   a) amaze   b) pounce   c) confirm   d) display

24. **diverse** interests
   a) parallel   b) kindred   c) distinct   d) equal

Circle the letter of the word that an antonym to the word. Then write a sentence using the word.

1. A **cordial** welcome
   a) friendly
   b) warm
   c) ungracious
   d) uncle

2. a **flair** for the dramatic
   a) tendency
   b) inability
   c) skill
   d) strength

3. a **vacant** seat on the bus
   a) abandoned
   b) active
   c) living
   d) occupied

4. a **significant** number of jobs
   a) monumental
   b) small
   c) unverified
   d) historic

5. **evade** the real issues
   a) miss
   b) address
   c) escape
   d) prevent

6. **rejoice** over unexpected victory
   a) agree
   b) suit
   c) possess
   d) grieve

7. **assist** the student with his lessons
   a) support
   b) hinder
   c) endorse
   d) overcome

8. **implore** the assistance of the donor
   a) compel
   b) reject
   c) research
   d) hire

9. **prosperous** economy
   a) flourishing
   b) unprofitable
   c) deadly
   d) virtuous

10. **universal** health coverage
    a) thorough
    b) limited
    c) spacious
    d) sizable

11. **absurd** argument
    a) silly
    b) fantastic
    c) wise
    d) amusing

12. **modify** his plan
    a) keep
    b) arrange
    c) conclude
    d) dispute

13. **remote** possibility
    a) fragile
    b) minimal
    c) significant
    d) eloquent

14. **impede** the Russian advance
    a) free
    b) delay
    c) help
    d) excitement

15. **muffle** her anger
    a) stifle
    b) exaggerate
    c) increase
    d) delete

16. **prudent** choice
    a) thoughtful
    b) advisable
    c) shrewd
    d) heedless

17. **invalidate** the test result
    a) nullify
    b) legitimize
    c) command
    d) clamp

18. the accident **demolished** the car
    a) overcame
    b) wrecked
    c) painted
    d) rebuilt

19. the pile of **discarded** tires
    a) combed
    b) frozen
    c) eliminated
    d) kept

20. a person of **delicate** tastes
    a) particular
    b) nice
    c) blank
    d) unpolished

21. speaking clearly and **deliberately**
    a) purposely
    b) advisedly
    c) thoughtfully
    d) unknowingly

22. **passionate** performance
    a) intense
    b) charged
    c) warm
    d) unemotional

23. **astound** the audience
    a) shock
    b) bore
    c) daze
    d) compress

24. **diverse** group of people
    a) perpendicular
    b) assorted
    c) mixed
    d) similar

Write ONE definition of each word and a sentence for it. Then write a synonym of the word and use it in a sentence.

1. CORDIAL

_____

_____

2. FLAIR

_____

_____

3. VACANT

_____

_____

4. SIGNIFICANT

_____

_____

5. EVADE

_____

_____

6. REJOICE

_____

_____

7. ASSIST

_____

_____

8. IMPLORE

_____

_____

Charades

Charades is a game where people act out a phrase without speaking, writing, or mouthing words. You can use sound effects to depict animals or machine noises, etc. but not words. The viewers try to guess which phrase is being played out. The goal is to try to act it out as clearly as possible so as many viewers can guess correctly.

No one may call out any answers or hints.

Once your names are called up to act out a charade, you have 20 seconds to begin. If you cannot come up with a charade by then, you lose no points, but are disqualified from the grand prize. If, after acting out the charade, any additional hints are given, you forfeit all points from that charade and are also disqualified from the grand prize.

As soon as the charade begins, viewers may start writing down their guesses.
No one may call out any answers or hints.
Anyone who calls out loses a point and is disqualified from the grand prize.

The viewers – quietly – write down their guess(es) on the paper in front of them.

As soon as time is up, no more guesses may be entered. Anything more written down does not qualify.

The teacher will announce the correct answer and ask for a show of hands by all who guessed correctly. **No one may call out at all!! Anyone who calls out at all, loses a point.**

Everyone keeps their own score and is honor-bound to be as accurate as possible. Scoring is as follows:
The players who act out a charade score two points each for the charade. If at least one viewer correctly guesses their charade, they score an **additional 10 points** each. If all the viewers manage to correctly guess it, they score an **additional 5 bonus points** each.

If you guessed the charade correctly, you score **1 point**. If it was your first guess that was correct, you score an **additional bonus 5 points**. If nobody else guessed it correctly, you score an **additional 10 bonus points.**

At the end of the game, no one may call out how many points he has.
The teacher will ask for a show of hands who has more than a certain number of points.
No one may call out how many points he has! Anyone who calls out, loses a point.

An idiom is a phrase that has a meaning different from what the individual words usually mean. The meanings of idiomatic phrases are usually found in the entry for the key word.

For instance, "flash in the pan" means "a sudden, seemingly skillful effort that fails."
> **flash** (flash) v. [ME *flaschen*, to splash; echoic] to send out a sudden, brief light, esp. at intervals – **flash in the pan** 1. a sudden, seemingly skillful effort that fail 2. one that fails after such an effort

The key word in the idiom is flash and under the dictionary entry for flash, the dictionary has the entire idiom with its definitions.

The source of this idiom has its roots in musketry, where preparing a musket or rifle for firing required a lengthy process which took over half a minute. First, gunpowder needed to be measured out and inserted down the barrel, followed by the musket-ball or bullet. Then it needed to be rammed all the way to the trigger with a ramrod. Finally, after cocking the striker, the musket was ready to be aimed and fired. When all that work was completed, sometimes the powder would go off in a flash, but fail to propel the musket-ball. All that resulted was the flash in the pan.

Other idioms are:
1. a hot potato
2. a knee-jerk reaction
3. a penny for your thoughts
4. actions speak louder than words
5. add insult to injury
6. as busy as a bee
7. at the drop of a hat
8. back to basics
9. back to square one
10. back to the drawing board
11. ball is in your court
12. barking up the wrong tree
13. beat around the bush
14. best of both worlds
15. best thing since sliced bread
16. bite off more than you can chew
17. blessing in disguise
18. break the ice
19. Burning the candle at both ends
20. button your lips
21. can't judge a book by its cover
22. chip on his shoulder
23. close but no cigar
24. cool as a cucumber
25. costs an arm and a leg
26. cross that bridge when you come to it
27. cry over spilled milk
28. curiosity killed the cat
29. cut corners
30. cut the mustard
31. cut to the chase
32. dead Ringer
33. dog eat dog
34. don't count your chickens before they hatch
35. don't give up the day job
36. don't look a gift horse in the mouth
37. don't put all your eggs in one basket
38. double whammy
39. drive someone up the wall
40. drop someone/something like a hot potato
41. every Tom, Dick, and Harry
42. excuse my French
43. face the music
44. far cry from
45. feel a bit under the weather
46. fish out of water
47. fly on the wall
48. from top to bottom
49. give the benefit of the doubt
50. get cold feet
51. get the run-around

52. get the short end of the stick
53. get up on the wrong side of the bed
54. gets under your skin
55. graveyard shift
56. have skeletons in the closet
57. having one's head in the clouds
58. hear it on the grapevine
59. hit the nail on the head
60. hit the hay or hit the sack
61. hold your horses
62. in full swing
63. in nothing flat
64. in the bag
65. in the heat of the moment
66. in the long run
67. it takes two to tango
68. jump on the bandwagon
69. keep a straight face
70. keep something at bay
71. kick the bucket
72. kill two birds with one stone
73. last straw
74. late in the day
75. let sleeping dogs lie
76. let the cat out of the bag
77. level playing field
78. like a headless chicken
79. living on the edge
80. make a long story short
81. make a mountain of a molehill
82. method to my madness
83. miss the boat
84. mum's the word
85. not a spark of decency
86. not playing with a full deck
87. off one's rocker
88. off the cuff
89. on the ball
90. once in a blue moon
91. open secret
92. over the top
93. picture paints a thousand words
94. piece of cake
95. put on airs
96. put wool over other people's eyes
97. red-handed
98. rule of thumb
99. see eye to eye
100. send someone packing
101. shake a leg
102. sit on the fence
103. small potatoes
104. smooth sailing
105. speak of the devil
106. spill the beans
107. steal someone's thunder
108. take with a grain of salt
109. taste of your own medicine
110. the whole nine yards
111. the sky's the limit
112. tickle someone's fancy
113. to hear something straight from the horse's mouth
114. turn a blind eye
115. whole nine yards
116. wild goose chase
117. wouldn't be caught dead
118. your guess is as good as mine

And their meanings

Try your best to match as many idioms as you can to their explanations by writing the number of the corresponding idiom. To make it easier for you, the idioms are in alphabetical order according to the first word of the idiom. There is one for each idiom, but some of them are similar, so be prepared to write more than one number for the meanings.

- An issue, usually a current and controversial topic, that makes everyone feel uncomfortable.
- To abandon as quickly as possible. As if having picked up a seemingly cold potato, you realize it is boiling hot.
- Having all the advantages.
- Cannot judge something primarily on appearance.
- When something is done badly to save money.
- don't make plans for something that might not happen
- believe someone's statement, without proof.
- To accomplish two different things at the same time.
- Used to say that someone missed his or her chance
- A way of asking what someone is thinking.
- Looking in the wrong place. Accusing the wrong person,
- deal with a problem if and when it becomes necessary, not before.
- You're not very good at something. You definitely can't do it professionally.
- To hear rumors about someone or something.
- Actions or communications need more than one person,
- to do or say something exactly right.
- The final problem in a series of problems.
- An assertion that, despite one's approach seeming random, there actually is structure to it.
- Meaning: no manners
- People's intentions can be judged better by what they do than what they say.
- To further a loss with mockery or indignity; to worsen an unfavorable situation.
- When an attempt fails and it's time to start all over.
- A good invention or innovation. A good idea or plan.
- Something good that isn't recognized at first.
- This idiom is used when something is very expensive.
- To take on a task that's way too big.
- Being inquisitive can lead you into an unpleasant situation.
- Do not put all your resources in one possibility.
- Very different from.
- To go to bed.
- Join a popular trend or activity.
- Keep something away.
- Meaning – do not disturb a situation as it is – since it would result in trouble or complications.
- Meaning – without any hesitation; instantly
- Avoiding the main topic. Not speaking directly about the issue.
- It is up to you to make the next decision or step.
- When you complain about a loss from the past.

- To succeed; to come up to expectations; adequate enough to compete or participate
- meaning – feeling slightly ill
- Overwhelmed by what is happening in the moment.
- To share information that was previously concealed.
- Come to the point – leave out details.
- Someone who lacks intelligence.
- When someone understands the situation well.
- A job, task, or other activity that is easy or simple.
- This idiom is used to say that two (or more people) agree on something.
- To take the credit for something someone else did.
- Everything. All of it,
- Would never like to do something.
- Meaning – an automatic response to something.
- Meaning – go back to the beginning.
- Carry a grudge. To look for a reason to be provoked.
- Coming close to reaching success, but reaching a disappointment due to failure.
- Meaning – identical to something or someone.
- Meaning – this refers to everybody and excludes nobody.
- Having to confront the awkward situation.
- Meaning – completely, thoroughly, totally
- meaning – receiving a series of excuses, delays, etc. This means you've been treated in a way that causes you to do much more than you really should by not giving you the answers you seek.
- Become frightened or nervous about something that you have to do.
- Working the night shift. Working at night. Origin: because in England people were sometimes mistakenly buried while still alive but unconscious and would sometimes be discovered trying to escape – there was a job working in the graveyard to be alert for such signs and rescue them.
- Getting the smaller share or worst portion.
- Currently happening at full speed.
- To die.
- Something that has happened at a very late stage.
- An equal and fair competition.
- Keep a secret and don't say anything.
- An unprepared action.
- To deceive someone
- to act superior.
- Being guilty of doing something and people know it.
- An insignificant amount of money, not worth doing something for.
- A basic rule that is usually, but not always, correct.
- To reveal a secret you are keeping.

- To interest someone in something
- crazy, demented, out of one's mind.
- Meaning – happens very rarely.
- A visual demonstration is far more descriptive than words.
- This is used when someone does not want to choose or make a decision.
- To hear something from an authoritative source.
- To have no idea, do not know the answer to a question.
- Meaning- that something happens to you, or is done to you, that you have done to someone else.
- Meaning – to be extremely busy
- meaning – a situation where people act ruthlessly in order to be successful.
- When you are given something you shouldn't be ungrateful.
- Meaning – a double setback from being able to do something.
- Meaning – an apology before or after using foul language.
- Referring to someone who oversees something without the people being watched noticing him.
- Meaning – in a bad mood
- meaning – immediately, straight away
- a secured or guaranteed outcome.
- Meaning – you should try not to laugh even though you find something really funny, especially from fear of being rude or giving away a secret.
- In a frenzied and uncontrollable manner. Origin – after a chicken is beheaded it usually jerks around for a while after being brain-dead.
- Meaning – eventually.
- Make something minor into a major issue.
- Something that is supposedly a secret, but everyone knows.
- Meaning – exaggerated or excessive.
- Send someone away; get rid of someone.
- To get active in the morning and out of bed.
- Meaning – easy to be in control of.
- To look the other way; to pretend not to notice something.
- To return to a simpler way of doing things. Without frills or fuss.
- To remove the tension at a first meeting or the opening of a party.
- To try to do too many things in too short a time so that you have to stay up very late at night and get up very early in the morning to get them done.
- To say nothing or stop talking.
- Calm and relaxed. Untroubled by heat or exertion.
- Get to the point without wasting time.
- To annoy and irritate someone.
- To be away from one's usual environment or activities.
- To be absentminded or impractical.
- Wait! Slow down!

- To make you annoyed or irritated.
- To keep secret a bad or embarrassing fact about oneself.
- To engage in risky or daring activities, often seeking excitement or thrill.
- Used when an object of discussion unexpectedly becomes present during the conversation,
- to view something, especially claims that may be misleading or unverified, with skepticism; not to interpret something literally.
- Used to say that there are no limits and that everything is possible.
- A search that is completely unsuccessful and a waste of time because the person or thing being searched for does not exist or is somewhere else.

AN IDIOM IS A PHRASE THAT HAS A MEANING DIFFERENT FROM WHAT THE INDIVIDUAL WORDS USUALLY MEAN.
YOU CAN OFTEN FIND THE IDIOM IN THE DICTIONARY UNDER THE ENTRY FOR THE IDIOM'S KEY WORD.

A hyphen is a little horizontal line that looks like a dash between letters. The difference between a hyphen and a dash lies in their purpose and function. The dash is a punctuation mark in a sentence – separating and connecting the two ideas, almost like a semicolon. The dash has a space before and after it. On the other hand, a hyphen has no space before and after it, and serves to separate and connect two parts of a word, or two words together.

Often, the meaning of a combination of words changes according to the way in which they work together. To clarify your writing, you need to convey to your reader how the words work together. The hyphen is you tool for that.

Consider the following sentence:

> Working twenty four-hour shifts (20 x 4 = 80 total hours) is not the same as working twenty-four hour shifts (24 x 1 = 24 total hours) or twenty-four-hour shifts (variable x 24 = variable total hours).

In the first part of the sentence, four and hour are connected, telling you that the shift under discussion is a 4-hour shift, and the quantity of these shifts is twenty. Twenty times four means a total of 80 hours. In the last part of the sentence, all the words before shifts are connected, telling you that the shifts are 24-hours long and we have no information about the quantity of the shifts (except that there is more than one of them). In the middle part of the sentence, twenty and four are connected telling you that the quantity of the shifts is 24, and the length of the shift is given as an hour. What a lot of information in the tiny hyphen.

In the following examples, consider the difference made by the use or omission of a hyphen:

> Bird eating spider (no more insect) vs. bird-eating spider (leftover feathers)
> small business manager (short person) vs. small-business manager (not a lot of money)
> two foot stools (at least six legs) vs. two-foot stools (not more than four legs)
> picture framing artist vs. picture-framing artist
> two year-old deer (both 1 year old) vs. two-year-old deer (single deer 2 years old)
> twenty one dollars (20 x 1 = $20) vs. twenty-one dollars ($21)

Rules for hyphens between words:

1. Join two or more words serving together as an adjective before a noun (compound adjective):
Hint: try the phrase with only a single one of the adjective words; if nonsense, needs hyphen.

> a one-way street
> state-of-the-art machinery
> chocolate-covered peanuts
> well-known author
> much-loved teacher
> long-term contract
> warm-blooded animal
> blue-eyed baby
> kind-hearted man
> lime-green shirt
> peer-reviewed research
> fourth-grade teacher
> face-to-face learning
> man-eating shark
> It is a dog-friendly restaurant

A HYPHEN IS A SYMBOL USED TO JOIN WORDS, YET KEEP THEM DISTINCT FROM EACH OTHER.

However when compound modifiers come after a noun, they are not hyphenated:

> The pretzels were chocolate covered.
> The speaker was well known.
> Is the restaurant dog friendly?

Also, if the first modifier is an ADVERB ending in -ly or the adverb 'very', it is not hyphenated:

> The quickly running athlete finished first.
> Finely tuned watch
> The clearly upset principal kept the students after school.

2. When forming original compound verbs, that are not already widely recognized:

> That slacker video-gamed his way through life
> The old queen throne-sat for seven decades.

3. When forming original, or little-used, compound nouns:

> His new diet makes him a no-meater.
> The slacker was a video-gamer.

4. When referring to time in a singular manner with a number more than "1":

>The baby was a two-year-old.
>But not needed if the time is in plural form: The baby was two years old.

5. When referring to a span of quantity:

>2:15-4:30
>120-140 people
>2018-2021

6. Whenever the hyphen can clear up ambiguity or a possible problem:

>The city of Chesterfield has little town charm. (merely a smidgen of town charm or a lot of small-town charm)

7. Use with compound numbers from twenty-one to ninety-nine:

>forty-nine
>sixty-three

Not with teens, which are written as a single word; nor with hundreds or more.

>Nineteen hundred twenty-five.

8. Hyphenate all spelled-out fractions. But not after "a" or "an":

>one-fifth
>five-sevenths
>one-quarter
>a fifth

Consider the following sentences, and determine where to place a hyphen. Sometimes it will depend on what you want the sentence to mean.

1. It's recommended you don't take down any load bearing walls when renovating.

2. The sign was five and two thirds feet long.

3. The five and two thirds foot long sign.

4. His interesting story was thought provoking.

5. His thought provoking story was interesting.

6. Fast acting medication can be useful when one has a headache.

7. The out of shape people signed up for the gym.

8. There are some beautiful looking plants in the garden.

9. We're looking for a pet friendly hotel.

10. The two word modifier needs to come before the noun to require a hyphen.

11. I only eat grass fed beef.

12. The alley was full of hungry looking cats.

13. Is that campground dog friendly?

14. The modern day miracle shocked most of the world.

15. The angrily behaving student was sent to the principal.

16. The top selling employee had the most sales for the month.

17. He wears clothes that are old fashioned.

18. The urgently needed doctor arrived in time.

19. The generous hearted people volunteered to help.

20. More than three fifths of registered voters oppose the suggestion.

21. We are eagerly looking forward to a much needed summer vacation.

22. The friendly little boy offered the stranger a cup.

23. The beautiful blue tefillin bag bore his initials.

24. They were playing with a small round ball.

25. The little used car barely held two adult passengers.

26. The little used car had an odometer reading of 8,000 miles.

27. Fewer than a third of the registered voters actually voted.

28. The seven and a half inch hot dog tasted strange.

29. The strange tasting hot dog was seven and one half inches long.

30. The parents ordered an extra special cake for the birthday party.

31. Her new apartment has on street parking.

32. Mario was known to be a self assured athlete.

33. He has a concealed weapons permit.

34. The student rented an off campus apartment.

35. The very elegant watch was old and large.

36. The new suit was a charcoal gray.

37. The Bar Mitzvah boy preferred the green embroidered leather Tefillin bag.

38. The majority scored between eighty two and ninety six on the test.

Some more rules of using hyphens, mostly in middle of a word.

1. To avoid confusion or awkward combinations of letters:

> re-sign a petition (vs. resign from a job)
> re-sent the message (vs. resent the message)
> re-cover the food (vs. recover from COVID-19)
> I have to re-press the shirt (vs. repress [meaning conquer])
> semi-independent (avoiding double I, vs. semiconductor)
> shell-like (avoiding double L, vs. childlike)
> still-life
> anti-inflammatory
> ultra-ambitious
> cross-stitch
> co-operate (vs. cooperate)
> co-owner (vs. coowner)
> re-elect (vs. reelect)
> anti-intellectual (vs. antiintellectual)
> drip-proof (vs. dripproof)
> bell-like (vs. belllike)
> de-ice (vs. deice)

SOMETIMES A HYPHEN IS USED IN MIDDLE OF A WORD FOR CLARIFICATION.

2. With prefixes EX- (meaning former), SELF-, ALL-, and -WELL:

> ex-husband
> ex-president
> ex-minister
> self-assured
> self-administered
> self-confident
> self-obsessed
> all-inclusive
> all-seeing
> all-knowing
> all-purpose
> well-being
> well-behaved

3. With the suffixes -ELECT, -STYLE, -BASED, and -FREE:

> mayor-elect
> president-elect
> restaurant-style (tortilla chips)
> lead-based (paint)
> mosquito-free (backyard)

4. Between a prefix and a capitalized word:

> pro-Trump
> pre-Civil War
> anti-Biden
> anti-American
> mid-September
> post-World War II

5. With figures or letters:

> t-shirt
> mid-1980s
> 25-cent stamp
> 12-foot Menorah
> x-ray machine

One of the most common punctuation mark is the comma. It functions as instruction to the reader to pause, and helps him organize his thoughts about the words you have written. It also sometimes changes their meaning. For example, there is a famous joke about a panda:

> The panda entered an eatery and ordered a sandwich. Upon completing his meal, he drew his gun and fired two shots in the air.
> "Why?" asked the confused waiter, as the panda made for the exit. The panda produced a poorly punctuated wildlife manual and tossed it over his shoulder.
> "I'm a panda," he said, exiting. "Look it up."
> The waiter turned to the entry in the manual and, sure enough, finds an explanation.
> *"Panda. Large black and white bear like mammal; native to china. Eats, shoots, and leaves."*

The final sentence fragment, as intended by the author, contains a verb (eats) with two direct objects of (shoots and leaves). However, the comma indicates that there is a series of three action verbs, instructing the animal to eat and shoot before leaving.

A similar type of difference can be noticed on the t-shirt that has the following quotation:

> Let's eat, Grandma vs. Let's eat Grandma

The comma separates *Grandma* from the command *let's eat*, letting her know that you are speaking to her; and prevents misunderstanding the intention of being a cannibal and eating the grandmother.

Rules for using commas:

1. Separate items in a list (three or more items):

> He wants peace on Earth, quality family time, great health, and no credit card debt for his Chanukah gift.
> I need to buy flour, eggs, vanilla, and butter for my cakes while shopping today.

2. Separate two or more co-ordinate adjectives BEFORE a noun (if their order could be reversed and they could be separated with "and"):

> The lazy, rebellious boy was suspended.
> The orange, yellow, and blue flowers were beautiful.
> The weary, emaciated man collapsed.

A COMMA WORKS TO HELP THE READER UNDERSTAND WHAT IS WRITTEN.

But not:

The happily singing boy hopped along the sidewalk.
The very pretty butterfly landed on the petunia.

A COMMA TELLS THE READER TO MAKE A SLIGHT PAUSE BECAUSE THE WORDS DO NOT HAVE SO MUCH TO DO WITH EACH OTHER.

---

3. After introductory words or mild interjections.

Sure, he is definitely unrealistic.
Well, that was an interesting presentation.
Yes, there are seven days in a week.

Examples of introductory words:

- In fact,
- Generally,
- Actually,
- Most importantly,
- Also,
- Furthermore,
- In addition,
- Additionally,

- Firstly,
- Secondly,
- Thirdly, etc.
- Finally,
- Meanwhile,
- Consequently,
- As a result,
- Anyway,

- First of all,
- I just want to say,
- After all,
- However,
- Although,
- On the other hand,
- In other words,

4. Set off words of direct address (calling the person to whom you are speaking).

Zevullun, why don't you help me?
Alex, would you please put the milk in the fridge?
Mr. Prime Minister, do you plan to change the energy vote?

5. Set off word(s) that interrupt the flow of a sentence.

The basketball player, as you can see here, plays better than all his opponents.
The makkos display, I think, is the more creative craft exhibition.
Will you, Dan, be able to finish on time?

410

6. Set off nonessential details of the sentence.

> Mr. Biden, the President of the United States, might have a 4th of July hot dog eating contest at the White House.
> Her grandmother, Mrs. Goldenwasserkin, made the best cheesecakes.
> The zebra, scenting the air and carefully scanning the path ahead, cautiously entered the water.
> The class clown, who has a wicked sense of humor, made us all laugh.
> Ben Williams, the captain of the team, was in their Math class.

7. When combining two independent clauses of the sentence that are joined with a conjunction.

> The dog chased three rabbits out of the woods, but they all got away.

8. Separate subordinate clauses[56] at the beginning of a sentence.

> Before eating three candy bars, he should have thought of the consequences.

Rewrite the following sentences, using commas and omitting unnecessary words.

1. We went to the beach and surfed and the park and played on the swings and then we went home.

_____

_____

2. When children come to school they need to bring pencils and erasers and scissors and a ruler and a briefcase.

_____

_____

_____

---

[56] Subordinate means that it cannot be used as a sentence on its own because it needs more words. The opposite is an independent clause, which can be used on its own.

3. The pansies were red and white and blue and black and yellow and purple.

_____

_____

4. Wonderful we always have such amazing parties.

_____

_____

5. His father the principal of the school was always harder on him than anyone else.

_____

_____

6. Consequently Paul always had to work harder than anyone else to be successful.

_____

_____

7. The mountains and the creeks and the shrubbery and the wildlife should be protected in this area.

_____

_____

8. Dad bought fudge and cake and ice cream in the store.

_____

_____

9. In the sky at night stars shine brightly.

_____

_____

10. Her best friend Shprintza lives far from her.

_____

_____

Review

Comma in a Series

Not all these sentences contain a series (three items or more). Put a comma where it belongs in each series.

1. The professor adjusted his Yarmulka shuffled his notes and began his lecture.

2. A jogger ran down the alley and onto my lawn this morning.

3. He stepped around the grass across the sidewalk and onto the curb.

4. Neither rain sleet nor hail shall keep away the U.S. mail.

5. A glass of milk a cup of tea or a mug of coffee will be fine.

6. Planning the itinerary buying supplies and packing emergency items are all part of good camping preparation.

7. I'll have pickles ketchup mustard and onions on this hot dog.

8. Her living room was cold dark damp and musty.

9. The poor child did not know how to walk or talk.

10. Who sent you why you came and what you intend to do are none of my concern.

11. Please put the cups jars and plates into the cabinet.

12. The young girl saw the mugging screamed loudly and cried about it for days afterwards.

13. I really don't care whom you see where you go or what you do.

14. He had a sense of humor a winning smile and a friendly nature that endeared him to most Americans.

Comma with co-ordinate adjectives

When the co-ordinate adjectives come before the noun, separate them with a comma.

1. We enjoyed the clean crisp smell of the mountain air.

2. Beth was a student whose intelligent conscientious mind earned her good grades.

3. Dr. Bean gave us a hard final examination.

4. She ate the sweet juicy apple with a vengeance.

5. The awkward shy teenager felt nervous about his first interview.

6. When the team failed to score, the bored restless crowd began to shout.

7. Miriam's light blue dress fluttered in the breeze.

8. The gentle kind giant helped Jack climb back down the vine.

9. We saw several large apples on the young tree.

10. Registration was improved this year by the addition of an efficient courteous staff.

Comma with introductory words

Use a comma to set off introductory words.

1. During the hot summer of 1984 the temperatures set records.

2. To get my records I had to send a check for $5.00.

3. To win you must practice hard.

4. After you complete the film you will edit it.

5. Wherever you go I will follow.

6. If the train is on time we will meet you.

7. Although the train is late we will still meet you.

8. He forgot his lines because he was tired.

9. Because she did not consult her calendar Merril missed her appointment.

10. I am copying this recipe because I want to make this dish someday.

11. To earn an "A" in Dr. Long's course one must work very hard.

12. After many days at the mine the workers were tired and angry.

13. As though nothing had happened she sat down comfortably.

14. Unless fiscal policies are changed the country will face a depression.

15. To get to my house make a right hand turn.

16. Before the war and bloodshed in that country the people were happy.

17. When Harriet finished the book she gave it to Harry.

18. Harriet gave the book to Harry when she finished it.

19. Even today the events surrounding his assassination are quite fresh in many ordinary citizens' minds.

20. However riding through Dallas on November 22, 1963 President Kennedy became the target for a killer.

21. To enjoy the pleasant weather and the Dallas scenery the president and Mrs. Kennedy chose to ride in an open convertible.

22. Finally realizing what had happened Secret Service men ordered the car to speed to Parkland Hospital.

23. Even today almost all who lived through those terrible shocking events can remember exactly where they were and what they were doing when they heard the tragic news.

Comma with nonessential words and phrases

Use a comma to separate nonessential words or phrases.

1. The man forgot however where he had placed his keys.

2. However the man forgot where he had placed his keys.

3. Mr. Jones the foreman at the plant is on vacation.

4. Mary Roberts calling out Joe's name ran down the street.

5. Calling out Joe's name Mary Roberts ran down the street.

6. Mary Roberts ran down the street calling Joe's name.

7. Amazed at the noise Boruch ran down the street.

8. The man who robbed the bank was caught today.

9. Sam Spider who robbed the bank was caught today.

10. Recognizing the thief the policemen arrested him immediately.

11. The student who writes the best paper will receive the best grade.

12. Alan Dershowitz a famous trial lawyer will represent the defendant.

13. The secretary realizing her bad situation tried to convince her boss to give her a raise.

14. Bees for example have four wings.

15. Mrs. Terry who wrote letters to George Bernard Shaw was a famous actress.

16. No you may not attend the game.

17. Idaho which is famous for its potato crop is located in the Midwest.

18. A man who writes mysteries is visiting the school this week.

19. Undaunted by the loss Georgette resumed her law practice.

20. Henderson Smith the mail carrier for our block always arrives on time.

21. The reason of course is obvious.

22. One measure however must certainly be the lasting impact of his death.

23. John F. Kennedy the 35th president of the United States was popular.

24. Doctors worked feverishly but Kennedy who had sustained a fatal head wound died at 1:00 p.m.

A **padded sentence** has useless words and phrases. The main idea is buried by unnecessary words. A sentence can be improved by eliminating the unnecessary words.

> ~~What I think is that~~ houses should have proper insulation.
> ~~The reason why~~ I can't attend ~~is~~ because I have to babysit that night.
> ~~What~~ Carol wants ~~is for~~ you to write the song.

Cross out the unnecessary words in each padded sentence.

```
OMIT
UNNECESSARY
WORDS!
```

1. What I mean is that the computer is a valuable machine.

2. Carlo will be the commentator and the reason is because he is a clever speaker.

3. War was avoided because of the fact that both countries agreed to compromise.

4. What I think is that the senator should not be impeached.

5. The thing is, this vaccine provides immunity from polio.

6. What I went to the doctor for was to have this imbedded splinter removed.

7. School was closed due to the fact that there was a snowstorm.

8. The reason why Leah seems impatient is because she is nervous.

Padded writing is sometimes clearly unintelligent as in the following example:

> Like a lot of people, I actually have the habit of actually adding a lot of actual padding words when I actually write. A common one I use is actually. These are actually rarely worth keeping, actually, and when I actually remember, I actually make some actual effort to actually find and actually delete them all.

Or it may seem to be super-intelligent, as in the following example:

> Although it was very and totally unnecessary for the tall skinny old and elderly man to walk down the wide broad street in the very wet rain, he slowly and deliberately managed to do this, making sure that he had a black wide umbrella above him the entire whole time so that not a single drop of water landed on his oily greasy short grey hair.

In any case, to write effectively you need to learn to eliminate unnecessary words.

Redundancy

Sometimes the extra words do not really confuse the reader or obscure the meaning. Yet extra padding words still slow the reader down and detract from the crispness of the writing. Test every word against its context. Ask yourself: "Will the text lose meaning if I remove this?" and "Is there already a word in this sentence that provided the meaning?" Look out for the following types of extra words:

1. references to time
   a) over the years
   b) currently   Mumbai is ~~currently~~ India's leading financial center.
   c) now
   d) from time to time
   e) to this day
   f) future   They planned their ~~future~~ response.

2. vague terms of size or number
   a) some   The highway expands to four lanes as it passes ~~some~~ built-up areas of strip development.
   b) a variety of
   c) a number of
   d) several
   e) a few
   f) many
   g) any   The scheme does not remove ~~any~~ government-funded programs such as Social Security, Medicare, and Medicaid.
   h) all   ~~All~~ seawater is salty.

3. words for which the meaning is already conveyed in another word or are easily recoverable from general knowledge
   a) its own   Each weapon has ~~its own~~ advantages and disadvantages.
   b) in those instances   ~~In those instances~~ when requests for assistance fall outside Eisenhower's scope, staff members attempt to locate other consultants.
   c) Subsequently   Iridion was released in North America on 29 May 2001, and ~~subsequently~~ in Europe on 21 September 2001.
   d) who come   The Center has worked to protect women ~~who come~~ from abroad.
   e) resulting   The cigar smoker burns the dried leaves of the tobacco plant but does not inhale the ~~resulting~~ smoke.

4. Useless filler words
   a) the point is
   b) basically

Some more sophisticated examples:

> While the journal had ~~relatively~~ low circulation numbers for its day, it ~~still~~ influenced popular opinion and was feared by the conservative administration.
> After *The Kroonland's* fitting out ~~was completed,~~ the ship sailed on its maiden voyage.
> ~~Born~~ the youngest child of a Mexican immigrant couple, she was singing on stage while still a junior high school student.
> A sign reads: ~~Visitors are warned to~~ take ~~every~~ care to avoid accidents.

In the following examples, cross out a single redundant word:

1. Last month, more than 40% of featured article nominations successfully passed.

2. They invaded the coast and brought along European diseases.

3. The manager has plans to accept the offer.

4. The least accessible forested areas were the last ones to be cleared.

5. Both the parents chose to educate their children in Beijing.

6. This sudden repetition had led to keen competition for Handei's future services.

7. The orbiter project, canceled in 2005, would have specifically targeted Europa, Ganymede and Callisto.

8. These two species are both members of the equine family.

9. After 1731 the opera was not staged again for more than 200 years.

10. There are three established methods available for the delignification of lignocellulosic[57] biomass.

    > This sentence can be much better rewritten by removing two words instead. And even better by replacing "the delignification of" with 'delignifying'.

11. Bruckner's Symphony No. 3 was a turning point for the composer; but he revised it several times in the years following the work's premiere.

---

[57] Ligmocellulose is a molecule in the structural cells of woody plants. Delignification is removing the lignin.

12. This question rarely arises outside of the soccer league.

13. The coastal region is an exception and it enjoys a flourishing tourist industry.

14. The field trips identified potential hot-spots in typical rolling mills, and the researchers have made some initial contacts with companies to gain permission for trials of their new cooling system.

15. Longer tonicizations may also include other secondary chords.

In the following examples, cross out two or more redundant words:

14. The B41 gold-nib fountain pen was originally released in 1966 and is still in production today.

15. This involves the provision of a reference section, complemented by inline citations for quotations and any material that is likely to be challenged.

16. Cystic fibrosis is a common hereditary genetic disorder that affects many different parts of the body.

17. This relationship had already existed before Adobe purchased the company.

18. Although Ottawa is one of the Ojibwe dialects that has undergone the most linguistic change, it is still mutually intelligible with other dialects.

19. These findings posed a great number of problems.

20. Recent analysis of available historical records show why the European settlement of Greenland failed.

21. After the punch-up at the grand final, the NCAA took measures to prevent major brawls from happening again.

22. In the year of 1988, there were renewed efforts to boost the government's popularity.

23. These aspects serve to distort what would otherwise be some of the attractive elements of the architecture, such as its structure and envelope.

24. As a result of making such decisions, poker players are able to maximize their odds and win more money.

25. More than 10,000 Avrohom Fried albums have been sold worldwide, including 7,000 sales in the U.S. alone.

26. Apart from the poets mentioned in the Kavirajamarga, later Kannada writers have referred to three poets as being eminent among their predecessors.

27. He contributed to research that led to the finding of a cure for malaria.

28. The majority of critics gave the film negative reviews.

29. The territory's path of evolution has been a challenge for the government.

30. Sport is a compulsory activity for all students; teams usually have training two times a week.

31. During a complex history, four local communities have tried to become the capital over the years.

PADDED SENTENCES HAVE UNNECESSARY WORDS. ALTHOUGH FLUFFY WRITING MAY SEEM ELABORATE, IT IS REALLY CUMBERSOME FOR YOUR READER AND MAKES COMPREHENSION DIFFICULT.

OMIT UNNECESSARY WORDS!

Lesson Eight

Different Kinds of Paragraphs

Key Concepts
- process of writing
- narrative paragraph
- first person
- third person
- descriptive paragraph
- explanatory paragraph

The **process of writing** involves prewriting, writing a first draft, revising and proofreading, and writing the final copy.

A **narrative paragraph** tells a story.

When the author is writing as if he is the speaker, that is **first person**.

Third person is when the author is writing as if he is someone else.

A **descriptive paragraph** paints a picture with words.

An **explanatory paragraph** explains something to the reader.

The success of a piece of writing often depends on the time you spend before you ever begin to write. This time is needed for prewriting, which is the planning stage for your writing. You will use a system of organizing your thoughts to be able to write smoothly. It involves gathering your thoughts and committing them to paper in a very tentative manner, without regard for grammar or spelling. Then it involves thinking over what you wrote down, removing ideas which don't belong, and possibly rearranging what you have written. You will be doing two basic things:

1. Deciding exactly what you will be writing about
2. Finding the best way to present your ideas

Begin by choosing and limiting a topic. After you choose the topic that interests you, make sure that you narrow it down to a manageable size. If you are writing a paragraph, make sure that you don't choose a topic that needs an entire essay. If you are writing an essay, make sure not to limit your topic to something that can be covered in a single paragraph.

Next, decide on your purpose. Ask yourself, *What do I want to say about my topic?* Do you want to describe it, criticize it, or explain it? Decide what effect you want to have on your reader. You can entertain, inform, explain, or persuade. Knowing what you want to say will help you decide which details you select. Knowing what you want to accomplish with your writing is important for the style that you use.

Gather the information that you will use for your writing. Make a list of specific details that you might use for developing your topic. Sometimes the details will be from your knowledge, memory, or experiences. At other times you will need to gather information from reference sources. List as many details or pieces of information as you can think of.

Look over your list of specific details and ask yourself these questions:
Are all of the details related to my topic and purpose?
Can any details be added that would make my purpose clearer or my writing more interesting?
Adjust your list as necessary. You may change one idea or several. You might even revise or change your topic.

Once you have completed your list, try putting the details into a logical order. If you are telling a story, you would probably want to present your details in the order they occurred. If you are describing a scene or an object, you might want to arrange your details in the order in which a viewer would noticed them. If you are presenting an argument, you might decide to organize your facts from least important to most important.

If you have taken time with the prewriting steps, you will then be ready to put your ideas together in a paragraph. This will be your first draft. As you write, leave space to enable you to make corrections later. Do not write too cramped together. It is a good idea to skip lines and leave wide margin so that you will be able to add improvements with clarity.

Remember that this is only a rough version, so you do not need to be too concerned with details such as spelling and punctuation. Instead, concentrate on getting your ideas on paper and making them flow together smoothly.

Write a good topic sentence that states the main idea of your paragraph. It should not be too broad to be covered in one paragraph. Make it interesting enough to engage your reader's attention. Then add supporting sentences based on the details that you already arranged in logical order. Keep your purpose in mind, but don't be afraid to drift somewhat from your plan. You will find that you have new ideas as you write.

Once the paragraph is written, it is time to revise and proofread your work. Revising means to check
the clarity of your writing and make improvement. You will want to fine tune your work by reading what you have written and asking yourself these questions.

- Did I stick to my topic?
- Are there unnecessary details?
- Could any points be added that would clarify or improve my writing?
- Does the writing sound interesting or boring?
- Do the ideas flow together smoothly?
- Would a different organization of ideas be better?
- Are any sentences out of order or confusing?
- Are there more precise or vivid words I could use?
- Did I achieve the purpose I set out in my writing?

As you answer these questions, make corrections and notes on your rough draft. You might even want to begin all over again rearranging your ideas or improving the way you say them. Writers often make several drafts of a piece of writing before they are satisfied.

Proofreading means checking the spelling, capitalization, punctuation, and grammar for mistakes. Pretend that you are reading something that another person wrote. It will be easier for you to catch mistakes if you do not keep in mind that you were the writer. Remember that the more mistakes you catch and correct, the better the final writing will turn out.

Finally, when you are satisfied that your writing is clear and correct, write your final copy. Write carefully. Make it as neat as possible. Indent the beginning of the paragraph. Leave good margins around your writing. Be proud of your work.

> THE PROCESS OF WRITING.
> PREWRITING – CHOOSE TOPIC AND PURPOSE
> PUT IDEAS ON PAPER
> ORGANIZE THEM
> WRITE FIRST DRAFT
> REVISE & PROOFREAD
> WRITE FINAL COPY

Before beginning to bake a cake, you must decide on the kind of cake you wish to produce. Your choice will determine the ingredients you use and the way that you combine them. If you wish to produce a marble cake, you will not be whipping eggs for a custard. If you are making a lemon pie, you will not be dissolving coffee for mocha icing.

Similarly, when you are going to write a paragraph, you must first decide on your purpose for writing. Do you want to tell a story? Do you want to describe something? Do you want to explain an idea or opinion? Your answer to these questions will determine the kind of paragraph you write and how you put it together.

Three major kinds of paragraphs are the narrative paragraph, the descriptive paragraph, and the explanatory paragraph. Each has a different purpose and gets put together in a different manner.

> YOU HAVE TO DECIDE WHAT KIND OF PARAGRAPH YOU WANT TO WRITE. YOU SHOULD APPROACH EACH KIND OF WRITING IN ITS WAY OF PREPARATION.

A narrative paragraph tells a story. When you tell your friend what happened on the way to school or about your experience at camp, you are telling, or narrating, a story. When you write a narrative paragraph you are doing the same thing with your writing. You would not want to begin at the middle or finish at the beginning. You want to say the events in the order in which they took place. This kind of organization is called chronological order. It is in the time sequence of the story.

When the author writes as if he were speaking about himself, that is first person. Your first reaction to being assigned to write a narrative paragraph might be, "What on earth can I possibly write about?" Think about all the things that have happened to you – funny things, serious things, exciting things, and unpleasant things. Then think about the things you imagine happening, either in the future or in a world of make-believe where anything is possible.

As you do your thinking, you will most likely discover several possible subjects for your paragraph. These relate to your real and imagined experiences. Each idea could be developed as a first-person narrative. In this kind of paragraph, the writer tells a story using first-person pronouns such as *I, we, us, me, my, mine*, and *our*.

One writer chose as a subject his first ride on a jet ski. Before he began to write, he took a few minutes to plan his paragraph. First he asked himself the following questions: How did I feel about taking the ride? Was I enthusiastic? Was I frightened? Whose jet ski was it? How did I get the chance for a ride? He wrote down the answers to these questions so that he would remember to include the ideas when writing the paragraph.

Next he thought about what he felt when he was actually on the jet ski. He asked himself these questions: Was it like riding a banana boat? a bicycle? How did I feel at the beginning of the ride? Did my feelings change? How did I behave during the ride? He added these ideas to his list. Then he wrote the following paragraph:

> I was torn between pain and pleasure when Uncle Volvy offered to take me out on the lake with his new jet skis for my birthday. Suppose I fell off? My hands felt clammy-cold at the thought. Bravely, I managed a weak smile. With fingers shaking, I buckled on the life-jacket and hoisted myself behind him. With a roar like a motorcycle, we took off into the waves. Gradually, I relaxed my knuckle-white grip and looked around. It was like skimming over the water on a sleek bumpy space ship. By the time we reached the other side of the lake, all my fears had been blown away by the force of the wind and waves around us. The jet ski seemed like an old friend, and I had been the first child in our family to ride it.

From the first sentence on, the writer involves the reader in his experiences. He vividly describes his reactions with phrases such as "torn between panic and pleasure," "hands felt clammy-cold," and "my knuckle-white grip." By doing so, he allows the reader to see life, for a few minutes, through his eyes.

Another example:

> I saw the flames coming from the basement window, and I knew there was no time to lose. Old Mrs. Taub, who was nearly deaf, was certain to be taking her afternoon nap. My hands trembled as I tried the front doorknob. Miraculously, the cool brass turned in my hand, and I entered the darkened house. Thick smoke was everywhere. My eyes burned, and my breath caught in my throat. I could feel sweat begin to pour down my back. I held my breath and felt my way to Mrs. Taub's bedroom. Feeling a surge of strength I didn't know I had, I lifted the frail old lady out of her bed and, stumbling, carried her to the front door. Through my eyes I could see the bright light outside. It guided me through the front door and into the fresh air. As fire engines approached, I sank to my knees, gasping for breath One look at the house, now engulfed in flames, told me I had not been a minute too soon!

Choose one of the following topics to write a first-person narrative paragraph about.

- the day I learned to ride a bicycle
- my first day in mesivta
- when I brought home a raccoon
- something exciting happened when I least expected it
- my most embarrassing experience
- the funniest Purim shtick I ever played
- the moment I awoke and knew something was going to happen
- the day I broke my limb
- a camping experience I will never forget
- my first speech and I tried not to show how nervous I was
- when I first put on tefillin
- last summer I did something I've never done before
- my first time davening before the amud
- tekiyas shofar on Rosh Hashana
- the first Yom Kippur I fasted

Write down the topic of your narrative paragraph.

_____

Next, brainstorm all the details that you can remember or imagine about the story. Ask yourself questions such as: How did I feel? What caused it to begin? What was I wanting? Who else was involved? How did I change from the experience? How do I feel about it now? List the answers to those questions here. Add as many details as you can. Ask yourself what would I want the reader to remember about my story? What would the reader want to ask me about it?

_____   _____

_____   _____

_____   _____

_____   _____

_____   _____

_____   _____

_____   _____

_____   _____

Look over your list of specific details and ask yourself these questions:

> *Are all of the details related to my topic and purpose?*
> *Can any details be added that would make my purpose clearer or my writing more interesting?*

Adjust your list as necessary. You may change one idea or several. If you need to add ideas, list them here.

_____   _____

_____   _____

_____   _____

Now go over your list of details and arrange then in chronological order. Put numbers next to the ideas indicating the time sequence of the events.

It is now time to write your first draft. Don't worry about spelling, grammar, or punctuation. Think of an interesting way to express your main idea that will engage your reader's attention. Then add supporting sentences that expand your main idea and tell the events in the time sequence that they occurred. Leave yourself sufficient space to revise and make corrections.

_____

_____

_____

_____

_____

_____

_____

_____

_____

_____

_____

It is now time to revise your writing. Carefully read over what you wrote and ask yourself the following questions:

- Did I stick to my topic?
- Are there unnecessary details?
- Could any points be added that would clarify or improve my writing?
- Does the writing sound interesting or boring?
- Do the ideas flow together smoothly?
- Would a different organization of ideas be better?
- Are any sentences out of order or confusing?
- Are there more precise or vivid words I could use?
- Did I achieve the purpose I set out in my writing?

As you answer the questions, make additions and corrections on your first draft. It is very helpful to use a different color ink or pencil so the changes can be easily noticed.

Then proofread it carefully, looking out for any spelling or grammar mistakes. Make sure you used the correct punctuation and quotation marks.

Now it is time to write your final draft. Make sure to write carefully and neatly. Avoid the need to erase anything. Remember to be proud of your work.

In a first-person narrative, the writer has a part in the action. In a third-person narrative, the writer mentally steps back from the action and relates something that happened to someone else. The subject of a third-person narrative can be a real or an imaginary event. As in all narrative paragraphs, the story in a third-person narrative unfolds in chronological order, in the time sequence in which the events happened.

Following is an example of a third-person narrative paragraph. Notice the use of the third-person pronouns *he, it, his its*, and *him*.

> Jimmy watched the cobra, waiting for a chance to master the deadly snake. Suddenly, the cobra's head hit Jimmy's hand, but it did not bite. It struck with its mouth closed. As rapidly as an expert boxer drumming on a punching bag, the snake struck three times against Jimmy's palm, always for some incredible reason with its mouth shut. Then Jimmy slid his open hand over its head and stroked its hood. The snake hissed again and struggled violently under his touch. Jimmy continued to caress it. Suddenly, the snake went limp and its hood began to close. Jimmy slipped his other hand under the snake's body and lifted it out of the cage. He held the reptile in his arms as though it were a baby. The cobra lifted its head to look Jimmy in the face; its dancing tongue was less than a foot from his mouth. Jimmy braced his hand against the curve of its body and talked calmly to it until it folded its hood. It curled up in his arms quietly.

The writer uses strong, specific verbs throughout the paragraph; for example: *hit, bit, struck, slid, stroked, hissed, struggled, caress, slipped, lifted, raised, braced, folded,* and *curled.* These actions help the reader visualize the encounter between Jimmy and the cobra. The reader "sees" the events as they were seen by the author.

When you write in third person, you are telling what someone else did. In order to do it effectively, you must put yourself in the other person's shoes. You must use your imagination to decide how you would feel if you were actually in the situation you are writing about. Here is another example:

> Jeffery entered the gym anxiously. He could see the list posted on the bulletin board. How he hoped his name would be on it! With breath held, Jeffery raced across the gym. He could see that there were five names beneath the heading "Opening Players." His eyes scanned the list, and then they filled with tears. He could barely see his way to the locker room. Jeffery ran to the back corner, slumped on the bench, and began to sob. How could he face his parents? And his friends? He had been so confident! This was the biggest disappointment of his life.

After beginning the paragraph with a topic sentence, the writer tells what happened in the order that it happened. He vividly describes what Jeffery was feeling and how he acted.

Choose one of the following topics to write a third-person narrative paragraph about.

- David was ashamed of his own behavior
- Gedalyah tried to run, but his legs had turned to water.
- When Nesanel learned that his great-uncle had left him a million dollars, he began to make plans.
- My uncle's experience in the army saved my life.
- Steve was in the bank when the robbers entered.
- The search for the lost child continued all night.

- When Hillel saw the accident, he rushed forward to help.
- The bicycle lay upside down, its wheels still turning.
- The veterinarian cautiously approached the wounded animal.
- Nechemiah's childhood had been filled with hardships.
- The two boys had been marooned on the island for a month.
- Hirsch was determined to win first prize.
- Azriel had always wanted to be a chazzan.

Write down the topic of your narrative paragraph.

_____

Next, brainstorm all the details that you can remember or imagine about the story. Ask yourself questions such as: How did he or she feel? What caused it to begin? What were they wanting? Who else was involved? How did he or she change from the experience?

How do they feel about it now? List the answers to those questions here. Add as many details as you can. Ask yourself what would I want the reader to remember about my story? What would the reader want to ask me about it? Do your best to put yourself in the place of the characters in your story and see it from their perspective.

_____   _____

_____   _____

_____   _____

_____   _____

_____   _____

_____   _____

_____   _____

_____   _____

Look over your list of specific details and ask yourself these questions:

Are all of the details related to my topic and purpose?
Can any details be added that would make my purpose clearer or my writing more interesting?

Adjust your list as necessary. You may change one idea or several. If you need to add ideas, list them here.

_____   _____

_____   _____

_____   _____

Now go over your list of details and arrange then in chronological order. Put numbers next to the ideas indicating the time sequence of the events.

It is now time to write your first draft. Don't worry about spelling, grammar, or punctuation. Think of an interesting way to express your main idea that will engage your reader's attention. Then add supporting sentences that expand your main idea and tell the events in the time sequence that they occurred. Leave yourself sufficient space to revise and make corrections.

_____

_____

_____

_____

_____

_____

_____

_____

_____

_____

It is now time to revise your writing. Carefully read over what you wrote and ask yourself the following questions:

- Did I stick to my topic?
- Are there unnecessary details?
- Could any points be added that would clarify or improve my writing?
- Does the writing sound interesting or boring?
- Do the ideas flow together smoothly?
- Would a different organization of ideas be better?
- Are any sentences out of order or confusing?
- Are there more precise or vivid words I could use?
- Did I achieve the purpose I set out in my writing?

As you answer the questions, make additions and corrections on your first draft. It is very helpful to use a different color ink or pencil so the changes can be easily noticed.

Then proofread it carefully, looking out for any spelling or grammar mistakes. Make sure you used the correct punctuation and quotation marks.

Now it is time to write your final draft. Make sure to write carefully and neatly. Avoid the need to erase anything. Remember to be proud of your work.

_____

_____

_____

_____

_____

_____

_____

_____

_____

THE NARRATIVE PARAGRAPH TELLS A STORY.

IT CAN BE IN FIRST PERSON, WHERE THE WRITER IS SPEAKING FOR HIMSELF OR HERSELF.
IT CAN BE IN THIRD PERSON, WHERE THE WRITER SPEAKS ABOUT OTHERS.

IT SHOULD BE TOLD IN CHRONOLOGICAL ORDER, THE SEQUENCE OF TIME.

The purpose of a descriptive paragraph is to paint a picture with words. A description appeals to one or more of the five senses – sight, hearing, smell, taste, or touch. Of these senses, sight and hearing are the most highly developed Therefore, most descriptive paragraphs appeal mainly to either sight or hearing, or to a combination of the two.

The success of a descriptive paragraph depends on the clarity of the picture created in the reader's mind. This picture depends on the specific words and details used by the writer.

Suppose, for example, that a writer described a new car as "beautiful." The reader would have only a vague idea of what the car looks like. On the other hand, if the writer used details such as "sleek, shiny blue doors," "gleaming, curved hood," "sharply squared trunk," chrome, spoked tires," and "sparkling mirrors," the reader would have a good mental image of the automobile.

Specific nouns, strong verbs, adjectives, adverbs, and descriptive phrases all help to create a clear picture in the reader's mind. Without them, descriptive writing is lifeless and ineffective. Read, for example, this sentence: "The bird sang in the tree." The nouns *bird* and *tree* are general. The verb *sang* does not provide the reader with a clue about how the bird sounded. The sentence lacks adjectives, adverbs, and descriptive phrases.

Compare the sample sentence in the preceding paragraph with this revised version: "The fat young blackbird chattered angrily in the gnarled, dead oak tree." In place of the general noun *bird* is the specific noun *blackbird*. The general verb *sang* has been replaced with the specific verb *chattered*. The adjectives *fat, young, gnarled, dead*, and *oak* and the adverb *angrily* have been added to the sentence. The reader now has a chance to see and hear the blackbird in the same way the writer did.

Many descriptions appeal to the sense of sight. The details in these paragraphs describe size, shape, color, appearance, position, and movement. Together, they create a visual image in the mind of the reader.

Read the following unskilled descriptive paragraph of an old man.

> By the time the boy had got to the house, the walking man was only halfway down the road. Jody could tell he was old; and, as he approached nearer, Jody saw that he was dressed in old jeans and a coat. He wore old shoes and an old hat. Over his shoulder he carried a sack. In a few minutes he had walked close enough so that his face could be seen. His face was very dark. He had a white mustache and white hair, dark eyes, and thin nose. There were no wrinkles in the face at all.

The paragraph is dull, uninteresting, and too vague to evoke much of a picture in the reader's mind.

Contrast it with this version, written by a skilled writer.

By the time the boy had got to the house, the walking man was only halfway down the road, a lean man, very straight in the shoulders. Jody could tell he was old only because his heels struck the ground with hard jerks. As he approached nearer, Jody saw that he was dressed in blue jeans and a coat of the same material. He wore clodhopper shoes and an old, flat-brimmed Stetson hat. Over his shoulder he carried a gunny sack, lumpy and full. In a few minutes he had trudged close enough so that his face could be seen. And his face was as dark as dried beef. A mustache, blue-white against the dark skin, hovered over his mouth; and his hair was white, too, where it showed at his neck. The skin of his face had shrunk back against the skull until it defined bone, not flesh, and made the nose and chin seem sharp and fragile. The eyes were large and deep and dark with eyelids stretched tightly over them. Irises and pupils were one, and very black, but he eyeballs were brown. There were no wrinkles in the face at all.

The paragraph is a vivid and interesting word picture of an old man. The writer carefully painted the picture with specific words and details, such as "heels struck the ground with hard jerks," "dressed in blue jeans and in a coat of the same material," "clodhopper shoes and an old, flat-brimmed Stetson hat," "a gunny sack, lump and full," "a mustache blue-white against the dark skin," "shrunk back against the skull," and "sharp and fragile." In addition, he drew the comparison that "his face was as dark as dried beef." Comparisons like this help to craft a clear image in the reader's mind.

By changing specific details, the author could completely change the picture drawn in a paragraph. The following paragraph is basically the same as the preceding one about a walking man. The details, though, are different.

By the time the boy had got to the house, the walking man was only halfway down the road, a short, fat man, very round-shouldered. Jody could tell he was young only because his heels struck the ground with short, quick, jerks. As he approached nearer, Jody saw that he was dressed in white duck pants and a coat of the same material. He wore dusty white shoes and a new black derby hat. In his right hand he clutched a bright red and black carpetbag, plump and full. In a few minutes he had walked close enough so that his face could be seen. And his face was white as blackboard chalk. A thin mustache, black against the white skin, drooped over his mouth, and his hair was black, too, where it showed at the neck. The skin of his face was puffed out so that it was difficult to define bone, and the nose and chin seemed lost in rolls of flesh. The eyes were small and pale blue, with thin black eyebrows arched above them. There were no wrinkles in the face at all.

Now, rather than seeing a lean, hard old man, the reader sees a short, fat young man.

Consider the following descriptive paragraph:

> The old man was thin and gaunt with deep wrinkles in the back of his
> neck. The brown blotches the benevolent skin cancer brings from its
> reflection on the tropic sea were on his cheeks. The blotches ran well
> down the sides of his face, and his hands had the deep-creased scars from
> handling heavy fish on the cords. But none of these scars were fresh. They
> were as old as erosions in a fishless desert.

The word picture is much more vivid than if the author had simply said that the man was
old and wrinkled, with blotchy skin. Underline as many specific details and sense words
that you can in the paragraph.

A DESCRIPTIVE PARAGRAPH CRAFTS A PICTURE FROM WORDS. IT USES MANY SPECIFIC DETAILS AND SENSE WORDS.

Choose at least six of the items below. For each of them list at least three descriptive details that could be used in a descriptive paragraph. Appeal to as many senses as you can.

- a park in summer
- a family simcha celebration
- your favorite animal
- a family trip
- kashering for Pesach
- biur chometz
- a busy restaurant
- a roaring fire
- a newborn baby
- a deserted beach

- the kitchen before supper
- a laundromat
- a barbecue or picnic
- cows grazing in a pasture
- a hospital room
- your street at night
- a carnival
- a gas station
- hadlakas ner Chanukah
- Hoshana Rabba Hakafos

1.

_____

_____

_____

2.

_____

_____

_____

3.

_____

_____

_____

4.

_____

_____

_____

5.

6.

The ideas in a descriptive paragraph must be arranged in some kind of logical order. In paragraphs that appeal to the sense of sight, the order usually is spatial order. Things are described in relation to other things in the same area or space.

Some descriptions are organized in loose spatial order. The first paragraph about the old man, for instance, presents details in three groups: 1. the details noticed from a distance; 2. the details Jody noticed as the man approached; and 3. the details Jody saw at close range. Within these groups, the details are given in the order that they caught Jody's attention. The writer does not bother to explain that the shoes are on the man's feet or that the hat is on top of his head. The space relationships are clear.

In some descriptions, particularly in descriptions of places, information about space relationships is essential. The following paragraph describes a scene at the edge of a river.

> The river ran smooth and shallow at our feet, and beyond it a wide sandy beach sloped upward gently to the edge of the forest, against which the rocks shone as white as weathered bones. The red soil bank on our side of the river, the silver sheet of water in front of us, the wet browns and greys of the sandbars, the whitewashed ramp of rocks on the opposite shore, the green forest front, and the pale purple of the Sierra Madre were like stripes of water colors. Across them strings of mules and donkeys moved with their loads, fording the river with their bellies awash. The drivers followed, their white *calzones* rolled above their thighs and the water up to their waists.

In this paragraph the author uses specific space, or direction, words to show the relationship of one thing to another. The words and phrases are: "at our feet," "beyond," "upward," "to the edge," "on our side," "in front of," "on the opposite shore," "across," "above," and "up to." These direction words allow the reader to picture the scene.

Consider another example.

> There was no underbrush in the island of pine trees. The trunks of the trees went straight up or slanted toward each other. The trunks were straight and brown without branches. The branches were high above. Some interlocked to make a solid shadow on the brown forest floor. Beyond the grove of trees was a bare space. It was brown and soft underfoot as Nick walked on it. This was the overlapping of the pine needle floor, extending out beyond the width of the high branches. The trees had grown tall and the branches moved high, leaving in the sun this bare space they had once covered with shadow. Sharp at the edge of this extension of the forest floor commenced the sweet fern.

Underline as many direction words, or relation words, as you can in the paragraph above.

The second most common kind of description appeals to the sense of hearing. The details in these paragraphs describe sounds rather than sight, as in the following example.

> The sound of a strange song floated in the air and seemed to be coming right out of the trunk of the tree. I stood there, turning my ears around in search of the source. The voice was light and unstrained, like some bird, and with a melancholy, human note. The sounds of the frantic children screaming for me to hurry with the ball faded into the background. My heart drummed fiercely, as I felt the presence of an unknown force.

The writer of this paragraph captures the quality of a sound with words such as "strange," "floated," "light," "unstrained," "melancholy," and "human." He also describes the screaming of the children and the drumming of his own heart, sounds whose sharpness and realism contrast with the strange sound. These details help the reader to share the writer's uneasiness.

Paragraphs that appeal to the sense of hearing are not necessarily organized in spatial order. The details, however, must be arranged in some logical order that is easy to follow.

In the following paragraph, the author crafted a word picture that makes you feel as if you are actually in the kitchen she describes.

> I close my eyes and remember my mother's kitchen. The cocoa steamed fragrantly in the saucepan. Geraniums bloomed on the window sills, and a bouquet of tiny yellow chrysanthemums brightened the center of the table. The curtains, red with a blue and green geometrical pattern, were drawn and seemed to reflect the cheerfulness throughout the room. The furnace purred like a great sleepy animal; the lights glowed with steady radiance. Outside, alone in the dark, the wind battered against the house.

Most of the details in the paragraph appeal to the sense of sight; for example: "tiny yellow chrysanthemums brightened," "red with a blue and green geometrical pattern," and "lights glowed." Two details appeal to the sense of hearing: "purred like a great sleepy animal" and "battered against the house." One phrase, "cocoa steamed fragrantly," appeals to a third sense, that of smell. The writer weaves these together to recreate a scene from her past for the reader to experience.

> IN A DESCRIPTIVE PARAGRAPH THAT APPEALS TO THE SENSE OF SIGHT, USE DIRECTION OR RELATION WORDS TO INDICATE SPATIAL ORDER – THE ORDER OF SPACE.

In each of the following pairs of sentences, choose the sentence that creates a more vivid image in your mind. Then write your own sentence that gives different details about the same subject.

1. branch
    a) The branch clicked against the window with the sound of snapping fingers.
    b) The branch made little noises as it hit the window.

   _____

   _____

2. dessert
    a) My mother made a delicious dessert last night.
    b) My mother baked a juicy apple pie last night.

   _____

   _____

3. sunburn
    a) Tzvi's sunburn felt as though his back were on fire.
    b) Tzvi's sunburn was painful.

   _____

   _____

4. flowers
    a) Abba gave Mommy some beautiful flowers.
    b) Abba gave Mommy a dozen long-stemmed pink roses for her birthday.

   _____

   _____

5. steak
    a) The steak was as tough as shoe leather.
    b) The steak was not as good as I had expected.

   _____

   _____

6. voice
   a) He had a voice that sounded like chalk squeaking against a blackboard.
   b) He had an unpleasant voice.

_____

_____

7. night
   a) The night wrapped us in black velvet.
   b) The night was extremely dark.

_____

_____

8. sandwich
   a) The sandwich filling tasted like old library paste.
   b) The sandwich filling tasted awful.

_____

_____

Choose at least seven of the items below. For each of them list at least three descriptive details that could be used in a descriptive paragraph. Appeal to as many senses as you can.

- pastrami frying in a skillet
- the noise at a game in the park
- a carnival
- a fire
- a baby crying
- a storm
- a group at lunch
- a jet taking off
- an excited puppy
- a deserted classroom
- chazaras hashatz
- a crowded bagel store
- hachnasas Sefer Torah
- dancing at a school Bar Mitzvah
- Tekias Shofar
- a chazzan chanting Keil Molei Rachamim
- singing at a chupa
- selichos
- waves at the beach
- your bedroom
- an outdoor market
- a campsite
- a traffic jam
- cars rumbling on a bridge
- a construction site
- a bridge at sunset
- geese flying
- a band playing at a wedding
- your favorite painting

1.

_____

_____

_____

2.

_____

_____

_____

3.

_____

_____

_____

4.

_____

_____

_____

5.

_____

_____

_____

6.

_____

_____

_____

7.

_____

_____

_____

SOME DESCRIPTIVE PARAGRAPHS APPEAL MORE TO THE SENSE OF SIGHT THAN OTHER SENSES. USE SPATIAL ORDER TO ORGANIZE IT.

OTHER DESCRIPTIVE PARAGRAPHS APPEAL MORE TO THE SENSE OF HEARING.

SOME DESCRIPTIVE PARAGRAPHS WEAVE ALL THE SENSES TOGETHER.

Choose one of the topics from the lists on page 440 and 446 to write a descriptive paragraph about, appealing to the sense of sight. Use either your personal experience or your imagination (or both) to develop the idea into a descriptive paragraph. Be sure to use descriptive details and remember that it should be in spatial order.

Write down the topic of your descriptive paragraph appealing to sight.

_____

Next, brainstorm all the details that you can remember or imagine about the situation. Ask yourself questions such as: How did it appear? Who was in the scene? What was being done? How did it feel? What other things were going on? Where were the details in relation to each other? List the answers to those questions here. Add as many details as you can. Use direction or relation words about the details that you list. Ask yourself what would I want the reader to experience about my scene? What would the reader want to ask me about it?

_____	_____
_____	_____
_____	_____
_____	_____
_____	_____
_____	_____
_____	_____
_____	_____

Look over your list of specific details and ask yourself these questions:

Are all of the details related to my topic and purpose?
Can any details be added that would make my purpose clearer or my writing more interesting?

Adjust your list as necessary. You may change one idea or several. If you need to add ideas, list them here.

_____	_____

_____   _____

_____   _____

Now go over your list of details and arrange then in the order that they should appear in your paragraph. Put numbers next to the ideas indicating their order.

It is now time to write your first draft. Don't worry about spelling, grammar, or punctuation. Think of an interesting way to express your main idea that will engage your reader's attention. Then add supporting sentences that expand your main idea and describe the scene in as vivid a manner as possible. Leave yourself sufficient space to revise and make corrections.

_____

_____

_____

_____

_____

_____

_____

_____

_____

It is now time to revise your writing. Carefully read over what you wrote and ask yourself the following questions:

- Did I stick to my topic?
- Are there unnecessary details?
- Could any points be added that would clarify or improve my writing?
- Does the writing sound interesting or boring?
- Do the ideas flow together smoothly?
- Would a different organization of ideas be better?
- Are any sentences out of order or confusing?
- Are there more precise or vivid words I could use?
- Did I achieve the purpose I set out in my writing?

As you answer the questions, make additions and corrections on your first draft. It is very helpful to use a different color ink or pencil so the changes can be easily noticed.

Then proofread it carefully, looking out for any spelling or grammar mistakes. Make sure you used the correct punctuation and quotation marks.

Now it is time to write your final draft. Make sure to write carefully and neatly. Avoid the need to erase anything. Remember to be proud of your work.

_____

_____

_____

_____

_____

_____

_____

_____

Choose another of the topics from the lists on page 440 and 446 to write a descriptive paragraph about, appealing to the sense of hearing. Use either your personal experience or your imagination (or both) to develop the idea into a descriptive paragraph. Be sure to use descriptive details.

Write down the topic of your descriptive paragraph appealing to hearing.

_____

Next, brainstorm all the details that you can remember or imagine about the situation. Ask yourself questions such as: How did it appear? Who was in the scene? What was being done? How did it feel? What other things were going on? What did it sound like? Who was speaking? How were they talking? Was there music? What other sounds were there? Where were the details in relation to each other? List the answers to those questions here. Add as many details as you can. Ask yourself what would I want the reader to experience about my scene? What would the reader want to ask me about it?

_____   _____

_____   _____

_____   _____

_____   _____

_____   _____

_____   _____

_____   _____

_____   _____

Look over your list of specific details and ask yourself these questions:

Are all of the details related to my topic and purpose?
Can any details be added that would make my purpose clearer or my writing more interesting?

Adjust your list as necessary. You may change one idea or several. If you need to add ideas, list them here.

_____   _____

_____   _____

_____   _____

Now go over your list of details and arrange then in the order that they should appear in your paragraph. Put numbers next to the ideas indicating their order.

It is now time to write your first draft. Don't worry about spelling, grammar, or punctuation. Think of an interesting way to express your main idea that will engage your reader's attention. Then add supporting sentences that expand your main idea and describe the scene in as vivid a manner as possible. Leave yourself sufficient space to revise and make corrections.

_____

_____

_____

_____

_____

_____

_____

_____

_____

It is now time to revise your writing. Carefully read over what you wrote and ask yourself the following questions:

- Did I stick to my topic?
- Are there unnecessary details?
- Could any points be added that would clarify or improve my writing?
- Does the writing sound interesting or boring?
- Do the ideas flow together smoothly?
- Would a different organization of ideas be better?
- Are any sentences out of order or confusing?
- Are there more precise or vivid words I could use?
- Did I achieve the purpose I set out in my writing?

As you answer the questions, make additions and corrections on your first draft. It is very helpful to use a different color ink or pencil so the changes can be easily noticed.

Then proofread it carefully, looking out for any spelling or grammar mistakes. Make sure you used the correct punctuation and quotation marks.

Now it is time to write your final draft. Make sure to write carefully and neatly. Avoid the need to erase anything. Remember to be proud of your work.

_____

_____

_____

_____

_____

_____

_____

_____

The explanatory paragraph is one of the most important kinds of paragraphs that you must learn to write. This is because you will probably do more explanatory writing throughout your life than any other kind. In an explanatory paragraph, you explain *how*, *what*, or *why*, as clearly as possible.

In a **how** paragraph, you are giving instructions how to do something or directions where to go. In this kind of paragraph you explain how something is done in chronological order, or time sequence of how to do it. You tell what to do first, what to do next, and so forth.

After reading a paragraph that gives instructions, the reader should be able to do or make something. Consider the following situation, for example. You have been invited to a Chinese banquet, where you will be expected to eat with chopsticks. A friend who is experienced in using chopsticks gives you these written instructions.

> Eating with chopsticks add an extra something to any Chinese meal. Learning to use chopsticks properly is not hard; after all, even a Chinese toddler can do it. First, hold the sticks in your right hand, one on top of the other. Grip them about a third of the way from the ends. Next, place the lower stick at the base of your thumb. Rest it also on the tip of your fourth (or ring) finger. Then, place the second stick between the tip of your thumb and the tips of you index and middle finger. Hold the lower stick steady, but move the upper stick so that together they act like "tongs." Remember to keep your hand relaxed and to hold the chopsticks lightly but firmly.

These instructions are detailed and well organized. They tell you exactly what to do and how to do it. After practice, you will be able to eat with chopsticks at the banquet.

Another example of a clear explanatory paragraph that gives instruction how to do something.

> Start with a ripe avocado. Cut through the outer skin carefully and separate the avocado in two parts. Remove the large brown seed. Wash the seed, or pit, and place it rounded side down in water or soil. The pit should be half covered. Keep the water halfway up the pit, or keep the soil evenly moist. When the pit splits and a stem emerges and reaches eight inches, cut the stem back to four inches in order to encourage a full plant.

When writing a **how** explanatory paragraph, you must be clear to use transitions, which are words that indicate a change from one thing or activity to another. Words like *first, start, next, soon, later, after, finally, in the end, secondly, lastly, while,* etc. are examples of transitions. In addition to being written in chronological order, it is important to make it easy for your reader to follow the order of the directions.

At the same time as you most focus on clarity for your reader, you have to avoid sounding too stiff, like a recipe book or a printout of traffic instructions. As with all paragraphs, craft your topic sentence to be interesting for your reader. Be creative when choosing transitions to keep your reader engaged and interested.

> # A HOW EXPLANATORY PARAGRAPH TELLS INSTRUCTIONS OR DIRECTIONS IN CHRONOLOGICAL ORDER.

Choose one of the following two easy-to-make homemade meals to write a **how** paragraph about: scrambled eggs or homemade pizza.

Write down the topic of your narrative paragraph.

_____

Next, brainstorm all the details that you can remember or imagine about the task. Ask yourself questions such as: What ingredients will be needed? What tools and utensils are used? Where will it be prepared? What are the steps that must be done? Is there other help must be arranged? What precautions should be taken? List the answers to those questions here. Add as many details as you can. Ask yourself what would I want the reader to be careful about? What would the reader want to ask me about it?

_____   _____

_____   _____

_____   _____

_____   _____

_____   _____

_____   _____

_____   _____

_____   _____

Look over your list of specific details and ask yourself these questions:

Are all of the details related to my topic and purpose?
Can any details be added that would make my purpose clearer or my writing more interesting?

Adjust your list as necessary. You may change one idea or several. If you need to add ideas, list them here.

_____   _____

_____   _____

_____   _____

Now go over your list of details and arrange then in chronological order. Put numbers next to the ideas indicating the time sequence of the events. Make sure to also choose smooth transitions to organize the flow of steps.

It is now time to write your first draft. Don't worry about spelling, grammar, or punctuation. Think of an interesting way to express your main idea that will engage your reader's attention. Then add supporting sentences that expand your main idea and tell the instructions in the time sequence that they should occur. Leave yourself sufficient space to revise and make corrections.

_____

_____

_____

_____

_____

_____

_____

_____

_____

_____

_____

It is now time to revise your writing. Carefully read over what you wrote and ask yourself the following questions:

- Did I stick to my topic?
- Are there unnecessary details?
- Could any points be added that would clarify or improve my writing?
- Does the writing sound interesting or boring?
- Do the ideas flow together smoothly?
- Would a different organization of ideas be better?
- Are any sentences out of order or confusing?
- Are there more precise or vivid words I could use?
- Did I achieve the purpose I set out in my writing?

As you answer the questions, make additions and corrections on your first draft. It is very helpful to use a different color ink or pencil so the changes can be easily noticed.

Then proofread it carefully, looking out for any spelling or grammar mistakes. Make sure you used the correct punctuation and quotation marks.

Now it is time to write your final draft. Make sure to write carefully and neatly. Avoid the need to erase anything. Remember to be proud of your work.

_____

_____

_____

_____

_____

_____

_____

_____

REMEMBER TO USE TRANSITIONS TO
CLEARLY INDICATE TO YOUR READER THE
CHRONOLOGICAL ORDER OF INSTRUCTIONS.
AT THE SAME TIME, MAKE SURE NOT TO
SOUND STIFF LIKE A COOKBOOK.

A second type of explanatory paragraph tells what something is and what it does. In other words, it defines a word or phrase.

A definition contains three parts: the term to be defined, the general class to which it belongs, and the particular characteristic that sets the term apart from the other members of the general class. This basic definition is the topic sentence of such a paragraph. The remainder of the paragraph is made up of supporting details. The details further explain the basic definition.

> A hurricane is a strong, swirling storm that usually measures several hundred miles in diameter. The eye of the hurricane, often measuring 20 miles wide, is usually calm and has no clouds. Around the eye, winds blow at 75 miles an hour or more. Death and destruction, unfortunately, are too often part of the hurricane's story.

After opening with the topic sentence that defines a hurricane, the rest of the paragraph tells more about it, explaining what it is. That is what makes it a **what** paragraph.

Choose one of the topics from the list on page 334 to write a **what** paragraph about.

Write down the topic of your explanatory paragraph.

_____

Next, brainstorm all the details that you can expand on your definition. Ask yourself questions such as: What makes it different from other members of the general class? What examples can you give? What similarities does it have? What else is it used for? What is known about it? List the answers to those questions here. Add as many details as you can. Ask yourself what would I want the reader to learn about my topic? What would the reader want to ask me about it?

_____   _____

_____   _____

_____   _____

_____   _____

_____   _____

_____   _____

_____   _____

_____   _____

_____   _____

Look over your list of specific details and ask yourself these questions:

Are all of the details related to my topic and purpose?
Can any details be added that would make my purpose clearer or my writing more interesting?

Adjust your list as necessary. You may change one idea or several. If you need to add ideas, list them here.

_____   _____

_____   _____

_____   _____

Now go over your list of details and arrange then in the order they should appear in your paragraph. Place numbers alongside the ideas to help remember the arrangement.

It is now time to write your first draft. Don't worry about spelling, grammar, or punctuation. Think of an interesting way to express your definition that will engage your reader's attention. Then add supporting sentences that expand your definition by including examples, facts, figures, or explanations. Leave yourself sufficient space to revise and make corrections.

_____

_____

_____

_____

_____

_____

_____

_____

_____

_____

_____

It is now time to revise your writing. Carefully read over what you wrote and ask yourself the following questions:

- Did I stick to my topic?
- Are there unnecessary details?
- Could any points be added that would clarify or improve my writing?
- Does the writing sound interesting or boring?
- Do the ideas flow together smoothly?
- Would a different organization of ideas be better?
- Are any sentences out of order or confusing?
- Are there more precise or vivid words I could use?
- Did I achieve the purpose I set out in my writing?

As you answer the questions, make additions and corrections on your first draft. It is very helpful to use a different color ink or pencil so the changes can be easily noticed.

Then proofread it carefully, looking out for any spelling or grammar mistakes. Make sure you used the correct punctuation and quotation marks.

Now it is time to write your final draft. Make sure to write carefully and neatly. Avoid the need to erase anything. Remember to be proud of your work.

The third kind of explanatory paragraph is one that gives reasons, also called a why paragraph. There are three general categories of why paragraphs: 1. why something happened; 2. why something is the way it is; and 3. why an opinion is believed.

In all three categories, the topic sentence should state the idea that needs the reasons. It should not elaborate on the reasons that will support it, but it should still be written in a manner to engage the reader's attention.

Once the topic statement is made, there are three ways to develop the paragraph. You can uses causes for why something is. Or you can smaller facts that explain a bigger fact. The other way is to present facts that are neither the cause of something nor explain anything; they merely lead one to develop an opinion.

The way to devote a why paragraph by using causes is often used when elaborating the circumstances that led to what happened. It might be a narration of an incident and resemble a narrative paragraph. Or it may be several incidents that each contributed to why it happened. This manner focuses on the cause(s) for why something happened, and does not use facts to explain the topic. Here is an example:

> I didn't do my homework last night. Right after school, I had softball practice, and we practiced for about two hours. Just before we finished the last inning, I was playing catcher. The pitcher threw a fast ball. I tried to jump aside, but the ball hit me in the stomach and knocked all the wind out of me. When I got home, I was so tired and so sick to my stomach, I just didn't feel like doing homework.

The reasons given in the paragraph explain why homework was not done, without explaining any facts that support that fact (until the end, when he says that he didn't feel like it). The entire paragraph is explaining the cause for the fact.

In this paragraph, the writer chose to devote the entire paragraph on the one incident that explains why he didn't do the homework. Another writer may have used a few short incidents that caused it. The paragraph would work the same way. The topic sentence states the fact, and the rest of the paragraph says the causes why that fact is true.

The way to develop a paragraph with smaller facts that explain the bigger fact works very well when you are trying to explain why something is so. The smaller facts explain the bigger fact of the topic sentence. This is an example of such a paragraph.

> Beavers do a lot of good when they build their dams in the right places. Beaver dams slow down the rush of water in brooks and streams. Brooks that otherwise would dry up in the summer flow all year round if a beaver dam is built across them. The trees and bushes near the brooks have enough moisture to grow well. Their roots hold the soil so that it does not wash away. Also, wells that usually go dry in summer hold water all year when beavers are put to work on nearby streams.

The writer did not give the causes for why the beaver does good work. (The cause is probably that he wants to have a place to live and catch fish.) He explains three facts that are true about beavers' dams. They are: 1. the dams slow down the flow of water; 2. trees and bushes near dams grow well, preventing soil from washing away; and 3. wells near dams do not go dry. Each of the smaller facts explain the more general fact stated in the topic sentence.

The third way of developing an explanatory paragraph begins with the statement of an opinion. The rest of the paragraph does not explain the causes for the opinion, nor smaller facts that comprise the bigger fact. It is developed by stating a lot of supporting reasons for why the opinion was formed. For example, consider the following paragraph:

> The frontier woman was, indeed, a special character. She proved her ability to uphold her end of the load even where physical endurance was required. She bore the children, cared for them when they were sick, and often taught them to read and write. She tended the garden, cooked the family's food, and preserve what she could for the winter. And when danger from wild beasts threatened, she proved herself capable of defending her family.

The writer states many facts that are not the cause of the opening opinion, nor are they the explanation of the general fact. They are the reasons that the writer believes this opinion.

A WHY PARAGRAPH TELLS REASONS FOR THE TOPIC SENTENCE.

SOMETIMES IT STATES THE CAUSE.

SOMETIMES IT STATES SMALLER FACTS THAT SUPPORT THE TOPIC.

SOMETIMES IT JUSTIFIES AN OPINION.

Choose one of the following topics to write a why paragraph about.

- mental training is more important than physical training
- everyone should have a hobby
- our school needs a better-equipped library
- one-man bands will never replace musicians
- general holidays should only be on Shabbos
- everyone should learn first-aid and CPR
- grades should be abolished
- baby-sitting is a job that should require training

- people eat more than once a day
- general studies is important
- boys (should) get less school vacation than girls
- drive on the right side of the road
- gym period is important
- the township provides garbage collection
- the busing system is messed up
- it is bad to get sick
- students cut class
- it doesn't snow in summer

Write down the topic of your why paragraph.

_____

Next, brainstorm all the details that you can remember or imagine about the topic. Ask yourself questions such as: What are the causes? What are the facts? What other facts or ideas are involved? How does it affect other things? How does it become affected by others? List the answers to those questions here. Add as many details as you can. Ask yourself what would I want the reader to understand about my topic? What would the reader want to ask me about it?

_____   _____

_____   _____

_____   _____

_____   _____

_____   _____

_____   _____

_____   _____

_____   _____

465

Look over your list of specific details and ask yourself these questions:

Are all of the details related to my topic and purpose?
Can any details be added that would make my purpose clearer or my writing more interesting?

Adjust your list as necessary. You may change one idea or several. If you need to add ideas, list them here.

_____   _____

_____   _____

_____   _____

Now go over your list of details and arrange then in logical order. Put numbers next to the ideas indicating their arrangement in your paragraph.

It is now time to write your first draft. Don't worry about spelling, grammar, or punctuation. Think of an interesting way to express your main idea that will engage your reader's attention. Then add supporting sentences that expand your main idea and tell the events in the time sequence that they occurred. Leave yourself sufficient space to revise and make corrections.

_____

_____

_____

_____

_____

_____

_____

_____

_____

_____

_____

_____

It is now time to revise your writing. Carefully read over what you wrote and ask yourself the following questions:

- Did I stick to my topic?
- Are there unnecessary details?
- Could any points be added that would clarify or improve my writing?
- Does the writing sound interesting or boring?
- Do the ideas flow together smoothly?
- Would a different organization of ideas be better?
- Are any sentences out of order or confusing?
- Are there more precise or vivid words I could use?
- Did I achieve the purpose I set out in my writing?

As you answer the questions, make additions and corrections on your first draft. It is very helpful to use a different color ink or pencil so the changes can be easily noticed.

Then proofread it carefully, looking out for any spelling or grammar mistakes. Make sure you used the correct punctuation and quotation marks.

Now it is time to write your final draft. Make sure to write carefully and neatly. Avoid the need to erase anything. Remember to be proud of your work.

_____

_____

_____

_____

_____

_____

_____

_____

Sometimes you will want to do more than simply express an opinion and tell your reasons for it. You may also want to persuade someone else to share that opinion as well, or to take action on an issue. In this case, you would write a special kind of explanatory paragraph called a persuasive paragraph.

To be convincing, a persuasive paragraph must be supported by more than your feelings on a subject. It must also be supported by specific information. This information can include facts and figures, examples, and incidents.

Your supportive material must be organized so that it is most effective. Usually, arranging your facts from least important to most important is the best way to organize them. That way, your best reason is the last one your readers will be presented with, and the one they will be most likely to remember. Good organization is often the key to a successful persuasive paragraph.

The use of persuasive techniques is also important. Some of these are:
- setting a hook[58]
  begin with a statement that piques the interest of the reader and softens him toward your persuasion
- asking rhetorical questions
  using statements to which the reader will agree with can make him more likely to agree with your persuasion
- creating a perception of popularity
  everybody likes to be liked by everybody – make the reader think that the popular opinion is like you are persuading

When assigned to write a persuasive paragraph, you might have trouble coming up with a topic. Think of something that has two possible sides to it. Maybe something controversial in the community or a neighborhood problem that needs to be addressed. Think of a conflict you may have heard of recently and see if you feel decidedly one way about it. If you come up with a topic that is not debatable, there will be no point in writing about it. For example, to argue that the sun shines by day is irrelevant.

Once you have selected a topic, make sure that you take a definite stance about it. Don't try to argue both sides of the debate. You are trying to persuade somebody, not educate them. Decide what your stance will be and think of how to state it in an interesting manner so that the reader will want to continue reading and have the chance of being persuaded.

The topic sentence of a persuasive paragraph should mention the topic you selected and state your definite stance about it. It also has to be interesting enough for the reader's interest to be engaged. Try to set the hook in the topic sentence or the one immediately after it. Setting the hook is when you make a statement that grabs the reader's attention in a way that he wants to continue reading about it.

---

[58] Setting the hook is a phrase used in fishing when the fisherman tugs at the rope in a manner to cause the hook to catch the fish, preventing its escape.

The following paragraph is a good example of a persuasive paragraph.

Plasticware is so much more convenient than real dinnerware. Who does not hate the tedium of washing dishes and sorting silverware after a long family meal? The time and effort spent washing, drying, sorting, and putting away all the dishes and silverware can be neatly avoided with the use of plastic disposable dinnerware. If you also used a disposable plastic tablecloth, the entire mess can be swept up in a single motion and merely thrown away. Mothers with young children need not be concerned lest an unruly or clumsy child accidentally break any of her delicate dishes, thereby maiming the entire set. There is no need to count each spoon to make sure that none were tossed in the trash by mistake. The slight cost in purchasing new disposable plasticware for the next meal is definitely worth it in light of the bother it saves.

The topic sentence begins with a statement about plastic dinnerware. It states that it is so much more convenient than real dinnerware. Someone could have argued that it is much more inconvenient because it is flimsy and gets blown away or for other reasons. The writer took a definite stance on the issue. The next sentence sets the hook. It asks a rhetorical question with the expectation that the reader will agree with. The rest of the paragraph mentions a number of conveniences.

The last sentence of a persuasive paragraph should reinforce the opinion stated in the topic sentence or be a call to action about it. An example of a call to action would be if the writer had instructed the reader to go out and purchase a new set of plastic servingware. Another possible call to action might have been to instruct the reader to use dinnerware at the next family celebration. In this case, the writer chose to reinforce the opinion set forth in the topic sentence that plasticware is better by dismissing any objection in light of its advantages.

> A PERSUASIVE PARAGRAPH SHOULD BEGIN WITH A TOPIC SENTENCE THAT STATES A DEFINITE STANCE ON A TOPIC. THEN SET THE HOOK BY MAKING A STATEMENT THAT DRAWS THE READER IN TO BEING PERSUADED.
>
> REMEMBER TO REITERATE YOUR STANCE IN THE FINAL SENTENCE OR CALL TO ACTION.

Choose one of the following topics to write a persuasive paragraph about.

- Should there be no school on Friday.
- Is spring (or summer, fall, or winter) the *best* season.
- No one should litter.
- Should students be allowed to wear hats during class.
- Is recycling the best way to help the environment
- Should school lunches be healthy.
- The more we read, the better writers we become.
- Students should/should not be able to have their own phones.
- Should schools have dress codes?
- If I could change one school rule, it would be …
- Is year-round school a good idea?
- Should we stop giving final exams?
- Is it better to be good at academics or good at sports?
- Which is better, private schools or public schools?
- Should every student have to participate in athletics?
- Do you think schools should ban junk food from their cafeterias?
- Should students be required to volunteer in their communities?
- What is the most important school subject?
- Are letter grades helpful, or should we replace them with something else?
- Do you think homework should be required, optional, or not given at all?
- Is it ever OK to cheat on homework or a test?
- Do you think college should be free for anyone who wants to attend?
- Bicycle riders should be licensed.
- The very best food of all time is …
- A course on emergency first aid should be required at every school.
- The school year is not long enough/too long.
- Which is better, book smarts or street smarts?
- Which animals make the best pets.
- Should all students have to learn a foreign language?
- Who faces more peer pressure, girls or boys?
- Should all Americans be required to vote?
- Which is better, giving or receiving?
- Is it OK to keep animals in zoos?
- Should we change the minimum driving age in the United States?
- Which is more important, happiness or success?
- Is democracy the best form of government?
- Should kids have set bedtimes or just go to bed when they're sleepy?
- Do you think the government should find a way to provide free health care for everyone?
- Is it better to save your allowance or spend it?
- Should we ban plastic bags and bottles?
- Which is better, living in the city or in the country?
- Should homeowners be required to shovel their snow?
- If I could make a new law, it would be …
- Who is the world's best athlete, present or past?
- What's the best holiday?
- Are professional athletes/musicians/ actors overpaid?
- Which is better, fiction or nonfiction?

- What is one book that everyone should read?
- Should you put ketchup on a hot dog?
- Is a taco a sandwich?
- Are clowns scary or funny?
- The best pizza topping is …
- Should we still consider Pluto a planet?
- Which came first, the chicken or the egg?

Write down the topic of your persuasive paragraph.

_____

Next, brainstorm all the details that you can remember or imagine about the topic. Ask yourself questions such as: What are the causes? What are the facts? What other facts or ideas are involved? How does it affect other things? How does it become affected by others? Why do I think it should be changed or remain the same? What should be done about it? List the answers to those questions here. Add as many details as you can. Ask yourself what would I want the reader to understand about my topic? What would the reader want to ask me about it?

_____   _____

_____   _____

_____   _____

_____   _____

_____   _____

_____   _____

_____   _____

Look over your list of specific details and ask yourself these questions:

Are all of the details related to my topic and purpose?
Can any details be added that would make my purpose clearer or my writing more interesting?

Adjust your list as necessary. You may change one idea or several. If you need to add ideas, list them here.

_____   _____

_____   _____

_____   _____

Now go over your list of details and arrange then in logical order. Put numbers next to the ideas indicating their arrangement in your paragraph

It is now time to write your first draft. Don't worry about spelling, grammar, or punctuation. Think of an interesting way to express your main idea that will engage your reader's attention. It must contain the topic about which you are writing and should state a definite stance about it. Next, set the hook by making a statement that will grab the reader's attention to be persuaded. Then add supporting sentences that expand your main idea and tell the events in the time sequence that they occurred. Leave yourself sufficient space to revise and make corrections.

_____

_____

_____

_____

_____

_____

_____

_____

_____

_____

_____

It is now time to revise your writing. Carefully read over what you wrote and ask yourself the following questions:

- Did I stick to my topic?
- Are there unnecessary details?
- Could any points be added that would clarify or improve my writing?
- Does the writing sound interesting or boring?
- Do the ideas flow together smoothly?
- Would a different organization of ideas be better?
- Are any sentences out of order or confusing?
- Are there more precise or vivid words I could use?
- Did I achieve the purpose I set out in my writing?

As you answer the questions, make additions and corrections on your first draft. It is very helpful to use a different color ink or pencil so the changes can be easily noticed.

Then proofread it carefully, looking out for any spelling or grammar mistakes. Make sure you used the correct punctuation and quotation marks.

Now it is time to write your final draft. Make sure to write carefully and neatly. Avoid the need to erase anything. Remember to be proud of your work.

_____

_____

_____

_____

_____

_____

_____